THE STINKWHEEL SAGA

Episode 1

David Beare   Andrew Pattle   Philippa Wheeler

Stinkwheel Publishing

Upper Cefn-y-Pwll Abermule
Montgomeryshire SY15 6JN

ISBN 0-9547363-0-3

Layout & photosetting by Andrew Pattle
Printed and bound by KDS Printing, Ipswich

Contents

Dedicated to my Dad, Louis, sorry he is not around to enjoy this.

Preface

"We have heard so much lately about the possibilities of the cycle assisted by a small motor which can be connected and disconnected at the rider's will, that by this time most of us who are devotees of the wheel have become interested, some more, some less, in the idea".

Cycling magazine, March 8th 1905.

"In my opinion, the power assisted cycle is the most villainous piece of machinery yet invented"

Councillor M D West, chairman of the Coulsdon and Purley Road Safety Committee, quoted by the Coulsdon & Purley Times, March 4th 1955.

Motor-assisted bicycles already existed by the turn of the 19th century, almost certainly as a result of early cyclists' unwillingness to overexert themselves. In this they were aided and abetted by enthusiastic engineers whose fascination with the internal combustion engine led them up many new avenues. In the case of powered bicycles, it was the quest for more speed than was possible from human legs that excited these men. Gottleib Daimler built a prototype motor cycle in 1885; by 1890 Messrs Hildebrand & Wolfmuller from Munich were offering the first series-produced machine to an eager public.

Cycling began originally as something of a fashionable occupation amongst the monied classes; few others were able to afford or could see the use of such a device. Many early purchasers had not indulged in much physical effort (except for riding a horse) before needing to disport themselves on the latest fad in order to keep up appearances with their peers. Fatter, unfit and wealthier cyclists of the day probably mulled over the prospects offered by Nikolaus August Otto's four-stroke internal combustion engine as a possible source of motive power to assist or even supplant pedal-power. Unfortunately, Mr Otto's internal combustion engine at that time was less than reliable or controllable. It weighed a lot, vibrated uncomfortably, had injurious rotating parts as well as becoming very hot and was in the habit of spraying the surroundings with oil, fuel and unpleasant gaseous emanations. An early motor cycle was a fearsome device, the courageous rider was in intimate physical contact with all the above and, more often than not, likely to be maimed by his mount without warning.

Engineering ingenuity being what it was in the late Victorian era, refinements to motors came not a moment too soon for the pioneers of motor cycling. Engines gradually became more compact, less leaky (though incontinent machinery would remain a great British tradition well into the 1960s) and power output per pound weight rose dramatically. Cycle frames and wheels had to become stronger and heavier in order to cope with the violence visited upon them by ever-more powerful engines. Drive to the rear wheel often entailed a long, flapping and incredibly dangerous leather belt arrangement, almost guaranteeing the removal of any clothing coming into contact with it while in motion. Chains became an alternative, dirtier and slightly more positive means of power transmission, so now the motor cycle rider had a choice of injuries; friction burns, abrasions and divestment from a broken belt or cuts and bruises from errant chains. Brakes were at best of little use, being simply a direct development of the cycle wheel rim brake, but then there was little traffic around in those days and at worst a rider could get kicked by the horse he had just run into.

A typical early motor cycle: Capt T W P "Will" Herbert as a young man on his Triumph motor cycle. He was killed in action on 2nd August 1917 and is buried at the Commonwealth War Graves Cemetery, Voormezeele.

Evolution was nonetheless rapid to the point where motor cycles soon departed on a tangent of their own to become very different, purpose-built designs owing little other than general layout to their ancestor, the bicycle.

Some engineers however were still determined to explore the possibilities offered by motorising normal bicycles. Perhaps the first to do so practically were the Swiss brothers Henri and Armand Dufaux of Route des Acacias, Geneva, who produced the forerunner of future clip-on[*] cyclemotor engine units around 1905, their *Motosacoche*.

Cycling magazine, in a report dated March 8th 1905, unfortunately committed a couple of major gaffes when reviewing the Dufaux brothers' invention:

"One of the most practical devices for applying motor assistance to a bicycle is the Motosacoche or Motor Wallet." My dictionary gives satchel, tool-bag, saddlebag or pannier as the meanings of *sacoche*, definitely not wallet. *"It is not quite a novelty - at any rate in the land of its birth, France, where it has been doing good service for some time."* The advert reproduced on the next page quite clearly states *"Société Anonyme (i.e. Limited company) H & A Dufaux, Genève"* as the maker. Their company had existed since 1899. The Paris address is that of their French *succursale* or branch of the company.

---

[*] The descriptive term "Clip-on" cyclemotor engine is believed to have been first used shortly after the end of World War II by Courtenay Edwards, motoring correspondent of the Daily Mail.

LA MOTOSACOCHE

Société anonyme H. & A. DUFAUX & Cie
GENEVE

CAPITAL : DEUX MILLIONS DE FRANCS

Groupe moteur amovible ayant la forme d'une SACOCHE
de cadre permettant de transformer une Bicyclette routière ordinaire
en une

BICYCLETTE A MOTEUR

Parfait engin de transport pour Touristes, Médecins, Officiers, Notaires, etc.
et même pour Dames.

SUCCURSALE POUR LA FRANCE :

41, rue Saint=Ferdinand, PARIS

LIVRE D'OR DE LA MOTOSACOCHE

Envoi franco du Catalogue sur demande.

1906

Course de côte d'Aix-en-Provence
(Bicyclettes à moteur)
1er, 2e et 3e Prix : LA MOTOSACOCHE

Course de montagne et de
consommation
407 kilom. en Styrie et Carinthie
(Autriche)
1er, 2e et 3e MOTOSACOCHE

2 juin 1907

Concours de côte du Val-Suzon
(près Dijon)
3 kil. 800, rampes atteignant 9 o/o.
Bicyclettes à moteur (chaines enlevées)
1er Motosacoche en 5 m. 37 s.
2e Motosacoche en 5 m. 41 s.
3e Motosacoche en 6 m. 17 s.

The brothers Dufaux devised the Motosacoche as a self-contained power unit capable of being installed on any bicycle. A reinforced leather casing designed to fit inside an average cycle frame carried their own designed and manufactured engine, fuel system and exhaust. Transmission was via a jockey-wheel tensioned leather belt to a rim screwed to the rear wheel spokes. It was simple, elegant, well engineered and decades ahead of the competition. Advertising (as above) noted a *"detachable motor unit having the form of a frame-fitted SATCHEL permitting the transformation of an ordinary road Bicycle into a MOTORISED BICYCLE. A Perfect engine for Tourists, Officers, Notaries and even for Ladies."*

In the correspondence page of *Power & Pedal* magazine, September 1955 edition, a Mr R B Moffatt of Whitley Bay wrote of his experiences using a Motosacoche a good many years

5

previously. Amongst his comments were: *"it had magneto ignition, which gave a lot of trouble, also air shields round the engine, pressed to a funnel shape for cooling. They were easily removed and were more often off than on. The drive was by twisted leather belt with a wire hook for the join. To tighten the belt one just gave it an extra twist or two."*

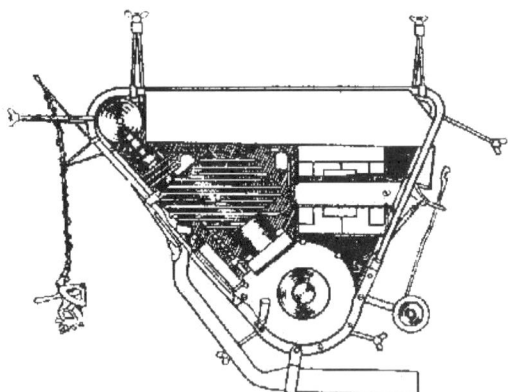

The Motosacoche was originally of 241cc capacity, later increased to 290cc.

Another visionary engineer who came up with his own version of the same idea a decade later was Gabriel Voisin. He was the creator and manufacturer of many successful World War I military aircraft, exotic sleeve-valve luxury cars, racing cars, the Biscooter minimalist micro-car, inflatable temporary aircraft hangars, prefabricated houses and the Motor Fly. Voisin designed his cyclemotor engine as a complete unit including the rear wheel, tyre, transmission and fuel tank, which would simply bolt into place on any bicycle, thus providing the owner with *"simple, economic power assistance"*. His concept from 1919 was 30 years ahead of the similar (commercially successful) post World War II Cyclemaster and BSA Winged Wheel machines.

A prototype Motor Fly with transmission by gears and horizontal cylinder. These gears proved horribly noisy and soon gave way to friction drive via a roller driving a Ferodo-faced ring. The rear wheel was aluminium. (Picture courtesy EPA/White Mouse Editions © 1991)

For the purposes of this survey we need to move forward perhaps forty years, through the industrialised horrors of one world war and the consequent civil, cultural and economic upheavals which followed the hollow victory of 1918, to a second global conflict. World War II was created largely by the vengeful restrictions visited on Germany following the Treaty of Versailles and made possible by an industrial society's ability to invent, mass produce and find excuses to use ever more efficient cost-per-death means of killing one other.

There is nothing like a good war to speed up development of new ideas, new technologies and provide the necessary funding. Politicians have always known this. Unforgivably, war also kills and emotionally destroys untold numbers of people, uproots and dispossesses millions more and devastates the surviving population for a generation, wrecks everything in the way and drains any country involved of its entire wealth. What is left after is penury, ruined infrastructures and countryside, lack of most basic resources and raw materials and a disillusioned and emotionally scarred people who have to learn to make do and live with much less than before.

So it was in 1945, when World War II ground to a close in Europe and the public at last began to be able to think of a better future. But returning servicemen without jobs, large swathes of Britain's industrial centres bombed to rubble (in addition, anything left standing was by then worn out and obsolete) and a country hocked up to the eyeballs to the Americans meant austerity was to be a way of life for a good many years to come. Universal mobility was seldom thought of in those days; most people needing to be somewhere else took the bus, train, walked or cycled. By a happy coincidence many talented engineers, who had been fully occupied in previous years designing and building new machinery with which to win the war, were now faced with a lack of work as reconversion to civilian life proceeded. Life became more stable and in turn confidence rose for the general public, many of these same engineers began to think in terms of using their skills to make travelling easier. Most of them possessed a push-bike of some kind and had to use it frequently, if not every day to go to work, so thoughts grew on motor-assistance for bicycles or possibly complete machines. Such thinking was far from new, but the time had come once again to revive ideas following the impoverishment of most of Europe by 1945.

Dreaming of motor-assisting bicycles was one thing, manufacturing them was entirely another. Firstly, while Britain had pre-war been one of the largest producers of motor cycles in the world, there was little or no tradition of producing small-capacity (below 150cc) machines as hide-bound UK legislators treated all motor cycles equally, whatever their engine capacity.

To quote *Power & Pedal* magazine's editor Frank L Farr in his leader column from September 1955, *"undoubtedly Governmental obstinacy based mainly on class prejudice (only the workers would ride cyclemotors) has maintained restrictions on the free use of under 50cc vehicles which discouraged the home market to some extent."*

Conversely, on continental Europe (where many countries had much larger rural populations and bigger distances to cover) relevant ministries, by means of light-handed legislation, had for decades encouraged manufacturers to produce simple small-capacity machines. Under-50cc cyclemotors could be ridden on the roads unfettered by anything but minimal insurance and without registration, licences or other bureaucratic nonsense, often at age 14. Hence these same countries had thriving design and manufacturing industries for cyclemotors before World War II and were to contribute many of the models available in the UK after the war, which is why few 1950s cyclemotors are 100% British in origin.

Post-1945, everything was in short supply or simply unavailable as politicians struggled to "export or die". Any manufacturer able to sell his products abroad (ideally to America for lots of US dollars to help pay off the National Debt) was given preference in the supply of essential raw materials such as steel, copper, rubber and of course oil and petrol. Such raw materials as were available would often be of execrable quality and limited durability. Aluminium conversely was plentiful and of good quality, a by-product of the wartime aviation industry's needs, so correspondingly large amounts of alloy were freely available post-war. Manufacturers of non-essential home-market products came a distant second in the queue and were unlikely to obtain what they needed without an extended struggle against obstructive faceless bureaucrats at the Ministry of Supply.

Nonetheless, a multitude of small, new and hopeless manufacturers, as well as large, old-established firms launched themselves into the breach. Their dream was that such products would find many willing customers prepared to part with cash for an often underdeveloped and recalcitrant machine, advertising having promised those customers a magic carpet whereas the reality was often very different. The importance of cyclemotors within the 1950s market can be judged by Ministry of Transport figures, issued for 1953. These gave the figure of new cyclemotor registrations as 35,164 out of a total for all classes of motor cycles (solo, side-car & three-wheelers) of 113,631. In other words, this new type of vehicle accounted for over one third of all new registrations in 1953 and was easily the largest single class.

Designers produced many technically ingenious complete cyclemotors and clip-on engine units within the severe limitations set by materials shortages, cost or legislation and it is extraordinary that so many of these have survived to this day. Perhaps, because little space was taken up, a cyclemotor could be consigned to the back of a shed or garage the moment there was any prospect an owner might be able to afford a motor cycle & sidecar combination for the family or, if really well-off, a Ford Prefect. The abandoned cyclemotor quietly disappeared behind lawn-mowers, flower pots, spare lumber, old tin trunks and junk, there to fester and rust for decades until a house move or family bereavement dragged it, cobwebbed and forlorn, into the light again.

On a personal note, it is difficult to explain why such an uncomfortable and unreliable means getting from A to B appeals today, at the beginning of the twenty-first century. Cyclemotors and motorised bicycles were never intended to be more than primitive labour-saving devices, destined for a short and brutal life, a stop-gap until prosperity and the means to purchase better modes of transport reappeared again. A fascination with elderly engineering, the challenge of bringing such devices back to life and riding them (a faltering engine, feeble ignition, precarious brakes, erratic handling, the smell of burning oil and pedalling a lot are a number of dubious pleasures) and revisiting times past are amongst some of the reasons.

Owning cyclemotors today also gives a rider the opportunity to dress up in silly period costume, wear pudding-basin helmets and attract elderly pedestrians who accost one with *"I had one of those you know in, oooh, let me see, 1953 it was, yes, it was an awful winter, the wife's chilblains had never been worse, I rode the blessed thing to my mother's funeral in January; Phyllis, our next-door neighbour who had that terrible complaint poor thing, said to me, don't you catch cold now, can't have two departures in one year ... we all had a good laugh at that I can tell you, but d'you know I never did, I always wore that Army greatcoat I bought down the road at the surplus store for three and six, it was marvellous, I wish I still had the old bike now, it smelled just like yours does and was always a bugger to start, still got my old coat though, the dog slept on it for years before she passed away..."*

In compiling a survey such as this, one difficulty is deciding which criteria to use in choosing machines to study; attempting to include all of them would result in an encyclopædia of massive size. Numbers of surviving models would seem a good starting point, dealing with the most survivors first and so on down the scale. This method also gives some indication of the robustness and durability of various designs, as well as their relative popularity at the time they were built and used.

Figures extracted from National Autocycle and Cyclemotor Club (NACC) archives in 1998 indicate roughly the following numbers of surviving cyclemotors owned by Club members, the approximate total number of machines produced by manufacturers (where known) is in brackets.

Cyclemaster	776	(181,000)
Trojan Mini-Motor	318	(75,000)
BSA Winged Wheel	203	(29,000)
Sinclair Goddard Power Pak	195	(65,000)
Ducati Cucciolo	95	(400.000)
Vincent Firefly	61	(7,000)
British Salmson Cyclaid	43	(6,000)
GYS Motamite/Cairns Mocyc	41	
Mosquito	33	
Cymota	31	
Berini M13	30	
Teagle	19	
Lohmann	18	
ABG VAP	12	
Tailwind	6	(6?)
Busy Bee	4	
Itom	2	
TI Powerwheel	1	(1)
Ostler	1	
ABJ Auto Minor	0	
Bantamoto	0	
Bikotor	0	(0?)

We have to assume that not all of the total in the first column indicate UK market-supplied cyclemotors, some will undoubtedly have been imported by enthusiasts decades after they went out of production, though the make could originally be bought here when current. Given the propensity for NACC members to buy anything resembling a cyclemotor to take home as a restoration project whilst on holiday in Europe, this has to be a fair assumption.

It would also be useful to define terms: what exactly are cyclemotors, autocycles and mopeds?

Cyclemotor: an engine unit designed to be fitted to a pedal cycle in order to motorise it and is also used to describe the resulting motorised machine. The term seems to have come into general usage by the late 1940s but does not appear to have been used before World War II to describe such machines as the French Cyclotracteur.

Another description, MAC (Motor Assisted Cycle) enjoyed brief popularity immediately after World War II but was soon ousted by cyclemotor. The term was not used where a machine was only available in motorised form.

Autocycle: originally, this meant motor cycle (probably as in autocar, motorcar) and lives on in the name of the Auto Cycle Union. From the 1930s on it came to mean a motor cycle with pedals, today it is understood as defining machines with pedals and an engine capacity of between 80cc and 100cc. A capacity range of 50cc to 150cc was accepted when under 150cc machines benefited from a lower road-tax band introduced in the 1931 Budget.

Moped: this is a legal definition of a motor cycle with pedals and an engine capacity of 50cc or less. Over the years changing legislation has altered this definition but for our purposes the 50cc-with-pedals identification suits our needs best. The word moped came into use by the late 1950s; earlier machines that fitted the moped definition were often called light autocycles. *Motor Cycling* magazine wrote a "Cyclemotor Manual" and had a go at introducing the French term *cyclomoteur* as a generic name for moped-type machines, Mobylettes and VéloSoleXes were at that time the only two machines readily available in the UK.

Concerning the VéloSoleX, many readers will question why this machine is not included. The reason is that the Solex was always sold as a complete cycle with engine whereas all the marques discussed here were originally supplied as clip-on units for fitting to push-bikes.

There are other accepted terms such as *vélomoteur* or BMA *(Bicyclette [à] Moteur Auxiliaire)* but these apply to French machines in continental Europe.

Whilst we are on the subject of definitions of terms, it would be appropriate to revisit pre-decimal British currency for the benefit of younger readers, those with short memories and International readers who have had the misfortune to be born outside the United Kingdom. Throughout this book we will need, for comparative purposes, to quote prices of machines when they were brand new and hence in 'old money'. Until decimalisation in 1971, British currency was denominated in pounds Sterling, shillings and pence. There were twelve pence in a shilling and twenty shillings in a pound Sterling, thus there were then 240 old pence in a pound as opposed to post-decimalisation (1972) 100 new pence in a pound. As an example, the price of a cyclemotor quoted in this text will be written as £24.10s.4d, (twenty-four pounds, ten shillings and fourpence or approximately £24.52p in modern money), whereas a lower priced item under a pound can be written slightly differently, eg: 10/6d (ten shillings and sixpence or approximately £0.53p).

To trap the unwary, items priced at over a pound could also be expressed in shillings alone, so for instance a coat priced at 75/- (shillings) actually cost £3.15s.0d. Then there was the guinea, value one pound one shilling and mostly used in the world of horses & horse-racing, though in early years of the 20th Century the motor trade was prone to quote prices in guineas. 'Motor

Copers' (car salesmen) were the linear descendants of horse traders and adhered to the same moral and business ethics: *caveat emptor*. Further Sterling sub-divisions were used, such as farthings (four to a penny) or ha'pennies (a half-penny), sovereigns, crowns, half-crowns, florins, bobs, tanners and threepenny bits, but these do not concern us here. This illogical and baffling method of currency denomination was deliberately opaque, very British and totally confusing to foreigners, the original intention all along.

Writing this work has been to indulge in a form of industrial archaeology, full of surprises at some of our discoveries, admiration at others and incredulity at many. Optimism was never in short supply in this industry. Period pictures from magazines, newspapers and photo-archives have been used throughout to illustrate the subject in question; we apologise in advance for the often-appalling reproduction quality. Many of these pictures were originally printed using a very coarse screen resolution with poor ink on worse quality paper and have not improved with time or the fading of old newsprint. Clean, original artwork or photos are almost impossible to find. Modern electronics can improve things up to a point, so we hope the pictures offer, if not sharpness, then at least a period feel to this book. We hope our readers enjoy the result.

You will just have to imagine yourself in 1952 at 37 Acacia Avenue, slumped in an overstuffed armchair in front of a small, fiercely hot coal fire, tartan carpet slippers propped up on a leather pouffe & smouldering gently, a pipe-full of Navy Shag glowing, glass of stout in hand, National Health specs focused on the latest issue of *Power & Pedal* or *Motor Cycling* whilst the Light Programme plays quietly on the wireless. Your spouse busies herself in the kitchen preparing your tea of Spam fritters and eggie bread whilst you avidly digest the latest news from the world of cyclemotors. Read on…

(I well appreciate the above imaginary scene and the general tenor of this work can be construed, in this 21st century 'PC' world, as extremely sexist and assumes all cyclemotor owners and riders to be men. This is definitely not the case. Many owners and regular users of cyclemotors were and are women who are every bit as capable riders and mechanics as men and who enjoy cyclemotoring just as much. I count amongst my friends several female cyclemotorists and apologise to them in advance for the rather masculine tone of the text that follows.)

Acknowledgements

I am tremendously indebted to co-publisher, editor and researcher Andrew Pattle, committee member of the National Autocycle & Cyclemotor Club, former editor of Club magazine *Buzzing* and now NACC Librarian. He has dedicated a huge amount of time to tracking down information used to describe the cyclemotors featured, together with a great deal of the period literature used. Without his assiduous fact-finding, encyclopaedic knowledge of cyclemotors, patient assistance, IT experience, enthusiasm and support, this survey would not have appeared in print at all, never mind in readable form.

Grateful thanks also go to *cyclomoteuriste par excellence,* intrepid traveller, Isle of Man racer and true cyclemotor enthusiast Philippa Wheeler who supplied much original material reproduced in this book. Her anecdotes and experiences as a cyclemotor owner and rider in the period that we are covering were invaluable, as was her assistance with text and corrections.

Most of the images used to illustrate this book have been gleaned from original factory manuals and publicity material, Power and Pedal, Motor Cycling and The Motor Cycle. Morton's Motorcycle Media Ltd kindly permitted us to repro some of their copyright cut-away line drawings. We have always tried to make contact to clear copyright but this is often difficult fifty years after certain magazines were published. If we failed to make contact, our letters failed to reach you or we have used an unattributed picture, please accept our apologies for not having been able to give full credit for copyright and use of photos & drawings. We will publish acknowledgements or corrections in future editions of this work.

We would like to express our appreciation to the family of George Murray Denton for allowing us access to their invaluable family archive and to quote and reproduce private correspondence. Thanks go to Patrick Knight, the Kelsey Publishing Group, Hugh Torrens and the Bath Industrial Heritage Trust for allowing quotes from their work on Joseph Day and the origins of two-stroke engines (and to reproduce pictures), Alan Cathcart for a superb Ducati history, Melvyn Lewis for detailed Cyclemaster history and Chris Draper and David & Charles for Salmson background information and illustrations. Thanks also go to G N Georgano for succinct historic descriptions of various car marques and models and to the British Motor Industry Heritage Trust, Rover Group and the University of Warwick Modern Records Centre for access to Crossley Motors Ltd company records.

Lastly, but far from least, thanks go to Lizzie for her support and patience in allowing me to stare at a computer screen unhindered for several hours a day for years.

Dave Beare,
Abermule, 2004

Joseph Day and the Two-Stroke Engine

Joseph Day was granted a patent in June 1892 for a *"crank-chamber scavenge two-stroke cycle gas engine"* that was very different from all previous two-stroke motors. These were usually large, cumbersome engines with a complicated arrangement of two connected pistons and cylinders. One was the power cylinder that ran the engine and whatever was driven by it; the other acted as a pump or charging unit to supply the power cylinder with explosive mixture. Consequently, all advantages of a two-stroke engine as we know it were lost. Granted there was no power-sapping valve-gear as on a four-stroke. There was a firing stroke every revolution as opposed to one in every two but the dual-cylinder arrangement doubled the rotating masses and there were many extra components to create friction and wear out.

What Joseph Day did was very clever. Instead of using a separate charging cylinder, he sealed off the crankcase and made that into a chamber where an explosive mixture could be introduced, collected, compressed and transferred to the working combustion chamber. (Remember, this was still the era of primitive open-crank four-stroke stationary engines where the only enclosed part was the combustion chamber; the crankshaft and con-rods flailed about nakedly.) His two-cycle, two-port stationary engine became something we would immediately recognise today: it was ultra simple, had only four moving parts (including a gas intake valve) and operated on the following principle:

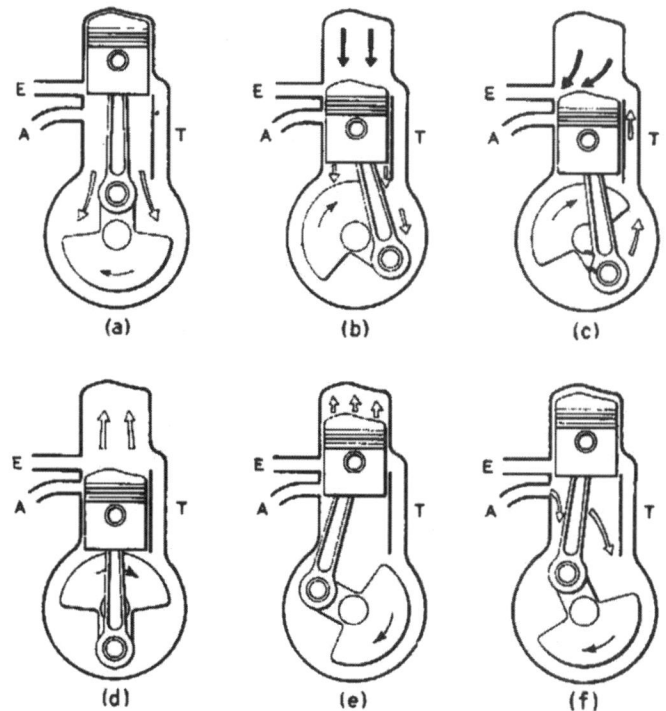

Cycle of operations in a two-stroke engine

A = Inlet
T = Transfer
E = Exhaust

(a)   (b)   (c)   (d)   (e)   (f)

Day was born in London, fourth son of the famous judge Sir John C F Day (1826-1908). He attended Beaumont College (now St John's Beaumont) at Old Windsor, Berkshire, from 1868 to 1873. Then, in 1873 and 1874, he attended the School of Practical Engineering at Crystal Palace, where he was one of its first students of engineering training. From there, he moved to Somerset to follow an engineering apprenticeship with the well-known engineering firm of Stothert & Pitt in Bath, between 1874 and 1877.

In January 1878, Day founded his own mechanical engineering business in the Victoria Ironworks, off the Upper Bristol Road, Bath, with the first of several partners he would be associated with. Early work was with machines for dressing leather hides and manufacturing concrete. Many small businesses like Day's became virtually satellite engineers to the much larger, well-established firms such as Stothert & Pitt. Progress was swift and by the late 1880s he was deeply involved with waterworks for the City of Bath. He also became entangled in the engineering required by mechanised bread making via his directorship of the Western Counties Steam Bakeries and Milling Co Ltd.

Although there is some evidence that his first engine was built in 1889, Day applied for his patent for a two-port two-stroke engine in April 1891. This was a consequence of the continuous litigation relating to the Otto 4-stroke engine patent in Britain at the time. Day set about his application after the Otto patent had lapsed in 1890; his justifiable instinct was to steer well clear of the lawyers.

"It seemed to me that all gas engines as then made were unnecessarily complicated and, therefore, expensive to produce and that the only chance of cutting in (to the engine market) was to devise something very much simpler" Day was quoted as recalling.

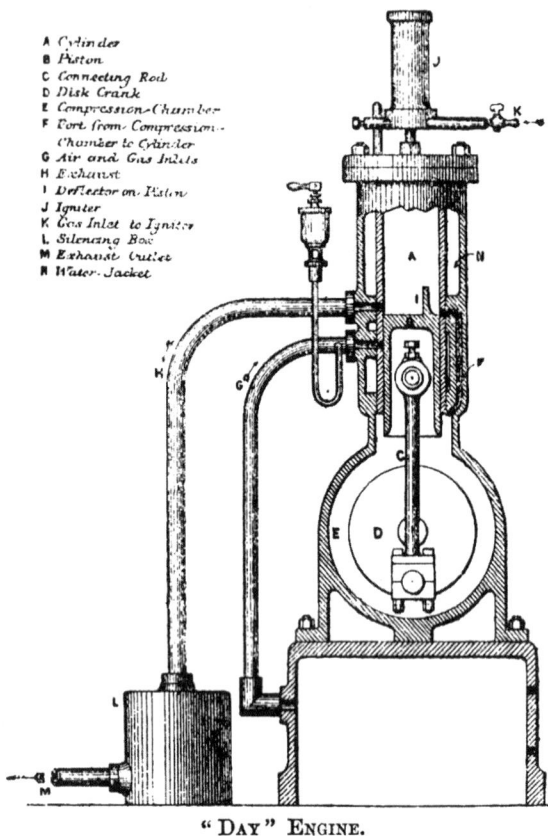

A Cylinder
B Piston
C Connecting Rod
D Disk Crank
E Compression Chamber
F Port from Compression Chamber to Cylinder
G Air and Gas Inlets
H Exhaust
I Deflector on Piston
J Igniter
K Gas Inlet to Igniter
L Silencing Box
M Exhaust Outlet
N Water Jacket

"DAY" ENGINE.

Joseph Day's new design also had the advantage of being able to run equally well in either direction. In fact his operating instructions stated that an operator, having got the engine ready for starting, simply spun the flywheel by hand in the desired direction and off it would go. On the subject of fuel economy (bearing in mind that at the turn of the 19th century a lot of stationary engines ran on town gas rather than petroleum spirit), the Day Gas Engine Company was prepared to offer a written guarantee that *"even in the smallest size the consumption of gas, at three shillings per 1,000 cubic feet, would not exceed one penny per indicated horsepower whilst the engine was running"*.

Such was the success of Joseph Day's two-stroke engine that by mid-1892 he had 60 to 70 men in his employ, producing engines as fast as they could. The reason for this demand was simple: a two-stroke engine gave power more evenly, had fewer parts and was therefore cheaper to make and sell and was generally more reliable than the Otto four-stroke equivalent. Just the qualities sought after by designers of small-capacity cyclemotor engines fifty years later.

(Kelsey Publishing Ltd/
Patrick Knight © 2002)

A whole range of engine sizes was soon on offer, from ⅛ to 12nhp (nominal horsepower), in single or twin-cylinder form. The twins were simply two single-cylinder engines joined together by a central flywheel, the first modular engine in fact.

(Kelsey Publishing Ltd /
Patrick Knight © 2002)

15

On 15th October 1892 an employee of Joseph Day's, Frederick William Caswell Cock, applied for a patent covering an improved version of the Day engine. This was granted and immediately signed over to Day, who saw the advantages of this improved and now completely valveless engine. Shortly thereafter production of the original engine ceased, to be replaced by the new design which had three ports (intake, transfer and exhaust), thus eliminating the old gas or fuel intake valve and reducing by 25% the moving parts, now down to only three.

Unfortunately, Day's company was beset by legal problems associated with the bread-making business that resulted in him being declared bankrupt in 1894. Production of his engines was taken over by the Millbury Pier Marine Engineering Company of Plymouth, but once he had obtained a discharge from bankruptcy in 1906, Day re-established himself by founding Day & Company of Barking, to produce marine engines. His business prospered somewhat better during the First World War, when many engines were supplied to the Army for use in pumping water out of trenches and it is believed the business survived until 1925-26.

Though he himself does not appear to have profited much from his creation, Joseph Day's legacy to engineers world-wide was immense; one has only to reflect on the vast number and types of machines which were and are all powered by two-stroke engines directly derived from that original patent. It was a gift gladly accepted by designers of nearly all sub-50cc cyclemotor engines.

Cyclemaster

THE MAGIC WHEEL THAT WINGS YOUR HEEL

The Cyclemaster remains today one of the most recognisable and successful clip-on auxiliary engine for bicycles and with good reason. It is a carefully thought-out and designed unit, comprising a complete 26" rear wheel assembly with tyre and tube, carrying within a much-enlarged hub shell a cleverly executed 25.7cc motor, clutch, final drive, fuel tank, carburettor and exhaust system, a marvel of miniature engineering. Fitting theoretically required nothing more than replacing an original rear wheel with the Cyclemaster unit and attaching controls to the handlebars, everything else was incorporated within the hub shell. Many other bicycle power units required mounting brackets, modifications or adaptations to the cycle such as cutting pieces of mudguard off and an often inconvenient siting of a petrol tank and feed hose.

Though it was deservedly successful in Britain, the Cyclemaster did not in fact originate in the UK, it was conceived in Holland and based on the pre-WW2 Saxonette. To quote *The Motor Cycle*, 10th April 1950:

"There was not a great deal to interest the motor cyclist at the Utrecht Industries Fair except for the fact that two new cycle attachments were shown. These are the Cyclemaster and the Berini and both have been designed by the Interpro Construction Bureau, the brains of which consist of two German engineers formerly with the Auto Union D.K.W. organisation. In close connection with the well-known firm of Hart Nibbrig and Greeve N.V. (agents for B.S.A., B.M.W. and many other motorcycle makes) the Interpro Bureau was founded some two years ago [1948] and its first design to reach the prototype stage was the Cyclemaster".

The two German engineers were originally detailed to help develop a DKW-designed two-stroke car, the prototype of which was hand-assembled by Pennock NV in the Hague, but this project proved too costly and never reached production. One of the two engineers, Bernhard Neumann, had a set of blueprints that originated from DKW pre-war. These showed a well-advanced design called the RadMeister: a small two-stroke engine entirely housed within a special rear wheel hub that could power a bicycle. Both men were still classed as prisoners of war in 1946, so the blueprints were handed over to the Interpro Construction Büro, an international organisation with American, English and French participation that had been set up to rebuild the Netherlands' industrial base after the war. *"Interpro Pats.Pend."* is found engraved on almost every Cyclemaster engine.

Those original DKW blueprints were then sent on to England. Mr Neumann, together with two colleagues from HNG, had adapted some elements from the DKW RadMeister idea to produce a very different clip-on cyclemotor engine of their own design: a front-wheel drive unit called the Berini (after **Be**rnhard, **Ri**nus and **Ni**co). This would be manufactured at a new factory called NV Pluvier Motorenfabriek. However, to return to Britain, a company called Cyclemaster (a translation of *RadMeister*) Ltd. was set up at 26 Old Brompton Road, South Kensington, London

SW17, to market the new unit. After some modifications had been made to the DKW design, it was put into production in September 1950.

The engine was, naturally enough, a two-stroke. Its 32mm bore and stroke gave a capacity of 25.7cc and power output of 0.6bhp: fairly minimal but remarkably good for only 25.7cc. The fuel tank carried 2½ pints and a petroil consumption of 280mpg was claimed. Of note at that time was the use of a flat-top piston and reverse-scavenging porting based on the Schnuerle loop-scavenging principle developed in 1925. Many manufacturers would remain wedded to the heavier deflector-top piston of dubious efficiency (first seen in Joseph Day's two-stroke patent from 1891) for years to come. The enlarged pressed-steel hub shell containing the engine carried louvres around the periphery. These faced forward so that cooling air was (in theory) forced across the cylinder and head, though most cooling was probably due to the movement of the cycle down the road.

Of particular interest on the induction side was the use of a spring-loaded steel rotary inlet disc valve placed inside the crankcase, attached to the right of the crankshaft. This *avant garde* technique was used decades later in very high-revving, high-output 2-stroke engines. Much more accurate control of the inlet mixture timing was possible than by use of the traditional piston-skirt timing. The disc valve gave a longer dwell with the induction port open, producing excellent overall efficiency, good low-down torque and a reduced tendency to the four-stroking endemic in two-strokes on light load or part throttle. The inlet porting arrangement was also ingenious: a long inlet pipe was cast integral with the right-hand crankcase half and, freed from having to be positioned at the base of a cylinder by the disc valve, was low-down and at the back of the engine.

As the piston nears the top of its stroke, creating negative pressure in the crankcase, an arcuate slot cut in the disc valve aligns with the inlet port in the crankcase side, allowing mixture to pass into the crankcase via a hole bored through the crank web. An additional benefit of this positioning was that fresh petroil mixture arrived first at the big-end bearing, thus ensuring optimum lubrication. Other engine details were equally well designed, the steel crankshaft was carried by three substantial caged ball-bearings, one housed in each side of the crankcase and the third outrigged in the primary drive case to support the drive sprocket. A Wico-Pacy Bantamag flywheel magneto was carried on an extension of this main-shaft and supplied HT current for ignition only. A caged needle-roller bearing big-end fitted into the steel con-rod, the piston gudgeon-pin is supported by a phosphor-bronze little end bush and held in place by circlips in the piston bosses. The slightly domed piston itself was of light-alloy and carried two rings.

Transmission from the crankshaft was by means of a primary roller-chain in an oil bath case connected to a wet, single plate, cork-lined clutch mounted on a counter-shaft. Final drive (incorporating a rubber block shock-absorber) was via a short secondary chain to the final-drive sprocket riveted to the rear inner face of the hub drum, the ratio being 18:1. This method of transmitting power to the rear wheel was far more reliable and durable than the various forms of friction drive via rollers to tyres used by many other makes, though more expensive to manufacture.

The whole Cyclemaster unit was incredibly compact. Not only did the engine, transmission, exhaust, carburettor and fuel tank have to fit within the circumference of the hub drum, but also be narrow enough to fit between the average bicycle rear forks. All-up dry weight was 35lbs, including the wheel assembly and tyre.

Cyclemaster Ltd was advertising the unit for £25 (including fitting) in December 1950 and by March 1951 was claiming no fewer than 570 appointed dealers. The actual manufacturer was EMI Factories, based in Hayes, Middlesex. The above photo shows a production unit which was supplied painted all-black. Early publicity pictures were of a prototype unit, which was finished in silver.

In publicity material, Cyclemaster justifiably went out of its way to describe and illustrate the many advanced technical features incorporated within its engine unit as compared to other, cruder confections on offer from competing manufacturers. Plain bearings were nowhere to be seen (except for a phosphor-bronze little end bush) and all rotating parts were carried by oil-lubricated ball-races in the interest of a long and trouble-free life. The clutch had its own adjustment screw in addition to the adjuster on the clutch cable, when even having a clutch at all was regarded as an unnecessary luxury by some makers of cyclemotor engine assemblies. The owner of a clutch-less cyclemotor was expected to stop and restart his engine constantly and in consequence suffered many an oiled spark plug and refusal to start, to the detriment of his journey times, peace of mind and physical well-being.

Another unusual feature of later Cyclemasters was a coaster or back-pedal brake incorporated into the rear wheel hub. The thinking behind this was that a conventional bicycle rim-brake on the rear wheel could soon become useless as a result of oil contamination from the engine, inevitably thrown outward onto the rim from the hub. Another advantage of the coaster brake was that it meant the Cyclemaster wheel did not have to be supplied with different rims to suit cycles with stirrup or calliper brakes. The coaster brake makes its appearance in a Cyclemaster advert published in *The Motor Cycle* magazine on 8th November 1951, inviting readers to visit stand no.56 at the Earls Court Motor Cycle Show, 10th-17th November.

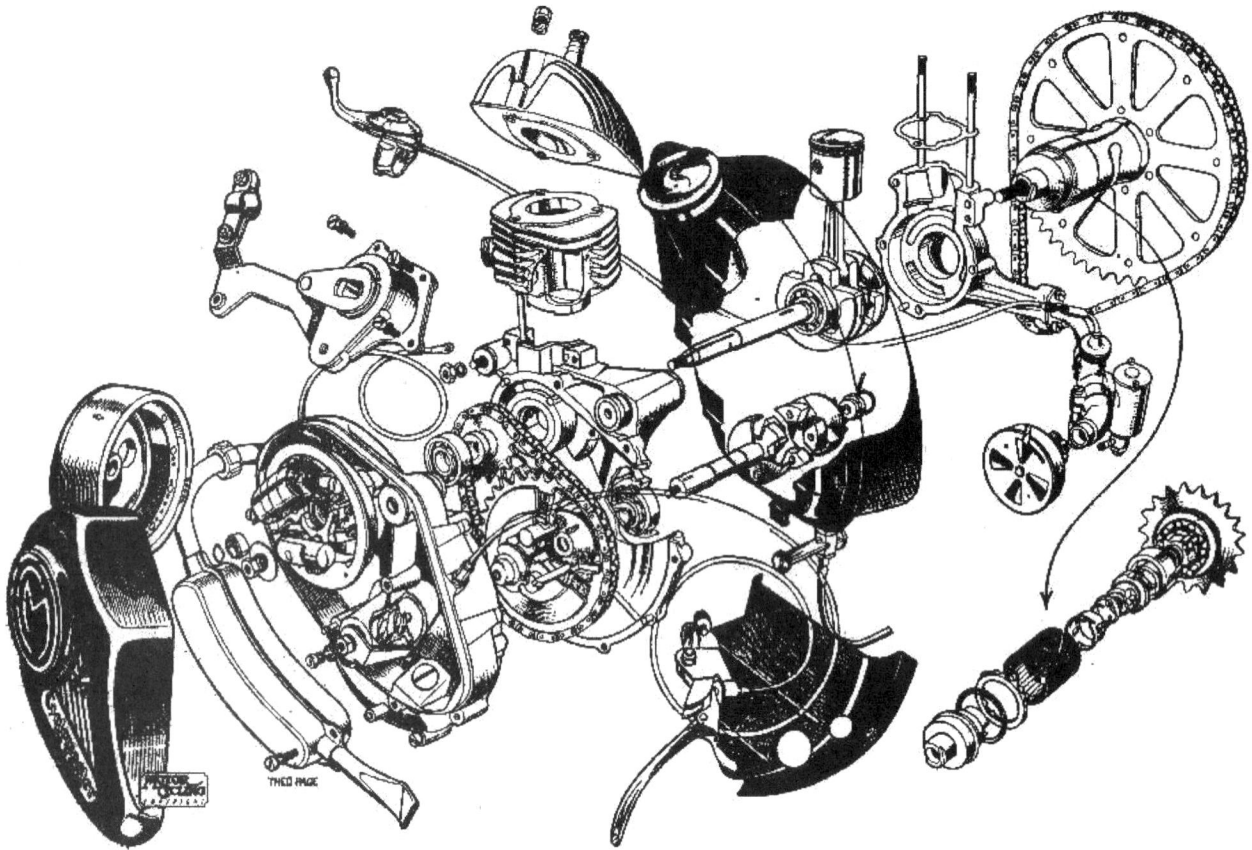

The above Cyclemaster 'ghost' view (from the pen of the incomparable Theo Page, a master of his art, published in *Motor Cycling* magazine) gives an excellent impression of the unit's layout; most of the engine assembly together with fuel tank fit comfortably within the 12½" diameter rear hub shell. The entire engine assembly is suspended from an integrally-cast boss behind the cylinder barrel. Torque reaction is taken by a bracket alongside the cylinder barrel, to which a clamp passing around the cycle frame lower fork is bolted. (Motor Cycling © Morton's Motorcycle Media Ltd.)

By Christmas 1951 Cyclemaster was claiming to have produced 40,000 units, as in the advert reproduced here, and had moved from the outback of South Kensington, SW17, to a more salubrious location at 38a St Georges Drive, Victoria, SW1.

happy Christmas

to

40,000 CYCLEMASTER OWNERS
and 720 CYCLEMASTER DEALERS
(in this country)

and thanks for your support !

Cyclemaster Ⓜ
THE MAGIC WHEEL THAT WINGS YOUR HEEL

CYCLEMASTER LTD., 38a, ST. GEORGE'S DRIVE, VICTORIA, S.W.I   VICtoria 6313

In addition to press advertisements, Cyclemaster Ltd also produced some very informative and well-illustrated brochures for customers on their product, a sample is reprinted below. Special mention is made of the *"efficient, economical and dignified"* power assistance furnished by a Cyclemaster!

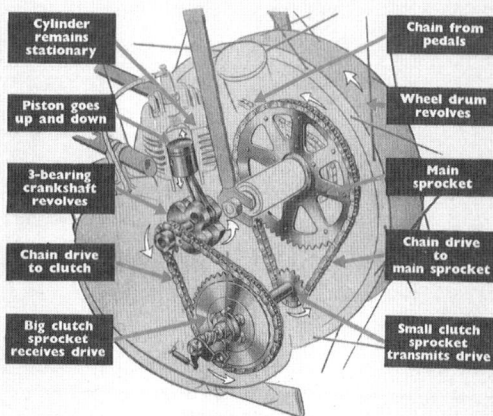

The Cyclemaster engine is fitted with a clutch, enabling the rider to keep the engine running at traffic stops. **A.** Clutch cable to handlebar lever. **B.** Adjusting screw. **C.** Clutch plates. **D.** Main drive sprocket. **E.** Clutch corks. **F.** Oil chamber.

The crankshaft operates in three ball bearings and is fully counter-weighted for smoothness and long life. The illustration shows **A.** Connecting rod. **B.** Big end and roller bearing. **C.** Fully counter-weighted crankshaft. **D.** Straddle mounting bearings.

There are two ball bearings on the clutch shaft, **A** and **B** in this illustration. The bearing **A** also takes up the end thrust of the shaft.

Smooth, vibrationless running and long life are also ensured by the cushioned drive. **A** and **C** are metal segments. **B** rubber cushions which give perfect smoothness.

SPECIFICATION

SIZE OF WHEEL	26″ × 1½″	FUEL MIXTURE	"Petroll" (1 in 25)
BORE	32 mm.	FUEL TANK CAPACITY	2½ pints (approx.)
STROKE	32 mm.	SPARK PLUG	K.L.G. Type F.50 14 mm.
CAPACITY	25.7 c.c.	FUEL CONSUMPTION	250-300 m.p.g.
R.A.C. RATING	.25 h.p.	IGNITION	Wico-Pacy Flywheel magneto
DEVELOPED H.P.	0.6 b.h.p. (approx.)	CARBURETTOR	Amal.
ENGINE SPEED	4,000 r.p.m. at 20 m.p.h.	CLUTCH	Single plate : sealed oil bath.
WEIGHT	28 lbs.		

CYCLEMASTER LIMITED, 38a St. George's Drive, Victoria, S.W.I

ASK FOR A DEMONSTRATION

£27/10/0 Fitted

(including wheel)

THE MAGIC WHEEL THAT WINGS YOUR HEEL

Cyclemaster

TAKES THE HARD WORK OUT OF CYCLING

Printed by The Leagrave Press Ltd., Luton and London

A REVOLUTION IN PERSONAL TRANSPORT

Private motoring is expensive, and likely to remain so for many years. Public transport is crowded and often inconvenient. A "full-up" bus may mean a long wait for the weary housewife ; or her husband tired out after a day's work.

Motor-cycles with their speed and weight are for the young—if they have the money. Thousands of people cannot endure the fatigue of ordinary cycling.

The Cyclemaster brings efficient, economical, dignified power-assisted cycling within reach of all. Using the Cyclemaster will change your whole outlook on life.

It is not a gadget, or an afterthought. There is no fussiness ; hardly any noise. It is a simple, powerful motor embodied in a wheel which just slips into the place of the back wheel of your own cycle. Go where you will, at your will—without effort.

PERFORMANCE

The trouble-free 25 c.c. engine will carry you at any speed up to 20 m.p.h. on the level. It will take you up most reasonable hills. On steep hills, you pedal easily to help it (no more effort than ordinary cycling on the level). On freak hills you get off and let it pull you up—instead of your having to push the machine.

NO SMELLS

There is no vibration ; hardly any noise, and as the motor is in the back wheel you get no fumes.

PETROL CONSUMPTION

250-300 m.p.g. According to conditions.

CONTROLS

Just two levers—one works the clutch ; the other the throttle.

TAXATION

The Road Fund Licence for Cyclemaster costs 17/6d. a year.
A Driving Licence costs 5/- a year.

INSURANCE

Full-insurance cover is 32/6d. a year.

LEARNING

If you can cycle it will take you five minutes to learn to use the controls.

There are over 40,000 Cyclemasters on the road and hundreds of testimonial letters have been received from owners.
A booklet reprinting some of these is available on request.

MECHANICAL DETAILS

The Cyclemaster drives through chains, and does not wear out tyres through friction. No reinforcement of the cycle is necessary.

FITTING & MAINTENANCE

Your dealer will fit a Cyclemaster wheel to your own machine. You can pedal it until you feel thoroughly at home. Details of any slight attention which the Cyclemaster may require are given in a simple-to-understand instruction book.

SERVICE

The Cyclemaster has this great advantage over cars and motor cycles—that in the unlikely event of trouble you can always use it as a pedal cycle. There are Cyclemaster dealers all over the British Isles, to give you immediate service if required.

SEE HOW IT WORKS

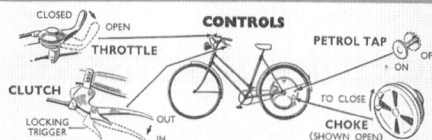

Cylinder remains stationary

Piston goes up and down

3-bearing crankshaft revolves

Chain drive to clutch

Big clutch sprocket receives drive

Chain from pedals

Wheel drum revolves

Main sprocket

Chain drive to main sprocket

Small clutch sprocket transmits drive

This much simplified diagram explains how the Cyclemaster engine works, but cannot show the many engineering features which make it the only sensible form of power-assisted cycling.

A detailed specification and illustrations of some of these features appear overleaf, and below is a diagrammatic layout of the simple controls, which all can learn to use in a minute or two.

CONTROLS

CLOSED / OPEN

THROTTLE

CLUTCH

LOCKING TRIGGER OUT / IN

PETROL TAP OFF / ON

TO CLOSE

CHOKE (SHOWN OPEN)

In use, the Cyclemaster appeared to produce the performance claimed for it in the manufacturer's publicity, judging by an advertisement placed in *The Motor Cycle* magazine, March 1951. This included *"sample extracts from hundreds of testimonials received"* quoting the following eulogies:

- *"The best investment of my life"*   *Huntingdon*
- *"I would not like to be without it"*   *Warwick*
- *"No praise too high for this little marvel"*   *Belfast*
- *"A masterpiece of Design"*   *Bristol*
- *"The finest auxiliary made"*   *Leicester*
- *"Makes light work of long hills"*   *Stockton-on-Tees*
- *"A grand asset to my business"*   *Bolton*
- *"Hills prove no obstacle to our tandem"*   *Peckham*
- *"Has become a Utility vehicle for the whole family"*   *Letchworth*

By 1952 however it was becoming apparent that the Cyclemaster's limited capacity of 25.7cc, and hence power output, was inadequate for many users. So, on 11th September of that year, *The Motor Cycle* published a road-test of a new model, now of 32cc capacity, which started from wheel number 73501. This was achieved by boring out the cylinder to 36mm (from 32mm), *"with the object of stepping up the power output without increase of piston speed"*. At the same time another improvement was made: lighting coils were now incorporated within the Wico-Pacy flywheel magneto. The thought that riders could now take advantage of increased power at night, their way illuminated by whatever feeble battery or dynamo lights the cycle carried, must have drawn the manufacturer's attention to the potential dangers of such situations!

At any rate, *The Motor Cycle* found *"the built-in lighting set is exceptionally good"* and *"at half-throttle speeds the light was strong enough to maintain daytime averages"* and the rear light provided a *"good warning glow"*. Road test fuel consumption was found to be 208mpg for *"steady country riding"*, dropping to 148mpg in town.

The larger capacity engine was found to allow tackling of 1 in 25 inclines with only *"the lightest of pedal assistance"* (LPA has over the years become a much loved technical term amongst the cyclemotoring fraternity). Price of a Cyclemaster had now increased to £27.10s.0d and outward appearance had also changed, from black to polychromatic grey.

The increased bore size of 36mm provided a larger bearing surface for the piston and was expected to extend the working life of this last. Despite improved acceleration up to 18mph, no noticeable change in fuel consumption was found. Further improvement came from Wico-Pacy, the Bantamag magneto being replaced by a Migemag 90 Mk1 with a machine-wound high tension ignition coil giving 50% more output than before and a better means of attaching the HT lead to the coil. The contact-breaker assembly was moved further away from the crankshaft bearing *"so that the magneto will not be affected by any slight oil-leak"*, which leads one to believe that this had probably happened in the past.

On September 19th, 1952, *Motor Cycle & Cycle Trader* magazine expounded further on changes made to the Cyclemaster, not only to the machine itself but also to the Company's sales and service departments. By this date Cyclemaster was claiming to have sold over 65,000 units and what had been a comparatively small company found itself in the happy position of needing to expand greatly in order to handle demand.

(Motor Cycle &
Cycle Trader
1952)

TUBULAR DISPLAY STAND which is now being circulated to dealers by Cyclemaster, Ltd.

In an interview with the *Trader,* Mr A F Palmer Phillips, a director of the Cyclemaster company, stated that they already had over 200 main distributors who served a further 800 agents. A new distributor sales aid was offered on loan or for purchase, a superb sectioned Cyclemaster unit in a tubular display stand (above) to entice new prospects once they were in the show-room.

Mr Palmer Phillips also mentioned the existence of a prototype stationary engine evolved from the Cyclemaster, which had a vertical exhaust and a three-pint fuel tank. Apparently one outstanding feature of this engine was the *"relative absence of vibration"*, but little seems to have come of the project. This must have been the Dutch-developed Type M16 or LandMaster derivative, which never seems to have been sold in anything but minute quantities.

Earlier in 1952 the Cyclemaster company took over much larger premises at 204-206 Queenstown Road, Battersea, London SW8 in order to establish a comprehensive spares and service depot. Total area of this new depot was 7,000 square feet, with more space to come once planning permission to erect additional buildings on the site had been obtained. Before the move took place, turn-around time for overhauling and testing wheels was between seven and ten days, after the move this was expected to be reduced to three to five days.

23

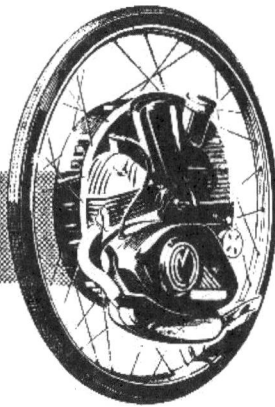

Cyclemaster believed in personal attention to the customer; a single fitter was responsible for the processes of dismantling, fitting replacement parts, reassembly and running on the test-bed of the customer's unit that had been sent to Queenstown Road for attention.

Power and Pedal magazine printed a road test report in February 1953 on the 32cc Cyclemaster to publicise the 100,000[th] wheel unit produced in December 1952.

THE HUNDRED THOUSANDTH WHEEL

The 100,000th Cyclemaster wheel unit came off the assembly line at the E.M.I. Factory at Hayes, Middlesex, in December, 1952.

In the picture are Sir Alexander Aikman, Chairman of E.M.I. and three directors of Cyclemaster, Ltd., Mr. Calcot Reilly, Mr. Palmer Phillips and Mr. J. D. Mc Gregor.

Manufacture of the Cyclemaster commenced in September, 1950

The road-test machine was a Mercury cycle[*], designed specially for use with a Cyclemaster and finished in the same polychromatic grey colour. *Power & Pedal* found an *"unexpectedly large increase in power that has resulted from the slightly greater cylinder capacity"* and, with the aid of a Smiths speedometer, clocked a sustained speed of 23mph on the flat. They found the machine smoother and less noisy at a steady 18 to 20mph. With *"wind astern or down a steady grade"* a Cyclemaster was capable of nearly 30mph without apparent stress or strain but *"speeds of this sort are not really in the cyclemotor world and the tests were made purely to check (and wonder at) the ability of the engine to rev"*. Some criticism was however levelled at a few aspects. Exhaust noise (probably due to restricted silencer dimensions within the wheel hub) was deemed excessive when running at wide throttle openings but *Power & Pedal* pointed out that the *"problem of silencing is one for the Trade as a whole to tackle and the Cyclemaster is no worse than average"*. Another noise source was found to be general mechanical racket amplified by the steel rear hub shell, but the fact that the unit was below and behind the rider made it *"seem unobtrusive from the saddle"*, which by the way was *"a large, soft Lycett"*. Further black marks were applied to the very irritating need, when starting from cold with the choke on, to dismount and return the choke to the open position after 50 yards or so. Finally, the Coaster-type rear brake which was *"not a real stopper even when the rider's whole weight was used on the pedal. It did, however, provide some useful slowing down on hills and showed no signs of fade through overheating"*.

In summing up, *Power & Pedal* found the Cyclemaster to be *"a sound, high performance specimen of the attachment unit"*. They thought it looked good, had a real clutch, the chain drive avoided any special consideration of tyres (such as would be necessary with roller-drive) and it provided excellent, reliable personal transport.

---

[*] Mercury Industries (Birmingham) Ltd., makers of the Mercury cycle, offered its 22 inch frame in either diamond or open pattern but supplied it with only the front stirrup brake, as a Cyclemaster by this time was fitted with a built-in coaster rear brake. Wheels were 1¾ inch fitted with 2 inch tyres. Number-plates, pump & licence holder were all included in the £13.19s.0d price.

Renno's cyclemotor dealers ran a series of unusual & eye-catching advertisements for the Cyclemaster in the motor cycling press, a sample of which is seen below. Note that Renno's also advertised the Mercury cycle, *"Built for the Job",* that was tested by *Power & Pedal* in conjunction with a Cyclemaster unit in February 1953.

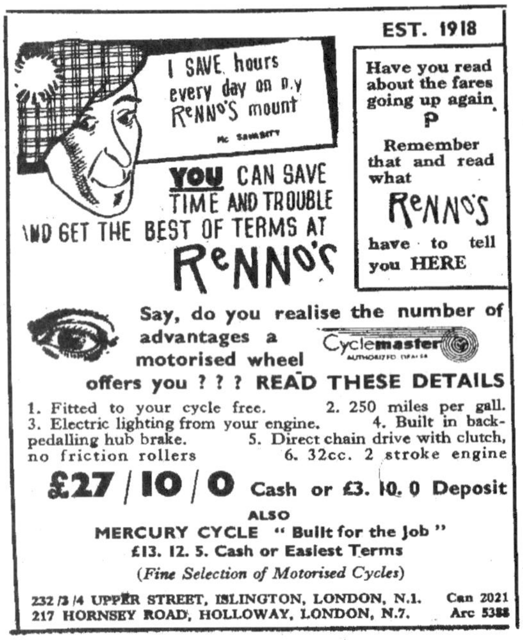

Cyclemasters were to earn an enviable reputation for reliability over the years, however, servicing was as important as build quality, especially if the machine was to be used as every-day transport. Most Cyclemasters were, so the factory Service Department issued bulletins covering routine items that could be tackled by an owner as per a few examples reproduced below:

- Clutch adjustment needs regular attention; the operating lever should have a quarter inch play at the tip before pressure from the clutch springs is felt.

- Oil level in the clutch chamber needs to be checked by inserting a screwdriver blade to a depth of ¾" through the "CM" cover and filler plug holes, oil should just show on the tip. If not, SAE140 oil should be added accordingly.

- Contact breaker points need to be set at 0.015" for both Bantamag and Series 90 magnetos, though up to a maximum of 0.018" is permissible. Spark-plug electrodes require a separation of 0.018" to 0.020"

- The secondary drive chain (from clutch shaft to wheel drum) should have not more than a half-inch free-play.

- The air-cleaner element should be rinsed in petrol, dried, then a little engine oil squeezed in to trap dust particles.

The factory also produced a small booklet entitled "Just in Case", given to customers on purchasing a Cyclemaster, with the advice "slip this into your wallet or handbag". It contained basic trouble-shooting information should a customer's engine stop or refuse to start.

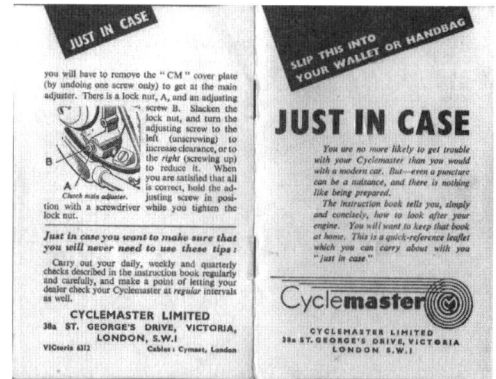

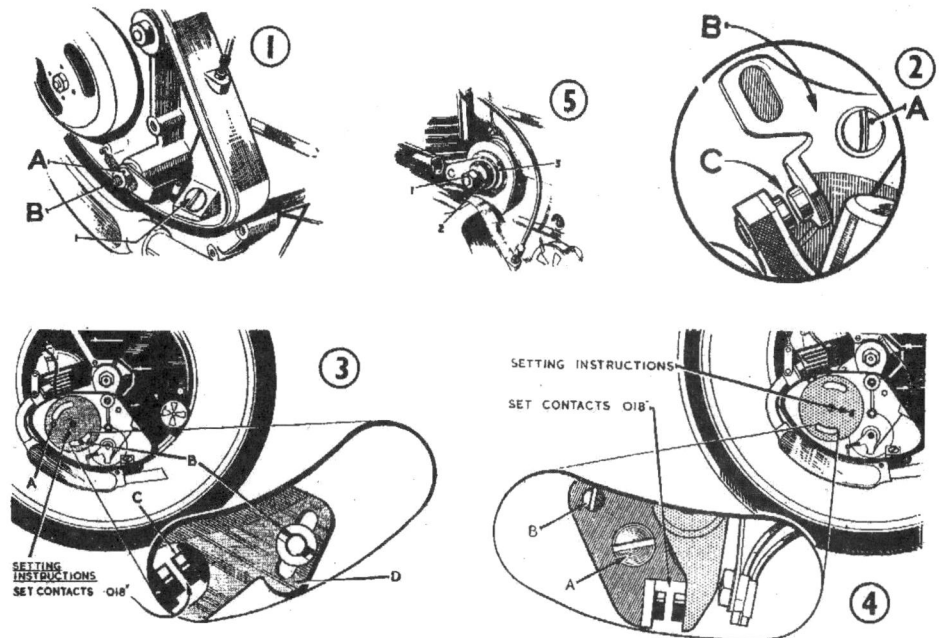

Cyclemaster manual

1); adjuster screw A unscrew to increase free-play, locknut is B.

2); Bantamag contact breaker, lockscrew is A, baseplate B, contacts C.

3); Series 90 magneto contact breaker, both locknuts A & B have to be slackened before baseplate D is moved.

4); Later Wipac series, slacken screw A, turn screw B to adjust contacts. Flywheel must be in position shown in illustration 4.

5); Secondary chain adjustment, slacken nut 1, slacken locknut 2, move eccentric 3 to adjust, retighten nut 1 and locknut 2.

Reliability was not the strongest suit of many a cyclemotor but the picture and extract from a press article below (written by the rider) proves just how robust a Cyclemaster was. Very diplomatically, no manufacturer's name is mentioned, though it very obviously is a Cyclemaster

Mr R C Button poses proudly with his *"power assisted pedal cycle of small capacity"*. He lived in Reading and travelled to Camborne, not far short of St.Ives, Cornwall, covering a total of 240 miles in 16 hours at a cost of 5 shillings.

From his uniform, he was either a bus driver or conductor but presumably wore more suitable attire for his journey.

This 'travel opportunity' seems to have come about as a result of Mr Button's determination to use his Cyclemaster to go on holiday, despite his workmates at the bus garage questioning its reliability on such a trek. He set off at 5:30am and travelled to Andover, where he picked up the A30, which then took him the entire length of his journey. His first refuelling stop occurred near Salisbury after 3 hours and 50 or so miles, when he filled up with one quart of mixture, the second near Chard at 12:35. He also took this opportunity to send a telegram home to let his family know *"so far, so good"* and commented on the steepness of a hill outside Chard with a 1 in 7 gradient over 1½ miles, causing him to walk for the first time.

The article concludes with comments about *"having to stop for tea and petrol"* still with 80 miles to cover, *"twists all the way until you get to Indian Queens at Gossmoor"* and finally *"I arrived at Camborne at 9.25pm., having been some 16 hours on the road without experiencing any trouble at all, not even a miss. Now, after having covered 240 miles, I had every confidence in doing the return journey in less time"*. Praise indeed.

Power and Pedal magazine continued to publish readers' experiences with Cyclemasters over the years. Another article, entitled *"Daily Work Routine with a Cyclemaster"*, published in February 1954, was written by *"a municipal officer controlling a number of employees scattered over a Borough of over 7000 acres"*. This owner put Cyclemaster number 70171 on the road *"at 5pm on 25th June 1952"*, fitted to a Raleigh cycle. Initially he had starting problems associated with ignition timing, causing the plug to need cleaning 24 times in one day, but this was soon rectified. Decokes were carried out at 1,300 and 2,200 miles but then he discovered a 2-stroke oil called TSL … which, by the way, was short for Two Stroke Lubricant.

(Could Slip Products by any chance be the same people who sold us that thick grey Molybdenum Disulphide muck we all poured into our clapped-out old banger engines back in the 1960s: Moly-Slip? Did it ever work?)

The above advert's testimonial says it all, over 5,000 miles without a decoke, though the exhaust port was reamed out every 500 miles or so using *"a small screwdriver with the piston at bottom dead centre and then blowing the carbon by running the engine for a few seconds before restoring the exhaust pipe ... the carbon is soft and easily comes out"*. Do not try this at home, dear readers. A further period recommendation came from the Invalid Tricycle Association's Sussex Newsheet, which found similar mileages possible between decokes and noted that TSL was *"the same consistency as olive oil at 70 degrees"* (Fahrenheit, of course, none of that Continental Centigrade business).

An interesting insight into 1950s cyclemotor riderwear is also provided by the same author:

"In winter I am attired in a Harris Tweed overcoat which is on the long side, double texture leggings and cap. The last two items are easily slipped off and left on the machine when visiting people. Gauntlet gloves - these stop a draught up the sleeves - and I always carry for wet weather an ex-army brown oilskin ... which goes over the overcoat in winter or raincoat in summer. Should the day be really bad I wear rubber boots and a pair of shortened leggings."

The anonymous writer concluded with an extract from his log-book, which showed that the machine had been on the road for 270 days in a twelve-month period, averaging 29.85 miles per day, apart from *"Sundays, Holidays & Illnesses"*, giving an annual total of 8,059 miles.

One aspect of high-mileage Cyclemaster usage that did become a cause for concern was the durability of the original fitment tyres. A Cyclemaster wheel was sold complete with a tyre, though company advertising never specified which make would normally have been supplied and it has proved impossible to identify from period photos. According to several readers' reports printed in the correspondence columns of *Motor Cycling* and *Power & Pedal*, to quote one typical comment, *"the walls could not take it"*. The legend *"inflate hard"* as found on standard-issue tyre side walls was *"an indication that the tyre is not up to the job"*. Various solutions were proposed, none of which entailed replacing the defunct tyre with another from the same source! One reader wrote of a 26×1½in Michelin Roadster which had *"done 9,000 miles without any trouble at 22psi ... and looks good for another 9,000 miles"*.

Perhaps the most unusual of all cyclemotorists using a Cyclemaster as motive power for his travels must have been a true Mad Dog and Englishman, Bill Greaves. Sadly, little is known of Mr Greaves's exploits in touring the world the hard way other than a photo printed below, taken in New Zealand. Mr Greaves had by then covered some 12,000 miles with his twin Cyclemaster engined cycle and camping-trailer, including tours of Jamaica and Australia. He must have grown to heartily dislike performing the task of dismounting to open the chokes on two motors on warm-up. The Yeti-scalp headgear is admirable.

The Earl's Court Motor Cycle Show opened in December 1954 to exhibit an ever-growing range of cyclemotors to the British public. Nearly a decade after the end of World War II, increasingly affluent and experienced riders were becoming more demanding and less inclined to tolerate unreliability or discomfort from their mounts. Many new, improved and innovative designs of cyclemotor were thus on offer from various manufacturers.

By 1954, Cyclemaster was in the enviable position of making and selling Britain's most successful clip-on cyclemotor engine unit but was also evidently thinking about the future. It would not have escaped its notice that sales of complete machines, designed and built with frame, running gear and motive power as a homogenous whole, were rapidly overtaking add-on engines for push-bikes. Thus was born the new Cyclemate, fruit of a collaboration between Norman & Cyclemaster and incorporating motive power from the well proven Cyclemaster engine unit. More information on this later in the chapter, but meantime further improvements were also being made to *"The Magic Wheel That Wings Your Heel"*.

No doubt mindful of frequent complaints about the inconvenience of dismounting in order to open the choke of a warmed-up engine, Cyclemaster announced the fitting of a BEC carburettor, developed by the Bletchley Engineering Co Ltd, which was *"specially designed for this machine and incorporating a starting device that needs no external de-control"*. Hooray. The price still remained at £27.10s.0d. In order to squeeze a little more money from their customers' pockets, Cyclemaster now launched itself into the consumables market (familiar to all of us living in the 21st century in the guise of computer printer ink cartridges, for instance; that's where the real profit is) and began advertising its own brand of 2-stroke engine oil.

Cyclemaster had been taking notice of other oil suppliers' adverts, such as TSL from Slip Products. TSL oil was sold for 5/9d a quart.

Thankfully, claims for this two-stroke oil are limited to how good the quality is, not the more usual issuing of dire warnings. These often implied that, unless a manufacturer's own branded lubricants were used, warranties became void, engines would wear out and then explode. It would all be the owner's fault.

More practically, better refined oils were less inclined to coke up an engine, thus the chore of decarbonising became a less frequent **occurrence**.

During the course of 1955, several structural changes took place within the company. Firstly, Cyclemaster Ltd separated from EMI, its manufacturer and took on production itself. Both administration and manufacturing were now grouped together and transferred to a new location,

Tudor Works in Chertsey Road, Byfleet, Weybridge, Surrey. The Cyclemaster Sales Office became something of an orphan, moving from leafy Surrey back to London to 154 Shepherds Bush Road in early 1956, only to close and move back to the Tudor Works again in August 1957.

Sales successes achieved by Cyclemaster in particular and the industry as a whole during the early 1950s was admirable, given the economic and manufacturing constraints which still applied in that period. Unfortunately, such visible success and corresponding growth in cyclemotor-related publications, accessories, parts, clothing, etc, advertising this fact awakened the unwelcome attention of that most feared of predators - the Chancellor of the Exchequer.

By early 1955 the British political landscape was changing fast: Churchill had finally resigned on April 5th at age 81, to be succeeded by his anointed successor, Anthony Eden, on April 22nd. The tight fist of R A Butler (popularly known as Rab Butler) had been at the helm of the Treasury since 1951 and would continue to be until he in turn was succeeded by Maurice Harold Macmillan at the end of 1955.

Chancellors of all political persuasions keep the hunting of new revenue-generating fields high on their agenda. It had not escaped Rab Butler's notice (nor that of his feared pack of hounds, the Treasury Civil Servants) that usage of motor-assisted bicycles and cyclemotors had increased dramatically in a few years and they were now a sitting target for some new taxation. Until March 1955 a cyclemotor engine, such as a Cyclemaster unit, was classified as a bicycle accessory and exempt from Purchase Tax (PT), though imported units were charged an Import Duty rated at 33⅓%. Then came Budget Day.

The Chancellor announced that henceforth cyclemotor units would be liable for Purchase Tax at 25%. Cries of great indignation arose from the specialist press, especially as Mr Butler had simultaneously announced a reduction of 25% in PT on fur coats, adding insult to pecuniary injury. *"Not only a piece of political ineptitude, it was a legislative act that bordered on the immoral"* thundered *Power & Pedal* in its editorial, adding *"the cyclemotor can mean an aid to efficiency and an end to drudgery. This is the instrument that the Government chooses to tax instead of fur coats and paper table decorations"*.

The main reason given for applying tax to cyclemotor units was to *"correct an anomaly"* which it might have done, but at the same time it created another, more serious one for imported cyclemotors. They were now classified with autocycles for taxation purposes and therefore subject to Purchase Tax, but they then should have come under the correspondingly lesser import duty rate of 22½%.

Her Majesty's Customs & Excise, with their usual flexibility, refused to alter the existing duty rate of 33⅓% on imported machines on the grounds that it *"would be difficult"*. No lack of trying there, then. The purchaser of an imported cyclemotor paid 33⅓% duty on the landed value and then 25% PT on top of that duty-paid price, a tax on a tax in fact. As is usual in these cases, all reasoned objections fell on deaf ears and no progress was made toward a sensible compromise, but then, it was such a good way of ensuring the decline of imports.

Cyclemaster had immediately to revise its pricing to take into account the application of Purchase Tax and published a new figure of £32.13s.11d in April 1955, achieved by dropping the pre-tax price to £26.8s. This was further reduced to £29.19s.2d, but by Earls Court time in November it had gone back up to £33.18s.3d.

The incorporation of *The Scooter* magazine into *Power & Pedal* in 1955 and the increasingly frequent appearance of adverts for new, complete cyclemotors must have chilled the blood of many a clip-on cyclemotor manufacturer. The days of the crude, old-fashioned motor-assisted push-bike were visibly numbered, the Cyclemaster amongst them. Customers were becoming relatively affluent, they were beginning to want increased comfort and weather protection, more power and sophistication from their cyclemotor ... or a Ford Popular if possible.

In truth, the era of clip-on cyclemotor engines was only ever going to be short-lived. Their demise was ensured by a torrent of new machines, many from the reconstructed European factories that were beneficiaries of American dollar largesse, which enabled them to re-equip with modern machine-tools and technology. The more liberal Continental legislation relating to cyclemotors also helped, whereas British manufacturers were still hobbled by restrictive, hidebound Nanny-state laws, scarce raw materials and obsolete, worn-out pre-war production machinery.

One newly-advertised cyclemotor representing the new wave that would sound the post-WW2 clip-on cyclemotor's death-knell was the Mobylette. That this was introduced by a French company, Motobécane, from a country the Allies had saved only 10 years earlier, just rubbed salt into the wounds.

MOTOBÉCANE   *Mobylette*

Motobécane, an industrial giant based at rue Lesault, Pantin, had been producing a wide range of motor cycles since 1922 (as well as bicycles) and was France's biggest manufacturer. Its master-stroke was to create the first simple, reliable, easy to use *cyclomoteur* that the general public was waiting for.

The Mobylette was an object lesson in how to design an integrated motor and frame combination from scratch, without compromises and hence with immeasurably better road-manners than those of a push-bike fitted with a clip-on cyclemotor engine unit. The AV3 was first seen at the Paris Salon in October 1949 and even then only just, as the display was concentrated on 125cc and 175cc motor cycles. The AV3 was tucked away behind a stand office. The rest is history.

Cyclemaster, together with many other British manufacturers, was well aware of how strong the European competition was becoming. The company probably did not have sufficient finance or factory space to develop its own frame and running gear, so collaboration with an existing cycle manufacturer was logical.

For the Cyclemate, Norman Cycles of Beaver Rd, Ashford, Kent was chosen, a company with roots going back to 1918. Originally started as a cycle repair business in Castle Street, Norman expanded mightily from the 1930s to early 1960s and at the height of its success was producing up to 5,000 bicycles, 600 mopeds and 120 motor cycles every week. Cyclemaster had already had dealings with Norman: Norman produced a special bicycle for the Cyclemaster unit (like the Mercury) and Cyclemaster had promoted this cycle via advertising.

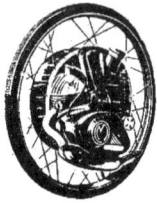

Cyclemaster continued to produce its rear-wheel power unit but sales slid inevitably into gradual decline as more and more customers wanted and could afford a better, one piece machine. Thus a new model, the Cyclemate from Cyclemaster Ltd. began appearing in the same adverts and the tax-inclusive price comparison was instructive: Cyclemaster £32.13s.11d, Cyclemate £48.19s.8d. Not a huge amount extra to pay for a factory-fresh autocycle.

Norman merged with Raleigh in 1960 and though the Norman marque continued beyond that date it was the Raleigh brand that most effort went into. There was also an earlier connection between EMI and Norman, the latter company had taken over production of the Rudge autocycle from EMI during World War II.

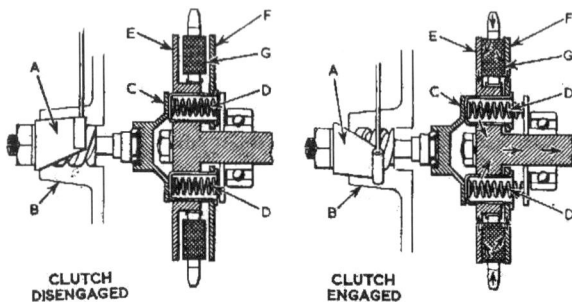

CLUTCH DISENGAGED   CLUTCH ENGAGED

SECTION THROUGH CYCLEMATE CLUTCH.

A. Clutch-operating mechanism.
B. Section of casting.
C. Clutch-release plate.
D. Clutch springs.

E, F. Clutch plates.
G. Plate with cork segments which transmit the drive.

Clutch operation on the Cyclemate/Cyclemaster engine was much more sophisticated than the average crank-and-pushrod affair fitted to most other units with a clutch. A coarse-pitch large diameter threaded sleeve rotated within a casting, smoothly and quickly engaging or disengaging the drive as required.

Power & Pedal, in its issue of December 1954, printed a survey of machines appearing at the Earls Court Show. Its opinion was *"likely to be even more successful on the market … a new built-for-the-job machine called the Cyclemate. The engine, primary chain and clutch are those of the Cyclemaster wheel but positioned in front of the bracket in the currently accepted autocycle fashion on a cycle specially designed for it. Twin top tubes swing from the steering head to rear hub of an otherwise conventional looking cycle frame … wide domed guards, carrier, number-plates, lighting set and 5-pint fuel tank … are all built in as part of the design. Hub brakes are fitted to both wheels … 2 inch tyres are fitted to 26"×1¾" wheels and the finish is an attractive green enamel on a rustproofed base."*

Despite its new baby, Cyclemaster Ltd continued to promote the *Magic Wheel* in the hope of squeezing out as many sales as could be garnered before the inevitable disappearance of clip-on engine units.

New markets were continually being sought by Cyclemaster in order to prolong production a little longer, as per the advert reproduced below, but this was straws-in-the-wind stuff and made little difference to the by then serious decline in *Magic Wheel* sales. Cyclemaster just had to pray that the Cyclemate would be as successful.

From August 1957 Planloc Engineering took over manufacture for a while but by 1960 Cyclemaster had been bought by Britax (London) Ltd, who also sold the Ducati Cucciolo. Production remained at Byfleet, though the Tudor Works had been renamed Proctor Works, but it was virtually all over for clip-on units. Demand had all but disappeared and only the Power Pak and Itom still survived as competitors by that date.

The final curtain fell on the Cyclemaster in 1961 after an honourable career and a fruitful one for the manufacturer, who by the end had produced some 181,000 units, a truly impressive total. Many owners graduated on to much better light autocycles but would always retain fond memories of their faithful, big-hearted little Cyclemaster, though still only of 32cc, it had always seemed able to perform like a 50cc competitor.

NORMAN Cyclemate

In its introduction to the Cyclemate, *Power & Pedal* wrote *"We have recently had the opportunity of visiting the new works of the Cyclemaster Company at Byfleet and of testing there an early number of the new Cyclemate autocycle. The engine and primary drive assembly of the new machines are practically identical with those of the wheel unit so that spares and service are already laid on throughout the country. The performance, therefore, is the same so far as speed and power are concerned. The handling of the machine, however, is very different from that of any cycle with attachment engine … Balance is perfect, steering and braking first class and comfort exceptional. This last is to a great measure due to the 2 inch balloon tyres which are designed to run at moderate pressures and provide not only rider comfort but also add to the road-holding and general handling qualities of the machine as a whole."*

"Hand-operated Phillips hub brakes fore and aft stop the machine quickly and smoothly either alone or together. The clutch is light and positive in action and the twist-grip throttle control has a ... range of movement that is comfortable ... Purring smoothly at its 22mph maximum, turning at walking pace in narrow circles or careering around over rough tracks and grassland, the Cyclemate inspired complete confidence in handling and seemed perfectly at home. It has a range of performance that will satisfy the needs of 80% of Britain's potential cyclemotorists and [is] a fine beginning to the light autocycle industry of Britain."

The magazine was evidently impressed by the new machine and also expressed high hopes that the 1955 Cyclemate could spearhead a new wave of British-origin autocycles, created to fend off a looming threat from European manufacturers. These benefited from more modern plant, more helpful legislation and less hide-bound thinking. They were hindered in their penetration of the British market only by a paper-thin wall of unfavourable Excise duties which, as massive production volumes on European home markets drove down costs, would eventually prove ineffectual against the rising tide.

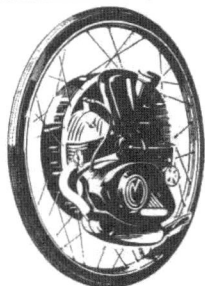

There is no denying that the Cyclemate was as good an autocycle as could be made in Britain in the mid-1950s with the facilities that were available. It combined the engineering skills of two experienced and successful manufacturers in an attempt to counterbalance the flow of imported Continental machines and declining public demand for the relatively crude clip-on units with an up-to-date British competitor. There was also an element of fear; both Cyclemaster Ltd and Norman Cycles Ltd were well aware that rapidly improving public fortunes, ten years after the end of World War II, meant their main market was moving upward fast and buying affordable small saloon cars instead of relying on motorised push-bikes. This upward movement left clip-on unit manufacturers with a rump market of less-fortunate customers who, for whatever reasons, were not able to climb the prosperity ladder so quickly. Cost was still King in the field.

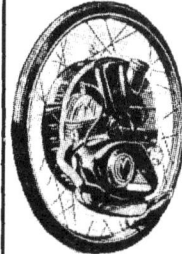

Sadly for Cyclemaster and Norman it was already too late; after an initial upward surge, the Cyclemate sales chart curve went flat, then declined steadily. The company tried a different tack, importing and distributing the excellent Dutch-built Berini autocycle which, in a nice twist of fate, was manufactured by NV Pluvier Motorenfabriek, originators of the DKW RadMeister-cum-Cyclemaster concept way back in 1946. This project had limited success, despite the Berini being a real high-performance integrated machine with no less than 1.8bhp output.

By late 1955 Cyclemaster planned to expand its range even further upward to take in the lower end of the popular scooter market. Unfortunately, instead of importing and selling an existing model it decided to do it the hard way and design and build its own machine from scratch: the Piatti *"All British Made Scooter"*.

The Scooter

EVERYBODY'S LOOKING AT *Piatti*
THE NEW 125 c.c.
The all-British made scooter

£104·10
Plus £25-1-7 P.T.

Including spare wheel, dual-seat, speedometer and luggage carrier.

Brilliantly new, brilliantly different—and its all-British made. The PIATTI is bound to be the centre of attraction wherever it goes.

For fully illustrated colour leaflet write to
CYCLEMASTER LIMITED
Sales Dept., 154 Shepherds Bush Rd. London, W.6

"The introduction of a new British built scooter would be an event of major interest itself, but in the case of the Piatti the interest is heightened by the originality of the design and the fact that it is produced by a firm which has already established a great reputation as a pioneer in the field of Cyclemotors. Cyclemaster Ltd have foreseen the logical development of this form of transport and the new scooter is created to meet the demands of this rising market". (The Scooter, August 1956)

40

A full review of the Piatti scooter would be out of place in this, a cyclemotor-oriented book, but a few facts are of particular interest. Cyclemaster Ltd engaged the services of one of the longest-established designers around, none other than Vincenti Piatti - creator of the hugely successful Mini-Motor clip-on unit amongst other things, to draw up its new scooter. The design was cutting-edge in many respects, a full monocoque pressed-steel frame, all machinery, electrics and suspension enclosed within the cigar-shaped frame-cum-body, cable-operated centre-stand and 3-stage rear suspension by tension spring to mention a few. The Piatti was also very low and rather small, carrying a rider and passenger rather swamped the machine. It was underpowered and undergeared, despite a 125cc engine, and very noisy, no doubt due to the amplification afforded by the bath-shaped frame. It was also spectacularly ugly and all the advanced technology in the world could not redeem this unfortunate feature. Sales never really took off.

Below, we offer you a picture of 1953's ideal family transport, a Mercury pillion cycle (designed for use with a Cyclemaster) and Trinder sidecar for the kiddies.

THREE-SEATER

THE new two seater *Mercury* cycle designed for use with the *Cyclemaster* engine has an interesting frame with twin curved top and seat tubes in one and a built-on carrier to support the pillion seat.

A.C.U. Trial at Wembley last April one of these machines appeared complete with sidecar and showed its paces, passengers up, to create much interest among the competitors and spectators.

The sidecar as shewn in this picture is a *Trinder* and we understand that the outfit is now available to order.

Postscript

The original DKW RadMeister design rootstock was very prolific and gave birth to several evolutions in different European countries. One was developed and manufactured in Britain as the Cyclemaster, described in the story we have just detailed, and another in Holland, where numerous differences to the UK version were apparent. What has now become known as the Dutch Cyclemaster was a very early version which, though it retained Bantamag ignition and an Amal carburettor, had a magneto cover with the CM logo of curved lines but no "Cyclemaster - Made in England" plate or back-pedal hub brake. The fuel tank had radial ribs and the side-cover two holes, for the fuel tap and filter.

One year after introduction, cylinder capacity went up to 32cc from 25.7cc, just as in the UK version, but the magneto cover now had a CM logo with straight lines and a "Cyclemaster - Made in England" badge.

A third variant evolved from the Dutch Cyclemaster via the German bicycle manufacturer Rabeneick, who got involved by supplying special cycle frames to the Dutch for fitment of Cyclemaster units. In 1952 Rabeneick announced its own version of the Cyclemaster, using the same frame originally sold to Holland but fitted with German-manufactured headlamp, rear lamp, wheels and saddle, these items being left off Dutch market frames in favour of locally produced equivalents. Engine capacity was 32cc, the magneto cover had straight lines, a "Made in Germany" badge and a Rabeneick logo replaced the British & Dutch "CM". Inside the magneto cover was a Bosch ignition system, though some German Cyclemasters also appeared with Wipac ignition and a corresponding cover with a "CM" logo. Only one hole was necessary on the side cover for the fuel tap; Rabeneick had replaced the Amal or BEC carb with a floatless Meco that had a filter incorporated. As an additional refinement, the silencer side-cover was removable to facilitate decarbonising. Rabeneick numbered its model the M14, just as the Dutch had, and also sold it under the brand name Taxi.

In an amusing cyclical symmetry, Rabeneick's Taxi version of the RadMeister/Cyclemaster was also produced under licence by Motosacoche in Geneva, Switzerland. Henri and Armand Dufaux had practically invented the clip-on cyclemotor engine with their *Motosacoche* of 1905 (see Preface for details) and here they were, fifty years later, going down the same old road again.

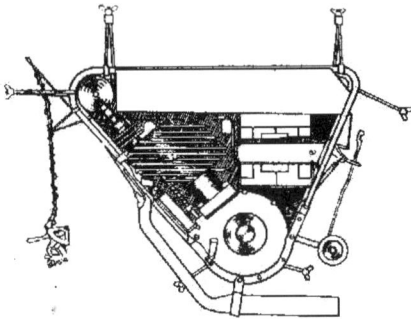

Yet another variant of the Cyclemaster was made in the Peoples Republic of China by the massive state-owned Flying Pigeon Cycle Works, though this was a straight pirated rip-off, not a licensed manufacturing agreement with Interpro.

Other Dutch progeny of the Cyclemaster & Berini engine family included the type M15 Boatmaster, suitable for powering small craft, and the ephemeral type M16 Landmaster, a very small stationary engine that, possibly because of this fact, is very rare indeed.

Little did DKW's designers suspect how successful their little cyclemotor engine would become post-war.

The Trojan Mini-Motor brought a revolution to power-assisted cycling when first announced on the British clip-on cyclemotor market in 1947, though the original design, inevitably, came from Europe. In fact, the basic Mini-Motor engine unit as first conceived in 1946 was to be a small, simple two-stroke industrial motor capable of driving portable lathes at the Bugatti factory in Molsheim, located in Alsace, south-eastern France. Vincenti Piatti was the engineer responsible for creating the *Mini-Motore* and it was he who also saw potential for adapting it to become a clip-on cyclemotor engine. The fact that his design of the industrial Mini-Motor was one of extreme simplicity (thus enabling the same basic unit to be readily adapted to many uses, as indeed it was) helped enormously in this task.

In Vincenti Piatti's native Italy immediately after the end of WW2 the demand for affordable motorised personal transport was huge, though road fuel of any kind was of appalling quality, expensive and scarce. An uncomplicated, cheap to produce and economical two-stroke cyclemotor engine had to be an excellent solution to most of these problems. The *Mini-Motore* therefore entered production in Italy and was, as expected, a great success.

That the Mini-Motor became such a success on the British market was down to a remarkable man and his foresight. George Murray Denton was on holiday in Switzerland in 1948 when by coincidence he saw his first *Mini Motore* in action. *"I followed a cyclist who not only free-wheeled downhill but shot uphill with no loss of speed and with only occasional pedalling. There was a device behind the saddle which emitted blue smoke and a noise like a bored-out wasp"*. On his return to England, George Denton carried out some research and discovered that Trojan in Croydon had taken out a licence and was already manufacturing and selling the Trojan Mini-Motor on the UK market.

Trojan was not strictly speaking the first British company to become interested in producing and selling the *Mini-Motore,* as an item published in *The Motor Cycle* magazine of 11th November 1948 reveals. Under the heading *"Details of an Italian Unit to be Manufactured in Britain"*, a company named Mini-Motor (Great Britain) Ltd of 1 Newman Street, London W1 was said to be shortly starting production of *"an Italian auxiliary engine"*. *The Motor Cycle* was evidently interested by this development as in its 25th November issue it printed another article entitled *"Mini-Motors from Italy"*. This concerned the epic voyage of three British Hercules cycles fitted with Mini-Motors ridden from Milan, via Switzerland, Paris and Calais to London. Riders were *"V Piatti, the designer, M Coco, a technical artist and C Gabardi-Brocchi, a journalist"* who had travelled the 800-odd miles from Italy to demonstrate their machines on, of all places, Selfridge's roof. No mechanical troubles had been experienced and the longest distance covered in one day had been the 200-odd miles from Paris to Calais. However, in *The Motor Cycle*, 2nd June 1949 issue, it was revealed that *"controlling interest in the Mini-Motor Co. has been taken over by Trojan Ltd"*. This is where our story begins.

A digression is required here as it is interesting to cover some of Trojan's history up to the late 1940s, this being a most unusual company, which manufactured an eclectic range of motorised transport for over 50 years.

Trojan was founded around 1904 by one Leslie Hounsfield as a precision engineering concern, though the name Trojan did not appear until 1910, when the company was rebaptised. Mr Hounsfield realised, as many engineers did, that motor cars would become an enormous business and decided to join the fray. He spent some six years in developing prototypes of what he hoped would be a very simple to drive, inexpensive to maintain, cheap to buy car and one which was, by contemporary standards, entirely unconventional. The first 2-seater Trojan of 1922 was named the Utility and was built on a chassis which, according to Georgano, consisted of *"a flat steel box, to which was attached a roomy, if hideous, open four-seater body"*. Suspension was by long, soft, cantilever leaf-springs at each corner, these were needed as until 1929 solid tyres came as standard, though motorists with piles (not of money) could pay an extra £5 for pneumatics.

A typical mild Northern day for a 1924 Trojan

The engine was a horizontal two-stroke, four-cylinder unit producing only 10bhp, connected to a two-speed epicyclic gearbox *à la* Ford Model T (no double-declutching on a crash box here) and final drive by duplex chains to a differential-less solid rear axle. Such power as was developed came at very low engine speed and hence pulling-power was colossal. A Trojan's hill-climbing abilities and economy of use soon became legendary and the car acquired a loyal following, especially in Yorkshire where hills and parsimony were respectively plentiful and inborn. By 1925 the Trojan was the cheapest four-seater on the market at £125 and also the slowest. Front-wheel brakes were never fitted but evidently not required by either drivers or vehicle. The only comparable unconventional car of the time to have captured a sizeable, faithful market for many years would be the German Hanomag *Kommissbrot* ("Army loaf", as it was symmetrical front & rear) which during the Great Depression was sold with wicker bodywork. Not a bad idea; so far, no substitute has been found for hot-air balloon baskets, for instance. Wicker does creak a lot though.

A 5cwt van version of the Utility car, built on the same chassis and sold at the same price, became very popular as a light delivery vehicle and many companies ran large fleets, including Messrs Brooke Bond, the tea company.

From 1922 to 1928, all Trojan cars were manufactured by Leyland Motors Ltd of Kingston on Thames, since Trojan itself did not have the factory capacity. They were unlikely bedfellows as

Leyland manufactured trucks and the luxurious Leyland Eight car. However by 1928 Trojan had taken over complete control of car production in Croydon but the market had become more sophisticated and ever fewer of their primitive cars were being bought. A brief foray with a more conventional Trojan (still using the same 2-stroke engine, but at the rear driving forward, still by chains), the RE 10hp, came to nought. By 1937, car production had ceased.

Post-war, Trojan again entered the commercial vehicle market by designing a more conventional medium-sized van, still equipped with a 4-cylinder version of the old 2-stroke engine, but it was slow and thirsty so a 3-cylinder Perkins diesel was substituted. This proved more acceptable and production continued with limited success until 1960, when Peter Agg purchased the Croydon factory in order to assemble Lambretta scooters there.

Come 1962 Trojan embarked on something of a wild expansion programme in an attempt to make something that would sell and acquired the manufacturing rights to the German Heinkel bubble-car, producing its own version, the Trojan 200. However, in the early 1960s BMC's Mini swept all before it and the bubble-car market had quickly vanished. Nevertheless, Trojan managed to make 6000-odd before production ceased in 1965. Concurrently with its acquisition of the Heinkel licence Trojan also bought the Elva sports car company and began production of the GRP-bodied Elva Courier Mk IV, something of a departure for a company that had made its name with the Utility! Elva sports cars had their roots back in 1955 when Frank Nichols designed and supplied bodies and parts kits for his very competitive Elva (from the French *Elle va*, she goes) build-it-yourself sports cars. These were not subject to the dreaded Purchase Tax provided they were sold in component form, however, the Chancellor soon rectified this oversight and instantly put paid to nearly all of the many kit-car concerns which had blossomed in the fifties, including Elva. By 1969 this Trojan venture had ended too, a victim of progress and overwhelmed by cheap, mass produced sportscars like the Triumph Spitfire and Austin-Healey Sprite/MG Midget.

Trojan soldiered on for a few more years, making parts for the McLaren racing car concern, the company still exists to this day though the factory was sold in the 1970s

That was then and this is now, back to our subject of the Trojan Mini-Motor.

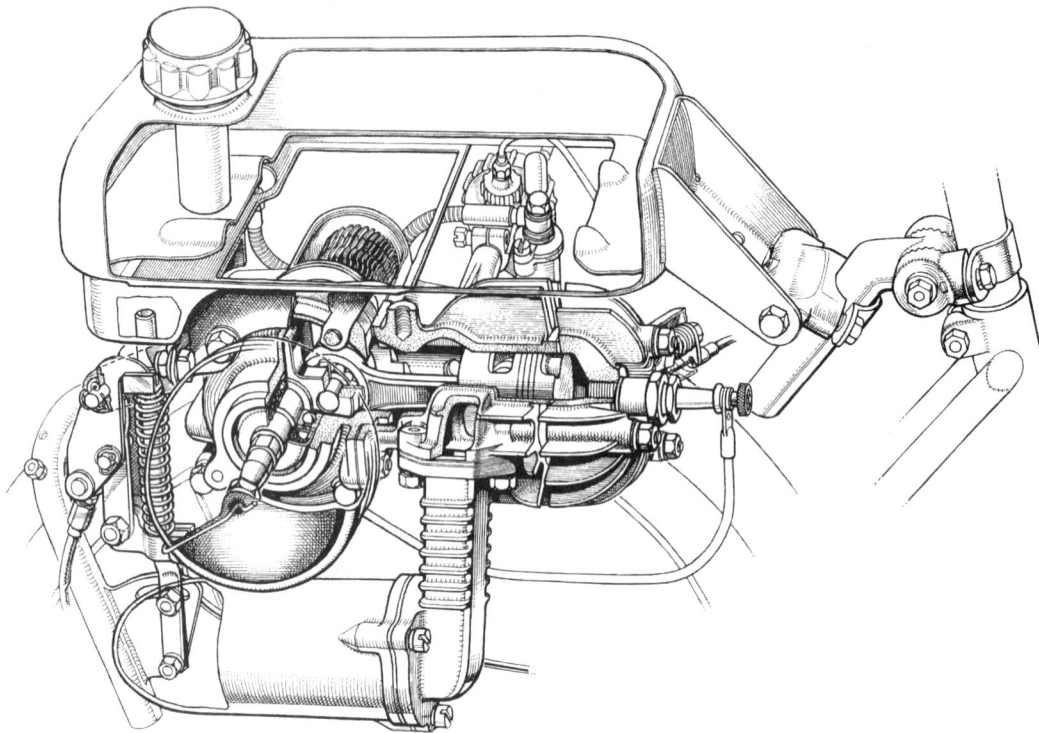

The above cut-away clearly shows the extreme simplicity of a Mini-Motor (in this case a later model, the Mk III, featuring a decompressor, altered engine mounting and ribbed iron drive roller not found on earlier MkI and MkII versions) which was one of the unit's great strengths. It was made from simple, tough parts and their number was kept to an absolute minimum. This also meant production costs were low. The unit is clamped to a bicycle saddle tube on the right. A steel crankshaft was assembled from three pressed-together components, carried by two ball-bearings while the big-end was by rollers, captive between the crankshaft halves.

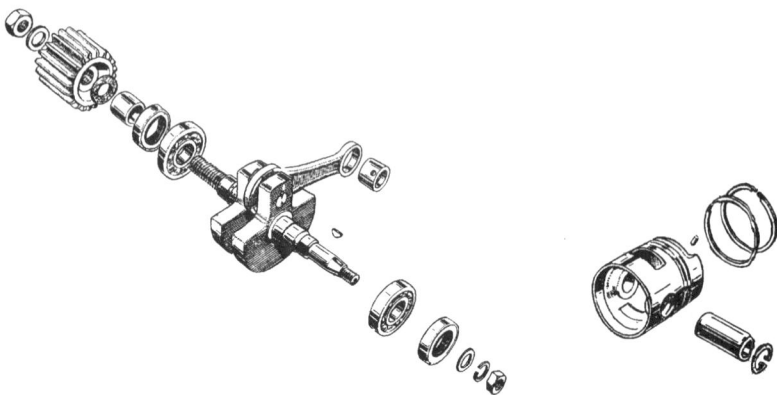

(Trojan Ltd.)

Little-end bearing material was phosphor-bronze, carrying an aluminium piston with two pegged piston rings. Pistons were fully machined at Trojan's works (as were crankshafts and cylinders) and featured two cut-out passages at right-angles to the gudgeon-pin axis which, in conjunction with recesses cast into the edge of the piston crown, provided accurate control of mixture flow timing from crankcase to combustion chamber.

Outrigged on the right-hand end of the crankshaft was a single-coil Miller or Wico-Pacy flywheel magneto (Miller equipped engines had a Z letter suffix to the engine number) providing HT current to the spark-plug (Lodge C14, Champion J8 or KLG F50), mounted centrally in the aluminium cylinder-head. Ignition timing was set at 29° or ⅛" on the piston before top-dead centre. Both the head and barrel (of cast-iron) were finned radially to maximise cooling, rather necessary given that there was no forced-cooling fan or shroud. The engine was located above the rear wheel and behind the saddle, so free airflow was somewhat obstructed by the rider's legs.

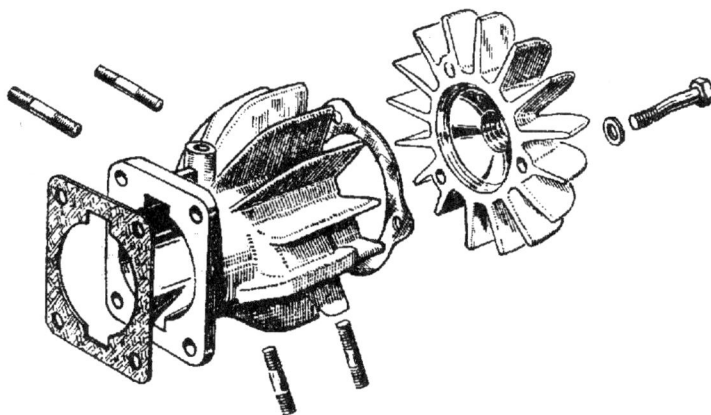

(Trojan Ltd.)

No clutch was fitted and hence no power-sapping and wear-prone primary or secondary chain or gear-drive trains were present. All of the available one brake horsepower was delivered by the Mini-Motor direct to your rear tyre by the drive roller, hence the unit being promoted by Trojan Ltd as the "Gearless Cycle Outboard". Technical details were archetypically European sub-50cc cyclemotor, indeed it seems likely Vincenti Piatti always had this use of his engine in mind when he designed it, there being no legislation limiting lathe motors to 50cc, or any other capacity for that matter.

Cubic capacity was therefore 49.9cc from a 38mm bore and 44mm stroke, the compression ratio being a lowly 5:8:1 in deference to the lack of a decompressor and in anticipation of indifferent to appalling fuel quality post-WW2. This lack of a decompressor was to prove something of an Achilles heel for Mini-Motors and the subject of much foul language and cursing in wet weather. Brake mean effective pressure at 200rpm was an equally low 50 to 55psi. Nonetheless, power output was quoted by Trojan as a respectable 1bhp @ 3,400rpm, maximum torque was 26.87 inch lbs @ 2,800rpm.

Fuel was supplied to the engine by a Trojan-manfactured Dell'orto carburettor that drew petroil mixture (20:1) from the 5-pint (2.84litres) capacity fuel tank. This tank (nearly always painted a bright blue) fulfilled a dual role as the structural frame for a Mini-Motor as well as carrying fuel. At the front was a welded-on bracket and a tubular support clamp which in turn attached to the saddle pillar and could be adjusted to fit virtually any bicycle frame. Beneath the tank were flanges to which the motor was bolted, the entire unit was then supported at the rear by a U-shaped steel hoop, which located on the bicycle rear wheel spindle and provided the means of engaging and disengaging drive. This infamous steel hoop would evolve though a number of different incarnations and would be fitted with various mechanisms for lifting or holding the motor unit against the tyre, none of which was to prove entirely satisfactory.

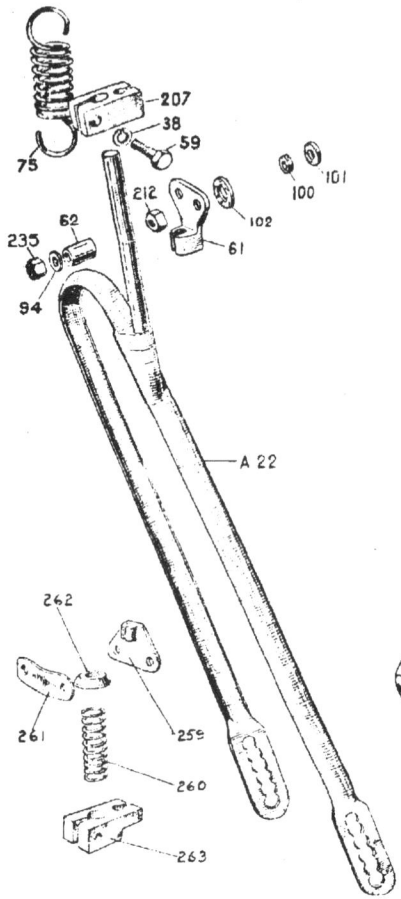

This first version featured a one-piece hoop with slotted lower ends (fixed to the wheel spindle) to allow for adjustment to different sizes of cycle wheels. The rod at the upper end passed between guide-rollers which were attached to the engine crankcase. Spring no 75 tensioned the tank & motor unit onto the cycle rear tyre; drive was disengaged via a handlebar lever and Bowden cable control.

Very few early Mini-Motors survive with this arrangement, Trojan continuously improved the hoop and mechanism design and conversion kits were produced to enable owners of older units to benefit from these changes.

More will be seen of this device later on...

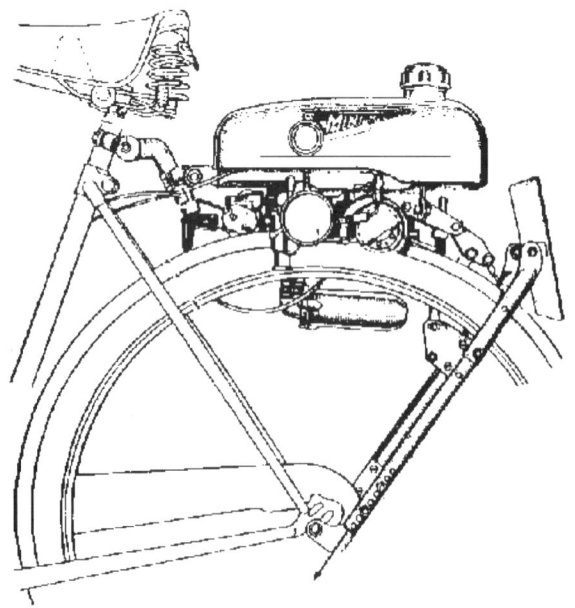

The Mini-Motor unit, ready to mount behind a saddle, weighed but 12½lbs (5.67kgs). It was supplied complete with a throttle control lever and engine-lifting lever and cables ready connected for quick installation by the owner or Mini-Motor supplier, and was priced at £21 retail, including Purchase Tax.

When George Denton returned from his Swiss holiday in 1948 he found that Trojan had already taken out a Mini-Motor manufacturing licence. So convinced was he of the potential shown by this clip-on power unit, he negotiated a dealership for Hampshire between Trojan and his employers of the time, Seals, where he was General Manager. This partnership sold some 400 units but George Denton wanted more involvement with the future of Mini-Motors. With great audacity (remember, this was just after WW2 and such an approach was unconventional to say the least) he wrote a letter dated 1st November 1951 to B Monk Esq of Mini-Motor (Great Britain) Ltd, Trojan Way, Croydon, which began:

"This is a difficult letter to write. If you will forgive little attempt at finesse, it will be easier. I would be very interested indeed in the job of Sales or Distribution Manager. From the time I first rode one abroad, I have been convinced of the need for the simplest form of motor transport. But I also believe it is going to require very purposeful sales management and more coherent advertising and presentation to keep Mini-Motor sales ahead of competitors."

Shortly thereafter he got the job, not least because George Denton was a successful motor cycle trials competitor and had a cupboardful of trophies as a result. He had every intention of using similarly high-profile riding exploits to promote the Mini-Motor name and increase sales.

Much of the information in this chapter comes from George Denton's family archive and so is an invaluable insider's view of the cyclemotor world.

A factory photo of a
MkIII Mini-Motor.

(Trojan Ltd.)

Production of Mini-Motor units began in 1949, engine serial numbers starting with a first unit of A1000, the prefix letter indicating the year of manufacture, A-1949, B-1950, C-1951, etc. Serial numbers 1000 to 5000 were to be found on the top face of the crankcase, magneto side, whilst serial numbers 5000 onward were underneath the crankcase.

Trojan's long experience as a precision-engineering concern meant that the factory in Croydon was well equipped to carry out most manufacturing operations in-house. Parts such as sparking plugs, magnetos, carburettors, ball-bearings and piston rings were bought in but all other components were made on site. Trojan's machine shop manufactured pistons and cylinders from cast blanks, machined and ground crankshaft components (4 parts) and pressed them together. Once each engine was fully assembled, it was set up on a test-rig on the north side of the factory that spun it for a 20-minute running-in period. A large electric motor ran 12 engines at once for this operation. Spark-plugs were then fitted, petroil mixture fed to the carburettors, exhausts connected to an extractor system and the same electric motor was used to start the engines which were then further run-in under their own power. Once this process had been completed successfully, the engines were removed from the test-rig, cleaned and ancillaries and petrol-tanks were fitted. Finished, tested units were now passed to the Stores as ready for despatch to customers.

Early users of the Mini-Motor found their mount to be surprisingly sprightly; the engine provided a good measure of hill-climbing power and gave around 20mph cruising speed together with 200-240mpg economy. One or two irritations soon manifested themselves: firstly, starting the engine in wet conditions was far from easy, especially with new, fairly tight units. The Mk1 cast-iron ribbed roller was a bit short on grip and the lack of a decompressor made matters worse, so a short balletic routine was needed to get the engine spinning. The drive roller was first dropped onto the tyre, and then the bike was wheeled backward until compression could be felt. Next, disengage the roller, mount the cycle and pedal off at good speed. The roller was then dropped back onto the tyre, the engine having to complete almost a full revolution before coming up against compression again, by which time drive from the tyre and flywheel inertia were hopefully sufficient to overcome this. With luck and some exertion the engine would then burst into life. A decompressor was soon offered as an option and later became a standard fitting, much to the relief of many riders.

A second irritation concerned that infamous hoop and the method of tensioning the drive roller to the tyre with a spring. This was perfectly acceptable engineering practice and weighed & cost next to nothing. However, in use it was found that uneven road surfaces were transmitted pneumatically by the tyre up to the roller, causing the entire engine unit to bounce up and down slightly against the tension spring and thus varying contact pressure with the tyre. This led to roller slip, a consequent loss of drive, tyre damage and the first of many improvements to the engine lifting and lowering mechanism. The next version inverted spring and cable so the cable held the engine unit down while the spring lifted it when the cable control disengaged drive, thus avoiding the bouncing problem.

A third version rear hoop was introduced with adjustments made via drillings rather than the slotted end of previous hoops, which soon spread under the pressure (and frequent removal and refitting of the rear wheel to mend punctures) of rear wheel spindle nuts, rendering the slots useless for their designed purpose. Correct adjustment of the hoop was then impossible without overtightening these nuts which in turn exacerbated the original problem even further.

This new design of hoop also made life easier for a Mini-Motor owner, the rear wheel could now be removed and replaced without disturbing individual settings for a particular cycle frame and having to readjust everything each time a puncture was repaired. An additional refinement was made to the guide rod, this was now adjustable for angle via a sector plate and made fitting an engine unit easier.

Adjustment on this version is much more positive, with two bolts & nuts anchoring the hoop to substantial brackets (397 & 398) fixed in place by the rear wheel spindle and supported by two backing-pieces (383).

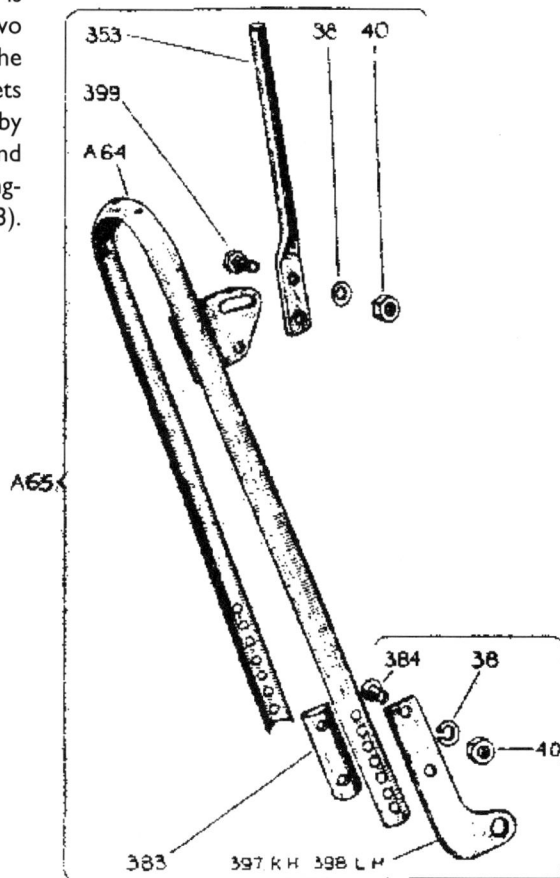

Staff working at the Mini-Motor factory were motor cycling enthusiasts keen to publicise the virtues and dependability of their product, so in 1949 three of them set off on a marathon proving journey. Their names were Nick Hands, Len Hurford and Harold Williams and they started from the Trojan factory in Croydon, rode down to Land's End, from there they rode north all the way to John O'Groats and then back to Croydon again. Sadly no record seems to remain of the total mileage covered by this intrepid trio (nor the time of year) but we would hazard a guess that it was at least a 2,350 mile round trip.

Some technical problems manifested themselves during the course of this long journey. Firstly the cast-iron drive rollers proved less than durable and wore out unexpectedly fast. Under dry conditions they also ground down bicycle tyre treads rather quickly. Messrs Hands, Hurford and Williams certainly rode for far more hours a day than the average commuter would, which may have contributed to the short tyre life they experienced. A second problem arose with bicycle free-wheel mechanisms: under normal cycling conditions these would free-wheel occasionally, not all the time as when under power. As a consequence they also wore out rather rapidly and it was also found that water was being squeezed off the tyre tread by the roller, running down onto the free-wheel, which did not take kindly to being lubricated with gritty water. A small shield was fitted in an attempt to prevent this happening.

Weather conditions were often atrocious and as a result the three-man team bought themselves bright-yellow sailor's survival suits. Thereby hangs a tale. One day, whilst riding through the Lake District on their way North, they stopped off for refreshments at a pub near Lake Windermere and, according to George Denton, *"thus garbed ... surprisingly, they were welcomed as heroes and liberally entertained. Slowly, the penny dropped, at that very time Sir Malcolm Campbell was attempting to lower the world water-speed record and our riders were mistaken for Sir Malcolm's mechanics!"*

The advert reproduced here is typical of so many published in contemporary motor cycle magazines such as The Motor Cycle, Motor Cycling or Power and Pedal. In this case it dates from 9th March 1950

The early 1950s were the heyday of clip-on cyclemotors but their glory was brief. Most dealers progressed from selling bicycles and cyclemotors to motor cycles proper, scooters and then, in some cases, cars.

On August 17th 1950 *Motor Cycling* magazine published a small article listing improvements made to the Mini-Motor, thus heralding the appearance of a MkII version. Trojan had taken notice of customer comments and had undoubtedly learned a lot from its staff members' marathon ride to Land's End, John O'Groats and back.

MINI-MOTOR
INSTRUCTION

FOR FITTING
AND USE OF

1951 Type of Drive Control and Decompressor

R. G. SINCLAIR,
Date 12th MARCH, 19.73.......
No. ....

A decompressor had been on offer as an accessory for some time in the life of the MkI but not fitted as standard. Now it was, much to the relief of many prospective customers. The crankcase halves were also modified, now being assembled using nuts and bolts, as below.

(Trojan Ltd)

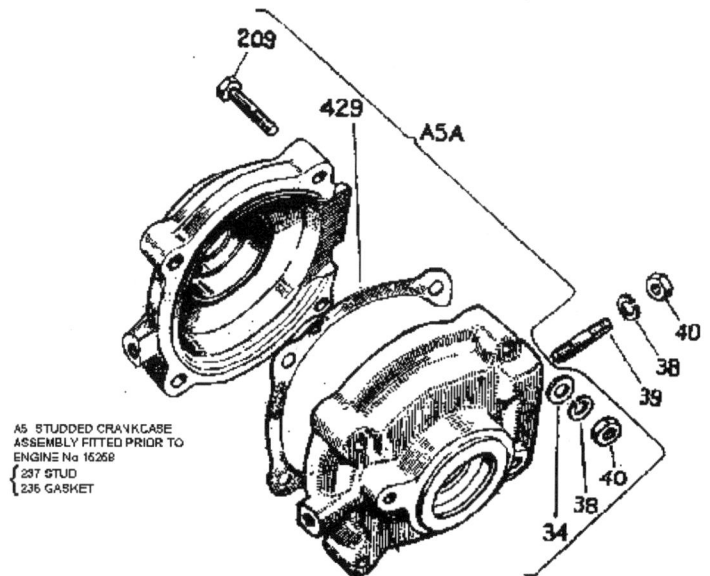

A5 STUDDED CRANKCASE
ASSEMBLY FITTED PRIOR TO
ENGINE No 15268
{ 237 STUD
{ 236 GASKET

Internally the engine had a stronger crankshaft assembly and a heavier flywheel was fitted. A new toggle-action lever controlled the engagement of the motor onto the rear tyre, this gave the rider improved traffic control since he only had to flick the lever to disconnect drive when a halt became necessary in traffic. Several modifications were also made to the Dell'orto carburettor (made under licence by Trojan): the 'strangler' or choke now had an integral lever and the float-bowl sludge-trap was redesigned and strengthened.

The stronger crankshaft assembly had been introduced for a good reason. It had become apparent that an epidemic of bent crankshafts was resulting from unskilled roller swapping. The original Mini-Motor crankshaft was a very simple and strong pressed-together assembly (see previous illustration) which carried the drive roller on one side and the magneto flywheel on the other. So long as the rotating masses did so in unison all was well, torsional stiffness was not a major requirement. However, unsympathetic mechanics (and owners) would hold onto the flywheel on one side and apply a large box-spanner to the roller retaining nut on the other side of the crankshaft and twist these against each other in an attempt to undo or tighten up the retaining nut. The result was that opposing forces applied in torsion from each end of the crank assembly could turn the crank-pin carrying the con-rod in one or other of the crank webs, resulting in an out of line, bent and now-useless crankshaft.

In the stronger version the crank-pin was drilled and pegged to both crank webs, thus virtually eliminating this problem.

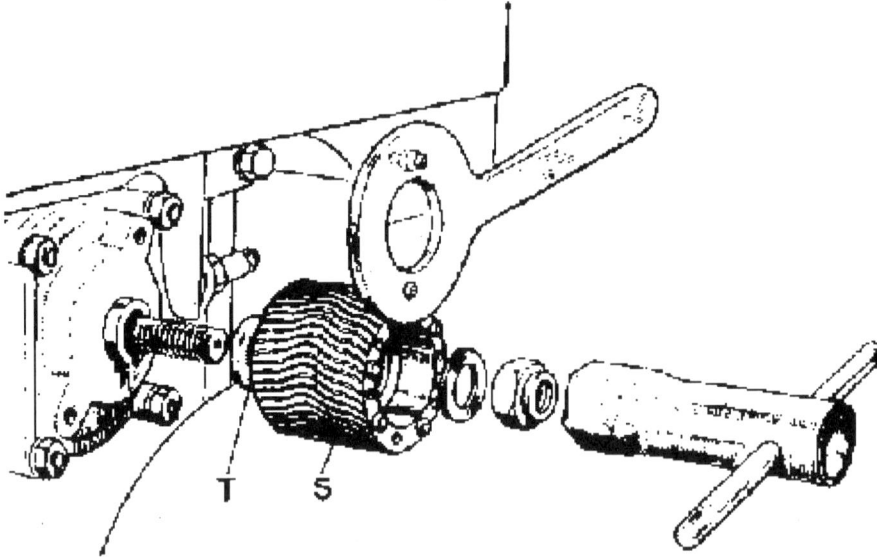

Fig. 5

Mini-Motor even issued an instruction carrying the above illustration, a special spanner was made with lugs locating in corresponding holes on the outside of the 'herringbone' roller, so all torsional forces were kept to the roller. A cautionary note was still made: *"the roller ... should come away quite easily and in this case it is permissible to grasp the magneto. If the roller will not unscrew easily it should be soaked in freeing oil and another attempt made"*.

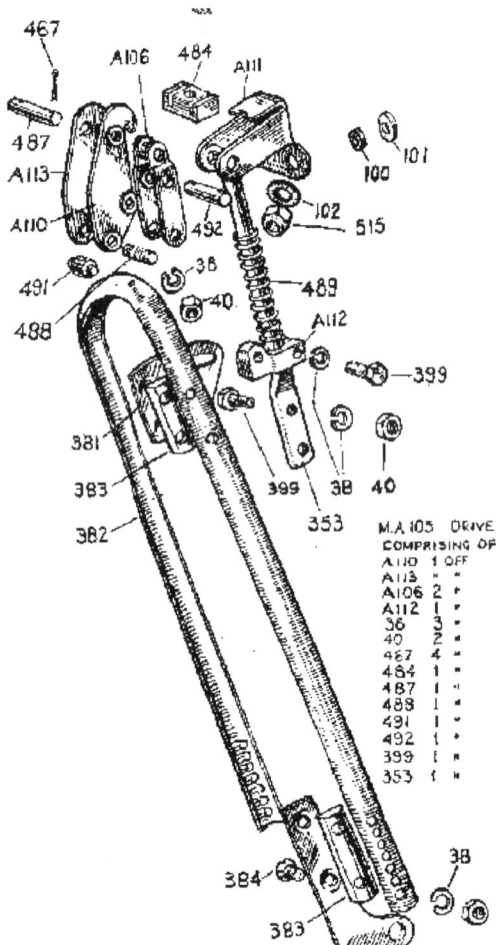

M.A 105 DRIVE
COMPRISING OF

A110	1	OFF
A113	"	"
A106	2	"
A112	1	"
38	3	"
40	2	"
467	4	"
484	1	"
487	1	"
488	1	"
491	1	"
492	1	"
399	1	"
353	1	"

The rear hoop and engine raising and lowering mechanism came in for an inevitable redesign at the same time. This new type now had a more positive 'toggle-action' mechanism, which was a great improvement on the old one. On an older version, if the cycle had been used with the engine disengaged and luggage was being transported on a carrier on top of the engine, the roller could sometimes bounce into contact with the tyre. The toggle-action mechanism gave greater support to the tank (via the new sub-frame) when the motor was in the raised position and almost eliminated this occurrence. This could now be said to be the ultimate, definitive rear hoop and mechanism.

Returning to the bicycle freewheel problems encountered by Trojan's intrepid riders, it soon became obvious that this was far from exclusive to Mini-Motors.

Power & Pedal magazine of February 1955 carried an article written by the editor, Frank L Farr, in his column "Comment, by Clip-on", entitled "Rear End Rollers", where he ruminates on the subject thus:

"The over-the-rear-wheel, roller driven engine remains with us in Britain because its representatives are relatively cheap and because they keep the petroil and noise behind the rider. Of course, all cyclemotors should be designed to keep petroil and noise to themselves, but pending this technical achievement these units are likely to remain with us, despite the disadvantages of their making up the space we want for baggage carrying and throwing mud over the chain, hub and freewheel … It seems clear that the various guards and deflectors do ameliorate the trouble but none of them has been able to beat the mud at its work of destruction. Freewheels are only lasting months instead of years and the mortality amongst three-speed hubs is disturbingly and expensively high. It is of interest to us therefore that the oil-bath chaincase, once the hallmark of bicycle quality, is coming back into favour again and on quite modestly priced machines. This is the only real answer to roller-slung mud and definitely a Good Thing for our clothes and our transmissions with any type of unit. A neat example that caught my eye at Earl's Court was the Armstrong 'Tourease' model, which, apart from the chaincase, makes a return to the lasting dignity of a black finish." Hear, hear.

This cartoon appeared in Power & Pedal, August 1955, drawn by Ray Evans

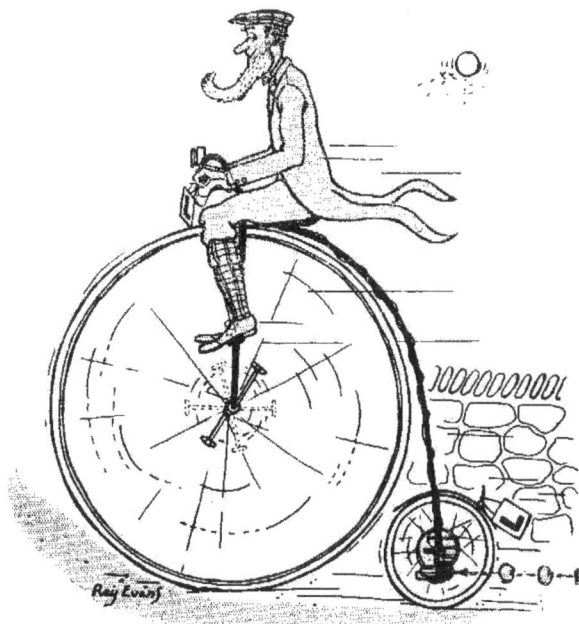

Gran'fer says they never had freewheel troubles in his young days.

The Great Freewheel Problem awoke the ingenuity of not a few inventors who designed alternative arrangements to wear-prone pawl bicycle freewheels. One which got beyond the sketch-on-an-envelope is reproduced in full below, in a news item printed in *Power & Pedal*, September 1955 and is probably the last word on this subject.

Bracket Freewheel

A COMPLETE answer to the old problems of freewheels under mud bombardment from over-rear-wheel roller drive engines is provided by a provisionally patented freewheel device to be incorporated in the chainwheel.

Apart from the advantages of protection against mud and grit the forward located freewheel is larger and more robust in construction than conventional types and runs at approximately one third the speed with a consequently greatly reduced rate of wear.

We have inspected a prototype and examined the patent specification and it appears that all the claims would be well justified in practice.

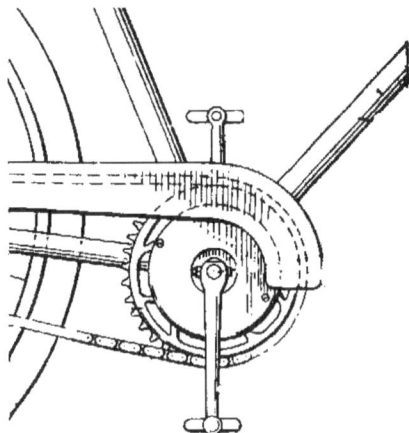

The patentee is Mr. A. H. Mayers, of the Maycoll Cycle Company 333-5 Kennington Road, S.E.11.

One thing not known is whether the Maycoll Cycle Company actually went into production with their device, bearing in mind that by September 1955 the clip-on cyclemotor market was already contracting as cyclemotorists converted to fully-built machines such as the Mobylette. The idea was not wasted however, its time came in the 1990s when Shimano made a modern equivalent for fitting to electric-powered bicycles.

In use a Mini-Motor proved to be tough, reliable and fast, all three advantages accrued through good, simple original design work from Vincenti Piatti and quality engineering from Trojan. However, some of Piatti's subsequent work was less successful, especially when he embarked on designing larger engines for James and Francis-Barnett. These soon gained a terrible reputation for internal condensation problems which resulted in the rusting-up of infrequently-used motor cycles. To quote George Denton: *"We almost dodged this trouble. A single-speeder powering a bicycle (Mini-Motor) soon got hot enough to vaporise any condensate, but a few customers, such as district nurses, house-to-house insurance collectors and would-be taximen 'doing the knowledge' did not get their motors hot. Priests with a home-pause-church-pause-home travel pattern also got mechanically rusted-up. One outraged customer complained direct to our managing director in terms so sulphuric that we went to investigate. 'How come', our critic asked, 'could any engine, fuelled and lubricated according to manufacturers instructions, completely rust up not once, but twice in a few months?' How was it used? 'Only up to the golf club and back', was the reply, 'That's why I cycle. Not worth getting the car out for such a short trip; I bought your contraption to save my legs'. It was tactfully explained that short distances were death to internal combustion engines and that his Rolls-Royce would suffer just as much with similar usage."*

A MkIII even-more-improved Mini-Motor then made an appearance in late 1951 and was duly road-tested by *Motor Cycle* magazine, a report being published in its 27th March 1952 edition under the heading *"Powerful Two-stroke Unit: Simple to Control: Excellent Hill-climbing Characteristics"*. The recently-standardised MkII decompressor was greeted thus: *"it was necessary only to pedal the cycle for five or six yards with the decompressor valve raised when, with one movement of the control lever, the decompressor was closed and the throttle opened to about the half-way mark, causing the engine to fire and take up the drive"*. Once warmed up, the engine gave *"perfect two-stroking … at any sustained speed between 15mph and the maximum available (approximately 29mph)"*. The best cruising speed was discovered to by around 23mph while overall fuel consumption for the test period was found to be 144mpg with a mixture of city and open-country use, somewhat less than the optimistic 240mpg quoted as achievable in Mini-Motor press adverts. A new drive roller material made an appearance on the MkIII, this was now carborundum-coated steel, no doubt introduced to improve wet-weather traction, but Trojan seemed to have some reservations about it. *Motor Cycle* mentioned that *"an additional roller is supplied with each unit; of cast-iron (the original type), it is intended for use in mainly dry climates"*.

This picture illustrates the third type roller, a ribbed steel affair introduced late on in the MkIII Mini-Motor series and known as the 'Herringbone' roller.

Trojan Ltd.

Mounting of the motor itself was also improved; from the MkIII the engine was held between side-plates that were clamped in place by nuts on the crankcase studs, whereas earlier models made do with a single bolt screwed into a threaded boss cast into the cylinder block and only two studs at the back of the crankcase.

Also announced by *The Motor Cycle* magazine in its Earl's Court Show review of 20th November 1952, almost as an afterthought, was a 75cc capacity version of the unit *"available to fleet owners"*. This larger capacity engine was a result of Trojan developing industrial variants of the Mini-Motor.

One of the first promotional outings for Mini-Motors was the Auto-Cycle Union (ACU) 9th National Rally on 12th & 13th July 1952.

The ACU rally Control Card no 551 shows that Mr Denton covered 150-odd miles and passed through 10 control points, amongst these were Derby, Nottingham, Lincoln, Gainsborough, Louth, Boston, Peterborough and Leicester. At the finish (Alton Towers, no doubt somewhat different then to today) he was given 305 marks for a theoretical B class award even though he was not eligible to compete as he was a factory representative. Of 822 entrants on the rally, 686 completed the course. The card also reveals that George's mount, JBY 313, was registered on 6th August 1950 and so was a MkI Mini-Motor.

In the early 1950s the ACU was an enthusiastic promoter of events for cyclemotors as a means of proving the true mettle of these little machines.

Long-distance trials and rallies were held annually and the motor cycle press accordingly wrote up long, comprehensive reports on such events, much to the delight of manufacturers such as Mini-Motor who fully appreciated the publicity value of their machines doing well. George Denton was an experienced competition rider who took full advantage of these opportunities, so Trojan entered the Auto-Cycle Union Motor-Assisted Demonstration Trial held on Sunday April 26th 1953. Three entries were official Trojan works Mini-Motors for George Denton (no 37), Alfred Pointer (26) and L J Hurford (39), with a further four privateer Mini-Motors also participating. The route of some 34 miles had a target time of 2 hours 4 minutes, starting and finishing at Wembley Car Park.

G M Denton, on his way home after the MCC Edinburgh Run in 1954, outside Hooley's of Nottingham, Mini-Motor distributors.

The ACU was founded in 1903 as the Auto-Cycle Club with the aim of fostering motor sport and became hugely successful, being renamed the Auto-Cycle Union in 1907 and adopting the role of governing body for British motor cycle sports. On the weekend of 11-12th July 1953 the ACU organised a Jubilee Year National Rally at Weston-Super-Mare, Somerset which included a road competition in celebration of their 50 years of existence. By 1953 membership had risen to 54,000 and some 750 Clubs were affiliated to the ACU. It still exists today and was renamed ACU Motorcycling GB in 2001.

George Denton participated in this National Rally, covered 303 miles in less than 21 hours and earned himself a bronze award. However, he was not riding a Mini-Motor but the Elswick-Trojan prototype, using a 49cc Mini-Motor 2-speed all-chain drive engine unit. It was registered in 1953 as JFW 601, George giving his home address at 35 Thornhill Road, West Croydon as the entrant. A full description of the Elswick-Trojan is given later in this chapter.

By mid-1953 the Mini-Motor clip-on engine unit had sold remarkably well, over 100,000 having been produced by Trojan in Great Britain alone, with many hundreds of thousands more being manufactured both in France (under licence) and by the original Mini-Motore company in Italy.

The advert alongside appeared in *Moto Revue*, Paris, October 1950 and claims "The bicycle outboard motor …the most powerful, economical and simplest … can be fitted in less than an hour".

Times were however changing fast for clip-on manufacturers and, as already noted in a previous chapter, rapidly increasing public prosperity was partly responsible for a worrying decline in sales, which affected Mini-Motor too. George Denton, was well aware of this trend, together with other problems affecting Mini-Motor own dealers. In a frank memo dated 12th April 1954, addressed to Mr Monk, copied to Mr Charles, (directors of Trojan) George Denton noted the following:

Mini-Motor Sales

"The present Season has advanced sufficiently for certain sales trends to emerge. They are;

1) *That so far this is a bad or very bad season for cycle sales and somewhat below average for cyclemotors.*

2) *That Mini-Motor sales are going down* (the typed text said "well" down, but GMD had crossed "well" out and substituted "going" in Biro)

3) *That it is almost certain that B.S.A., Cyclemaster and Firefly combined are outselling Mini-Motor and Power-Pak in a greater proportion than the corresponding types did last season. Put simply, the "semi-built-ins" are preferred to "clip-ons".*

4) *That where the Min-Motor (sic) and standard Power-Pak are on offer side by side, the latter outsells the former by about 5:1.*

Amongst other points GMD makes are: *"newly-appointed dealers are failing to 'get away'"* and *"some of the oldest and best are seriously alarmed at the sales resistance they are meeting from the public and are urging us most insistently for an entirely new model".* He notes that it *"has become very difficult to appoint fresh stockists"* and also *"dealers have pointed out that Mini-Motors command a comparatively poor second-hand price"* and *"more Mini-Motor owners sell to buy other makes than the owners of other makes do".*

One response Trojan made to this increasingly alarming situation was to embark on the development of a new model of cyclemotor, the Elswick-Trojan moped, in conjunction with the Elswick Hopper bicycle company. It participated in the ACU National Rally in prototype form and was most definitely of the "semi-built-in" type. The fact that it was already running around in July 1953, well before GMD's wake-up call to his directors in the memo of April 1954, showed that some at Trojan were taking events seriously.

(Trojan Ltd.)

The engine unit illustrated above was first seen at Earl's Court in November 1952 and aroused considerable interest. It was very evidently a serious re-engineering of the ugly-duckling Mini-Motor into an altogether more elegant 2-speed moped engine and gearbox swan and aimed squarely at manufacturers such as Elswick, who wished to join the rush to produce mopeds.

It was to be offered in both capacities (49cc & 75cc) and featured primary-drive by ⅜" chain in an oil-bath to the cork-lined clutch with a two-speed gearbox at the back. A ten-tooth final-drive sprocket was suppled, to take a ½"×0.305" drive chain. Overall dimensions were 15" long, 8½" wide and 8¾" high; weight was 18¾ lbs.

However, the above factory photo of the prototype Elswick-Trojan shows the wrong tree was already being barked up. It had all the hallmarks of a classic Great British Lash-Up: various parts-bins had been raided and the whole lot cobbled together. The Elswick Hopper bicycle company had come up with a nice new frame for the moped, cables and wires were festooned around, some fancy extras like front suspension and a couple of gears thrown in and we can take on the likes of Motobécane and their Mobylette in the commercial arena, can't we? I don't think so. Granted it was a prototype, but it looked a mess to start with. Continental European cyclemotors by this time were often of a very homogenous, modern, clean design and featured 'styling', a concept alien to most British engineers (we were still in greasy Barbours and boots territory here) who regarded such trivialities with the same deep suspicion as under-arm deodorants for men.

The outcome was sad and inevitable, the Elswick-Trojan remained a single prototype, never going into production, despite having attracted a certain amount of interest from *Motor Cycling* magazine in its report of the ACU rally. Mention was made that the manufacturer was to be Elswick-Hopper Ltd in Barton-on-Humber (indicating that Trojan were to supply the engines only) and that the prototype had coupled brakes operated by the right-hand handlebar lever, a thumb-operated lever changed the two gears and Webb sprung front forks were fitted. The engine didn't look very modern or integrated compared to such current European motors as the monobloc JLO G50 2-speed unit illustrated below, which shows what an integrated engine should look like. It even incorporated vestigial legislation-friendly pedals.

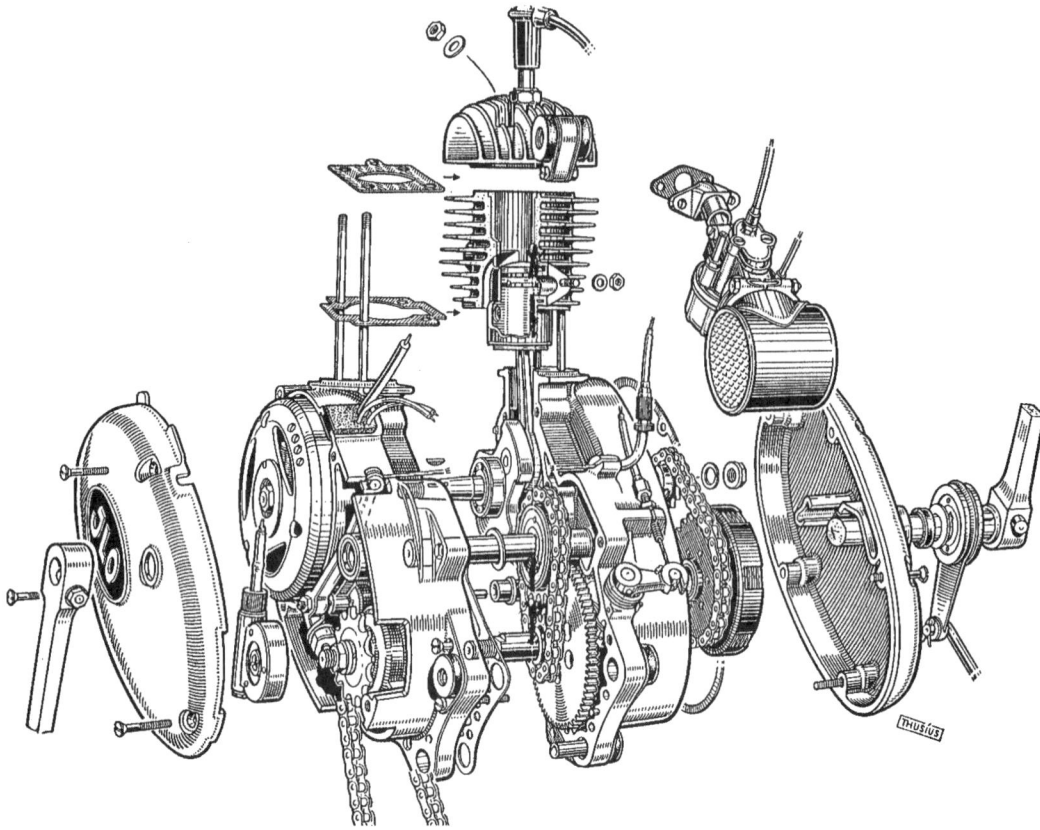

Potentially the Elswick-Trojan could have been the first British moped on the market but insufficient development money and vision were available to take on the European giants at their own game. The deciding factor was a sudden, catastrophic, loss of nerve by Elswick management, who took fright at the prospect of making and selling an entirely new product which, in their view, was perhaps less than satisfactory. There were also rumours about the unreliability of the new gearbox attached to the Mini Motor engine. Elswick had got as far as producing frames with wheels and brakes, buying in tyres, chains and saddles and commissioning engine development with Trojan when they decided to cancel the whole project.

Trojan was then left with a new engine & gearbox unit but nothing to put it in so, rather than let it go to waste, the company made contact with Raleigh in Nottingham with a view to encouraging a similar project to the recently-deceased one with Elswick. The prototype was demonstrated to Sales staff at Raleigh, who were generally enthusiastic, but final approval for such an idea had to come from Raleigh supremo George Wilson.

His opinion was entirely negative and rather sniffy: *"Cycling is a healthy and invigorating pastime to be enjoyed without licence or special skills by everyone from school age to dotage. Raleigh make the best bicycles in the world. Motorising would be a step in the wrong direction".*

It would surely be too cynical to recall how, very soon after this episode, Raleigh management made that very step in the *"wrong direction"* by ripping off their collective nighties, jumping into bed and indulging in unseemly mechanical activity with their new Gallic lover, Motobécane. The resulting progeny, a plethora of Raleigh-badged Mobylettes, kept the company afloat for a good many years. However, before the Motobécane tie-up Raleigh had dipped one toe in the water by launching a moped that followed the Elswick-Trojan principle in being little more than a lady's bicycle with an engine attached. Raleigh was to build this engine under their Sturmey-Archer marque (of bicycle hub-gears fame) but first had to get someone to design it, so they engaged … Vincenti Piatti no less.

A second attempt at producing an equivalent to the old Elswick-Trojan was later made by Raleigh in the form of the Wisp, but the less said about that the better. Oh, all right then: how the Wisp came into being is an intriguing if slightly irrelevant story. A few years after Raleigh had shown such astute judgement with regard to the Elswick-Trojan moped they did it again when a nice young man called Alex Moulton came to them with a prototype for a small-wheeled bicycle. Rebuffed by an arrogant management, Alex Moulton proceeded to undertake production himself and subsequently took the 1960s' bicycle market by storm with his rubber-suspended small-wheel Moulton cycles. Raleigh was forced to cobble together the dreadful RSW16 bicycle in an effort to compete with Moulton and then compounded its error by fitting the RSW16 with a Mobylette engine, thus giving birth to the unlamented Wisp.

Even though sales had begun to nosedive, the engineering department at Trojan continued to incorporate improvements into production Mini-Motors in the hope that this trend could be slowed or reversed. They also began seriously looking at alternative industrial uses for their now well-proven little engine. Had it not started life driving lathes?

Display by Boston Motors of Boston, Lincs, an important Mini-Motor dealership that also sold James, AJS and Royal Enfield motor cycles, as well as bicycles. A Tri-ang child's tricycle is also visible.

The Mini-Motor sales department began emphasising how cheap the clip-on unit was: a MkIII being advertised for £18.18s retail, *"an honest effort to get our product down to a price you can afford without sacrificing reliability or efficiency"*. Special payment terms called *Take it Easy* were on offer, requiring a down payment of only two pounds, plus 15 shillings fitting charge, tax and insurance, giving an on-the-road figure of £5.10s. Fuel economy was still being claimed as *"more than 200 miles to the gallon with speeds of up to 25mph"*. At least Mini-Motor adverts did not pull the same trick as competitors Sinclair Goddard, makers of the Power Pak clip-on unit. They managed to prove that running a Power Pak was actually cheaper than walking, this feat being achieved by quoting a military test on Army boots which indicated these were good for 300 miles marching before needing repair, at a cost of 12/6d. Sinclair Goddard calculated that the equivalent cost of 300 miles travel with a Power Pak came to 11/3d, *ergo* it was cheaper than walking.

By now, in late 1953, Trojan was up to a MkV version of the Mini-Motor. This featured several redesigned parts, notably the engine itself now being mounted on a sub-frame, which carried both the fuel tank and motor, as opposed to earlier types where the engine was mounted directly onto the tank, which functioned as a monocoque frame. The tank itself was now no longer load-bearing and of brazed instead of welded construction. It was rubber-mounted to the new sub-frame. A more robust front attachment bracket was also fitted.

The Motor Cycle magazine, in its 19th November 1953 Earl's Court Show report (which gloomily mentioned that only seven cyclemotor manufacturers were displaying their wares as opposed to eleven the previous year) said of the new tank that *"the familiar blue finish has given way to a striking new polychromatic gold colour scheme"*.

George Denton's Sales department had meantime been exploring several other avenues and twisting arms in the engineering department, some of the fruits of their communal labours went on display at Stand 136 in Earl's Court. The Trojan industrial engine versions of the Mini Motor, in 49 and 75cc capacities (some with fan cooling) could be seen, as well as a box tricycle model of 75cc.

A 75cc Mini-Motor powered box-tricycle is illustrated above. These were often used by High Street shops for short-hop light local deliveries. They were also employed as an early version of the now well-known 'Mr Whippy' ice-cream van, as in this cartoon by 'Lee'.

The new, larger 75cc capacity had been achieved by increasing the bore from 38mm to 44mm, the stroke of 38mm remaining the same for both capacities. Output increased from 1hp to 1½hp at 3,000 rpm, torque from 20 to 30lbs in at 2,500rpm. Both engines could be ordered with two or three-bearing cranks, were able to run clockwise or anti-clockwise as required and could be mounted horizontally or vertically.

A whole series of different accessories were on offer in a very comprehensive Industrial Engine Catalogue: a variety of angles and layouts of inlet tubes, vertical or horizontal carburettors with bottom or top fuel feeds, various exhaust pipes and silencers, numerous different fans and starting pulleys (for rope starting), mounting flanges or even a fuel tank, stand and cowl unit, as below.

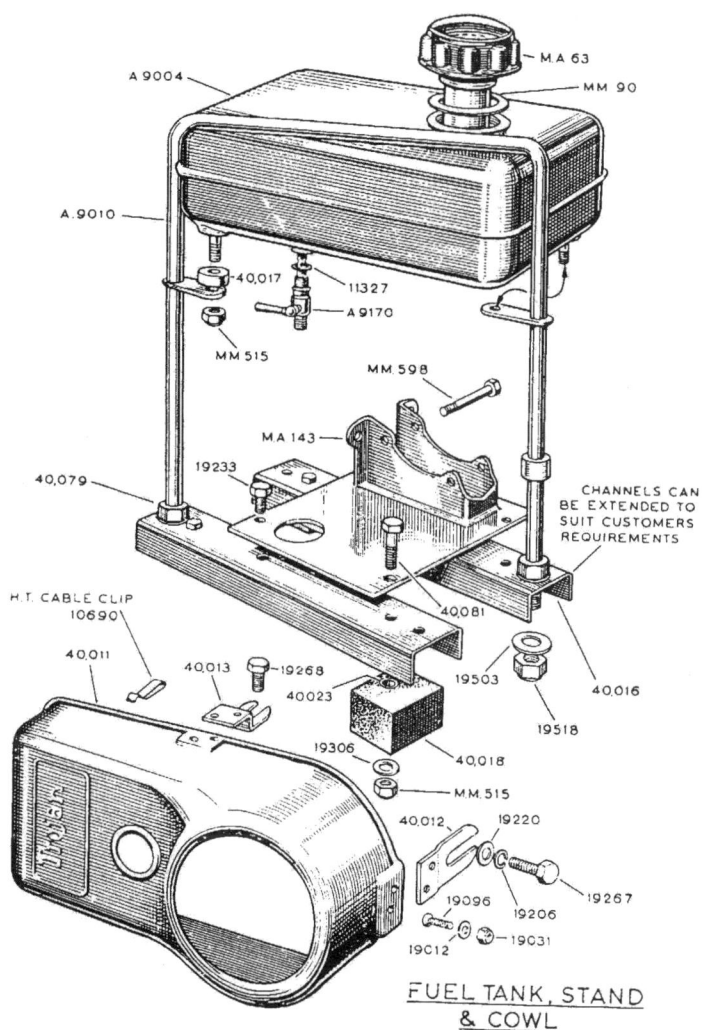

FUEL TANK, STAND & COWL

Once the Sales department had got its communal imagination in gear and the bit between its teeth there was no stopping it. Some six months before the appearance of industrial engine versions of Mini-Motors, in April 1953, an unusual advert appeared in *The Ironmonger* magazine. It depicted a lawn-mower powered by the Mini-Mower. This surely must be the *ne plus ultra* of cyclemotor engine adaptions and leads one on to the frightening speculation that, if a Mini-Motor powered bicycle was capable of 28mph, would a Mini-Mower powered suburban push-mower go as fast? Mind the Hollyhocks, Henry!

Just in case you don't believe any of this, see below.

The Mini-Mower attachment, also publicised as the Moweriser, was something of a technical *tour de force*. It had benefited from a great deal of engineering skill in adapting Trojan's simple clip-on roller-drive cyclemotor engine to fit an average cylinder mower and take the strain out of mowing. But, why? It was very doubtful whether your average Mr Smith of Acacia Avenue, owner of a tiresomely slow but steady small push mower (as seen in Moweriser publicity photos), would lash out the cash to the tune of £19.18s.6d for one - even if he had a big garden. Anybody with a decent acreage of lawn would usually risk life & limb and mow it with some evil monstrosity from the likes of Allen, Suffolk or Ransomes (see your local Steam Rally for details).

So, another engineering feat from Trojan that no doubt cost a great deal to develop and probably never recouped the original outlay, never mind make a profit for the company. It was a shame really, the idea of a clip-on mower attachment might have appealed to many impecunious mechanically-minded people, just the sort who might already had a Mini-Motored bicycle in the garage but hadn't yet managed a Ford Popular on the front drive. Unfortunately they would probably not have had twenty quid spare to spend on a powered mower attachment. Another wrong tree barked up.

Meanwhile, sales of the standard Mini-Motor bicycle attachment continued to decline, though George Denton valiantly attempted to keep his product in the public eye by competing regularly. A golden opportunity was provided by The Motor Cycle Club (MCC), which had organised a London-Edinburgh Run since 1904 and was celebrating its Golden Jubilee Sporting Motoring Event, a 50th anniversary edition of the Run in 1954. The start took place at the GPO (General Post Office, back in the days when we actually had one), St Martins le Grand, London, from 8pm on May 21st and finished at 7pm on May 22nd in Edinburgh, 397 miles and 23 hours later. In order to complete the distance within the time limit, an average speed of 17.26mph had to be maintained, no time allowance being made for refuelling, repairs or rest. Most participants on such an event rode proper motor cycles more than capable of a 40 to 60mph cruising speed; to enter a 49cc motor-assisted push-bike incapable of reaching 30mph flat-out seemed extremely foolhardy. GMD's Mini-Motor was by far the smallest capacity solo motor cycle entered, the next engine size up were two 150cc LE Velocettes (Harold Karslake rode one), then a 197cc Francis-Barnett (not suffering from Vincenti Piatti's condensation problems on a run of this length) and so on up to a 998cc Vincent.

For George Denton this was his eighth 'Edinburgh' so he had a fair idea of the challenge he had set himself. It was an extraordinary feat and a very, very close-run thing but he managed to finish the course in 23 hours 58 minutes, no doubt by riding the entire route virtually non-stop. He was already 48 years old and had ridden his first 'Edinburgh' in 1930, 24 years earlier. Weather conditions had been far from perfect; three-quarters of the route were ridden in mist, drizzle or rain and against a trying, stiff headwind for 200 miles north of Stamford. GMD calculated his overall fuel consumption to have been 160mpg.

The publicity value of such an exploit was priceless: GMD had pre-prepared a circular letter (dated 25th May 1954) to all Mini-Motor dealers, *"anticipating another Mini-Motor success"* and advising them that *Motor Cycling* and *The Motor Cycle* magazines would be writing about his exploit, as well as the possibility of him being on the BBC's 'In Town Tonight' programme. Dealers were invited to send the first three paragraphs of his letter, written as a news item, to their local paper. Failure was not on the agenda for George Denton.

This photo, believed to have been taken in Nottingham, shows GMD on his way home from the London-Edinburgh Run. Cars visible are a Ford V8 Pilot (right), a Sunbeam Talbot (behind the Keep Left sign) and two Bedford lorries.

Despite his best efforts to turn around the decline in sales, clip-on cyclemotor engines had had their day and so, in a letter dated 14th October 1954 addressed to Major W T Charles, GMD concluded:

"Earlier this year I expressed an opinion as to what I felt were the poor prospects of the Mini-Motor if it were to be carried into the coming season in its present form. This is not a view that can properly be held by the Mini-Motor Sales Manager and I therefore ask to be released from that appointment at the end of this year."

Presumably his resignation was accepted as, with GMD's departure at the end of 1954, the fire went out at the heart of the Mini-Motor company. Nobody is sure exactly when production ceased but *The Motor Cycle* magazine's Earl's Court Show report of 17th November 1955 indicated Mini-Motors were still available, though now priced at £21.14s. The end by then could not have been far off and best estimates are that Trojan shut down the assembly lines during 1956. One Mini-Motor (no.74807) is known to have been registered in 1958 but this was in all probability from a dealer shifting old stock. Assuming this was a late model, (engine numbering being sequential), we can estimate that in total some 75,000 Mini-Motors, including industrial engines, were built at Croydon between 1947 and 1956.

The *"bored-out wasp"* did Trojan proud.

Question and Answer

Address your queries to Q & A, and enclose SAE if postal reply is required: Full information must be given if our replies are to be helpful.

As a Mini-Motor curio, we offer this little gem from Mr L E Furminger, published in *Power & Pedal*, October 1953. One wonders how present-day Traffic Police would view a cyclemotor carrying two numbers and tax discs.

Q   Two Engines

I have a *Philips* Cycle, and have a *Minimotor* on it, and have just bought an *Itom Tourist* cyclemotor and have had that fixed on.

My cycle has two tax Discs, and two lots of number plates, to cover same. I am running it on the *Itom*, but when I get to a steep hill, I put both motors on, and it goes up quite easily. Can you tell me if it is illegal, to have two engines on one cycle, also when I re-tax it could I get the cycle taxed for 17/6 a year, as even a 98 c.c. autocycle is only 17/6.

L. E. FURMINGER

A *It is perfectly legal for you to have two engines on your machine provided the total cubic capacity does not exceed the limit of the taxation class, 150 c.c. If you go over 100 c.c. you will also have to fit a speedometer.*

You do not need double licences and number plates. One log book should be surrendered to the licensing Authority who will enter particulars of that engine into the other log book, making one registration of the power installaton of the machine. You will receive a rebate on the surrendered licence.

If you later remove the second engine you must report this to the Council and if it is disposed of the new owner must re-register it as new.

Don't forget your insurance cover will have to be extended for a 98 c.c.

An interesting post-script to the Trojan Mini-Motor story concerns an announcement published in *Motor Cycling*, February 7, 1957, headed "Talbot Moped". The text went on: *"Another all-British mo-ped (sic) will shortly be marketed. The makers, H.J.Talbot & Son, 7 Central Hill, London S.E.19, tell us that it will have a 49cc Trojan engine and belt-cum-chain transmission. Finish will be in gunmetal grey with a cream panelled tank and the price will be under £50. Production is expected to start in 10-12 weeks."*

This was followed by a further announcement dated 28th November 1957 which elaborated on the previous press-release: *"the 49cc Talbot has an open, pedal cycle type of tubular frame. The front wheel is carried in a Webb sprung fork. Power unit is a fixed-gear Trojan two-stroke mounted in front of the bottom bracket. Two-speed pedalling gear with separate chain drive is featured and the gear change is of derailleur pattern. Low gear is intended for assisting the engine, such as on steep hills".*

The above was accompanied by a rather small indistinct photo of the *"mo-ped"* centre section (not worth reproducing here), containing the very familiar radially finned Mini-Motor cylinder head projecting out from some token panel-work, it all looked rather Heath-Robinson.

Power & Pedal meanwhile in March 1957 expressed the opinion that the British Talbot was *"aimed at the true motorised cycle market, a machine of unusual interest"* but that was about it. The same magazine page included a photo of *"the new, ultra-modern"* Sachs-engined Achilles Lido 2-speed moped, a Continental symphony of swooping curves, chrome and duo-tone paint-work, printed alongside the rather drab, utilitarian Talbot, which stood no chance against such competition, even though the Achilles Lido was being sold by Curry's for 50% more at 75 guineas.

We believe the Talbot vanished without trace or probably never progressed further than a few prototypes, which meant the hoary old Mini-Motore engine was finally dead.

The Chimp and the Mini
"Perhaps an all-time winner in the readers' photographs competition" published in the April 1953 edition of Power & Pedal. Taken by Mr R G Neale of Mitcham, Surrey at London Zoo in December 1952.

Winged Wheel Bicycle

By the 1950s, BSA (Birmingham Small Arms) Ltd. of Small Heath, Birmingham was one of the world's biggest motor cycle manufacturers and a giant compared to all other British cyclemotor makers. Why the company bothered with the Winged Wheel at all is a mystery. It was first shown in private to dealers at the 1952 Earl's Court Show, but BSA was behind: clip-on cyclemotor engines were already at the height of their success and the market was about to be invaded by mopeds. It was of small capacity (35cc) and also comparatively expensive, though there was some justification for this.

(© Morton's Motorcycle Media Ltd.)

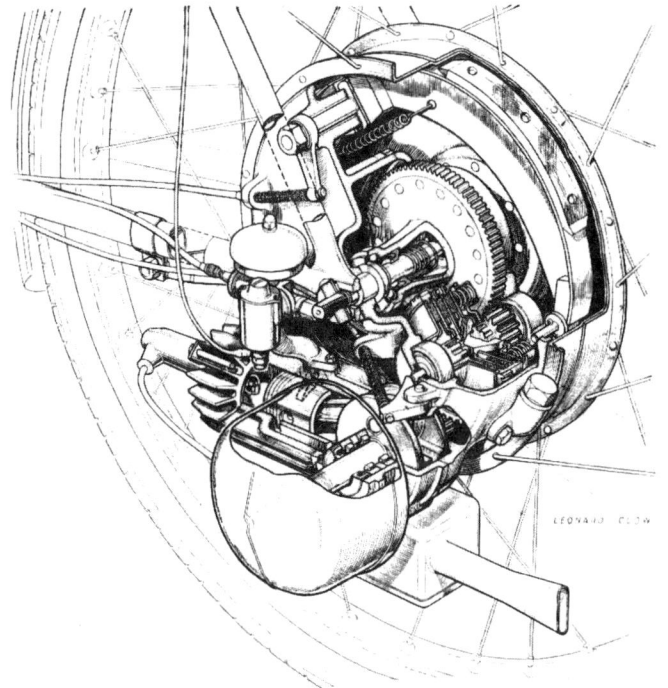

To examine the history of BSA in detail would require a book as long as this, but a brief outline of the company's background is interesting. Established on June 7 1861 as the Birmingham Small Arms Company Limited, it grew to become a large industrial conglomerate in the mid-to late 20th Century. The roots of the group go back much further than 1861, to the year 1689 in fact.

King William III was worried that his only reliable source of military weapons was Holland and that he also had some grounds to believe England would be vulnerable to invasion. Overhearing these concerns, Sir Richard Newdegate, an MP for Warwickshire, replied that amongst his Birmingham constituents there were many fine gunsmiths. As a result, the Government placed a trial order with five of the leading smiths for the supply of 200 snaphance muskets a month, "*at seventeen shillings per piece, ready money"*. King William had found an alternative supply and such was the success of this arrangement it continued for over 150 years. At the time of the Crimean War, fourteen master gunsmiths joined forces and formed The Birmingham Small Arms Trade Association, which shortly after became a Public Limited Company. As an emblem of their craft, the sign of three crossed rifles was adopted and has since become the internationally recognised Piled Arms trademark.

A 25-acre site was bought at Small Heath and, within two years, the factory was operational, turning a profit of £7,000 in 1866. Unfortunately for BSA, wars were in decline and, by the late 1870s, it was forced to shut down for a year. The future was looking very bleak. A small contract enabled the company to reopen briefly and then Fate took a hand, in the form of Mr E C F Otto. He had invented a strange bicycle with two large wheels either side of the rider and was looking for a manufacturer. He demonstrated the bicycle by riding it along the Boardroom table in front of the Board of Directors, who were so astonished they agreed immediately to go into production.

1881 Otto dicycle
(© Science Museum, London)

Other more conventional bicycles and tricycles soon followed and within a few years BSA was supplying most British and foreign bicycle manufacturers with cycle parts of the highest quality. The first complete machines were motorised bicycles. By the end of the 19th century, all transportation work was dropped in favour of a massive increase in armaments production created by the Boer War, when the company supplied thousands of rifles to British forces.

In 1907, BSA set off on a new course: that of car manufacture. Small and medium-sized cars were made to begin with. These were originally designed by E E Baguley of Ryknield, in capacities from 2.5 to 4.2 litres and they sold in moderate numbers. By 1910 however, BSA realised this range was not a success and thereupon bought the *doyenne* of car companies, Daimler, in order to drop its own designs and instead produce a small, cheaper 2 litre Daimler. The car in question had several unusual features that became hallmarks for many subsequent designs: a Knight sleeve-valve engine, worm drive transaxle and transverse rear springing. Daimler was founded in 1893 by F R Simms as The Daimler Motor Syndicate in order to exploit Gottlieb Daimler's motor patents, the company became active in Coventry, Warwickshire in 1896 as the first commercial motor car manufacturer in Britain.

BSA never shrank from a challenge and in 1910 had also embarked on manufacturing its own range of motor cycles. These were to become a world-wide success for 55 years and led the company to claim *"one out of every four motor cycles in service throughout the world is a BSA"* in its press adverts.

BSA's first motor cycle, produced in 1910

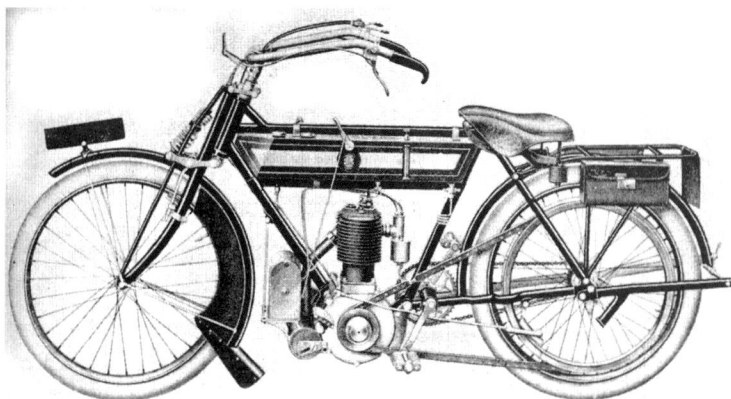

Come the Great War of 1914-1918, BSA was totally dedicated to manufacturing munitions and huge quantities of service rifles, machine guns, military motor cycles and folding bicycles for use by troops. Post-WW1 the company manufactured the Wall Auto-Wheel for a short time, an early foray into attachment cyclemotors.

A 1922 B.S.A. 10hp two-seater coupé, it retained a worm-drive axle but with conventionally positioned gearbox and British Hotchkiss air-cooled V-twin engine. This model sold reasonably well until 1924, (Photo The Daimler Co Ltd)

The 1920s and 30s were thin times again but BSA somehow maintained a lot of redundant factory space out of a sense of duty while continuing to manufacture a range of cars at its Coventry plant.

A 1936 BSA fwd three-wheeler. This ingenious and successful design by F W Hulse was introduced in 1929 with a BSA developed version of the Hotchkiss air-cooled V-twin, followed by a water-cooled 4-cylinder 1100cc power unit in 1933. Front brakes were inboard & double transverse leaf IFS.
(Photo © G N Georgano)

By 1927 Daimler had progressed from making small 2-litre Panhard-layout saloons to the vast 7-litre, 12 cylinder double-sleeve valve engined, worm-drive axled limousines that were to be so popular with the Royal Family for the next thirty years. BSA's own cars were more low-rent, encompassing small to medium saloons and a quirky front wheel drive 3-wheeler powered by an ex-Hotchkiss air-cooled V-twin. They were nonetheless successful and continued to be made up to 1939.

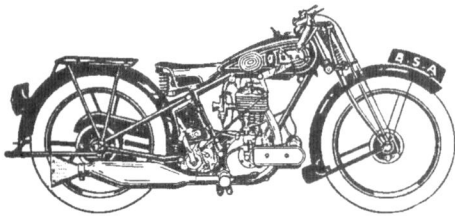

493cc BSA (sv) 1929

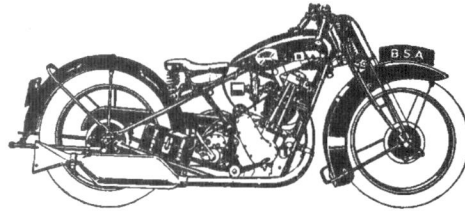

497cc BSA (ohv 'Sloper') 1928

(© Erwin Tragatsch/Hamlyn/Quarto Encyclopedia of Motorcycles)

246cc BSA (sv 'Roundtank') 1924

The retention of factory space paid off handsomely at the advent of the Second World War. By the end of 1945 BSA had become a massive engineering enterprise, owning factories in Birmingham, Redditch, Coventry, Sheffield and Co Durham as well as many dispersal units and shadow factories.

The Small Heath administration alone controlled 67 factories employing 28,000 people who had used 25,000 machine tools to manufacture over half the total of small arms supplied to Britain's forces during the war. Other products included half a million Browning machine guns used in Spitfires and Hurricanes, one and a quarter million service rifles, 400,000 Sten guns, ten million shell fuses, 3½ million magazines and 750,000 anti-tank rockets. Moreover, we haven't even mentioned the military motor cycles and bicycles that were supplied in great quantity to British and Colonial armed forces.

```
                              ┌──────────────┐
                              │   BSA Ltd    │
                              └──────────────┘
```

Small Heath Administration	BSA Tools Ltd Burton Griffiths & Co BG Machinery Ltd BSA Grinding Machine Co Ltd BSA Automatic Machine Co Ltd Arthur Andrews Ltd	William Jessop & Sons Ltd J J Saville & Co Ltd Bromley, Fisher & Turton Ltd	The Daimler Co Ltd Lanchester Motor Co Transport Vehicles (Daimler) Ltd Birtley Co Ltd Hooper & Co Ltd Barker & Co Ltd

Cycle & General Finance	BSA Cycles Ltd	BSA Cars Ltd	BSA Guns Ltd	BSA Radio Ltd	Monochrome Ltd of Redditch

Ixion Cycles Ltd	New Hudson Ltd	The New Rapid Cycle Co Ltd	Sunbeam Cycles Ltd	Eadie Manu-facturing Co Ltd

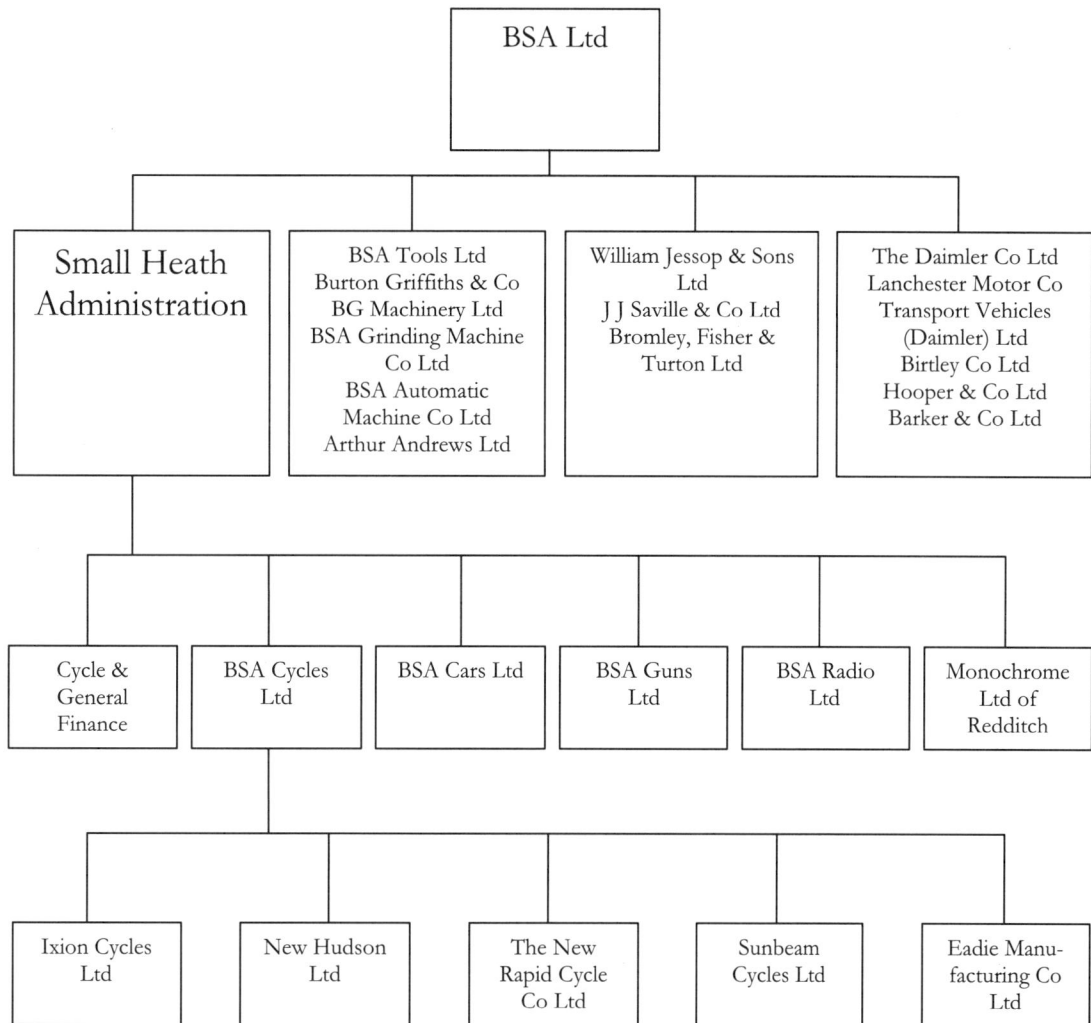

"When a firm with such an old-established name and reputation in both the cycle and motor cycle worlds as the BSA Company was first rumoured to be entering the cyclemotor field, there was a wave of genuine interest, not to say excitement, over a public far wider than that of the potential riders." Thus spake *Power & Pedal* in October 1953.

The Winged Wheel was to be one of the more elegant of cyclemotor engine units. No short-cuts had been taken with the engineering side of things, something that was only to be expected from such a long-established quality motor cycle manufacturer. What was on offer to the public in 1952 however was not BSA's first attempt at a cyclemotor. A revealing small report entitled "Bicycle Power-Drive" that was published in *The Motor Cycle* magazine of 3rd October 1946 describes:

"A patent (No 580,067) covering the driving mechanism from an engine to the road wheel of a bicycle has been granted to the BSA Company and Mr John Fletcher. The arrangement comprises two friction wheels - one on each side - which bear on the undersides of the rim of the rear-wheel of a bicycle. By pivoting the engine unit, mounted near the bottom bracket of the bicycle, the friction wheels may be brought into contact (with) or moved off the road wheel rim and are easily detachable to allow the cycle wheel to be removed. Each engine mainshaft carries a sprocket directly connected by enclosed chain to each friction wheel."

An aside: the following paragraph on the same page is rather alarming, being headed *"Rocket Assisted Speedway Machine To be Ridden at Wembley Tonight"*. It continues, *"An experimental rocket-assisted machine will be ridden by Bill Kitchen during the interval at Wembley Speedway tonight (Thursday). The machine is the outcome of experiments by Professor A.M.Low, assisted by Mr.Alec Jackson; the latter has already tried out the machine. There will be four rockets, controlled by handlebar switches".* The very same Prof Low was to carry out the noise-tests at ACU Cyclemotor Trials. One wonders how it ended and if the rockets shut down in time.

To return to BSA's first thoughts on a cyclemotor with Patent No 580,067: *The Motor Cycle* magazine picked up the story too, in the *Comments by Ixion* page. He notes; *"I am rather tickled with the BSA patent for an improved form of friction drive, presumably intended for autocycle use. The root idea is as old as the hills - that is to say it originated on motor cycles around 1900".* He contemplates whether the BSA system using two friction wheels would be better than the older, single wheel type and concludes, *"The scheme should have real possibilities".* Nothing further came of it and, as far as our research indicates, no illustrations were published to show how it worked, nor did it ever appear in production.

Instead, BSA went back to the drawing board and, in conjunction with a Mr V J Stohanzl, came up with another cracking idea, a lot more bizarre than the first. This too was granted a patent (No 581866) for a *"ratchet drive for power-assisted bicycles"* and it would be best if you carefully read the following description (from *The Motor Cycle*, 5th December 1946) as it is not very easy to grasp.

"Below the bottom bracket of the cycle is a tiny engine, which may be slid backward until a flange on the inside of the flywheel makes contact with the rear tyre. The engine is thus started. On the outside of the flywheel is an eccentric which by means of a tension wire is connected to a one-way ball type clutch on the hub of the rear wheel. An arm from the outer member of the clutch is connected through a bracket to a quarter-elliptic spring on the fork tube. When the engine is running the outer member of the clutch is, say, pulled clockwise by the tension wire. The fork tube spring is therefore loaded until the eccentric turns far enough to relieve the tension wire. This allows the fork tube spring to react and drive the rear wheel through the clutch." All clear so far then? Below is a picture that might help:

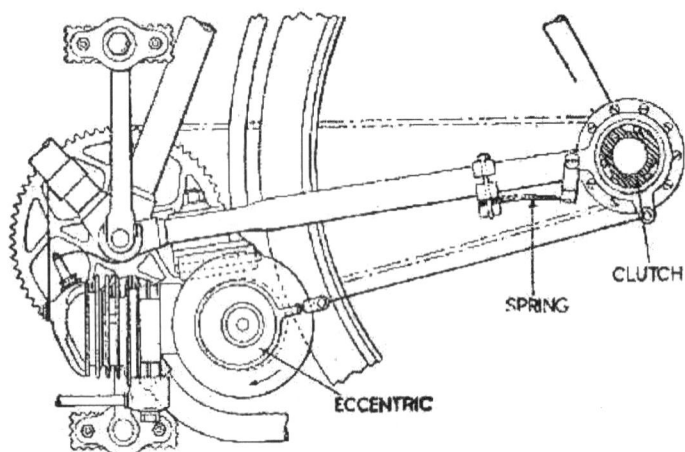

This was evidently not the way to go either as the spring was providing the driving force, having been tensioned by the motor, and probably useless against a headwind or an incline. Why not just drive the wheel directly with the motor and eliminate all the other mechanisms?

BSA's engineers were beginning to think aloud in 1946 but seemed initially unsure where to start with their project. It might have been a case of looking at the rather more extreme possibilities first, dismiss those, then get back to more conventional engineering which should prove economical and reliable. Probably the first thing they did was to size up what the competition was already selling in the market-place and decide where to go from there: whose good ideas to purloin, which clip-on unit seemed powerful, was it reliable, how easy would it be to manufacture and was there any profit in it? It all went quiet for a few years.

On May 7th 1953 *Motor Cycling* and *The Motor Cycle* magazines, in the true spirit of competition, simultaneously published detailed reports on the recently introduced BSA Winged Wheel Model W1, sub-titled *Small Heath Factory addition to the Ranks of Auxiliary Engines for Cycles* and *Ingenious Power Unit Which Incorporates Gear Drive Through a Three Plate Clutch* respectively.

BSA had designed an exceedingly well thought-out cyclemotor unit. They probably took their lead from Cyclemaster (introduced late 1950) and decided on the motor wheel approach whereby the Winged Wheel would be sold as a complete unit. This comprised the motor incorporated into the hub with rim and tyre (usually a Dunlop Carrier 26"×1¾") included, together with a separate fuel tank and carrier and handlebar controls for throttle & clutch.

(La Vie de la Moto)

A motor incorporated into a cycle rear wheel was a very old idea; the earliest known attempt was the Millet from France. Félix Millet was granted patent no 194,933 in 1887 for a bicycle equipped with a five-cylinder radial engine incorporated into the rear wheel; the crankshaft functioned as the wheel spindle whilst the cylinders rotated around with the wheel. Heaven knows how such things as carburation and ignition were meant to function as none are illustrated. Unless of course it was a steam engine - or a diesel. Such rudimentary technology would probably never have worked but Millet persisted and built a similarly powered tricycle in 1889 that actually ran, albeit very slowly and with many difficulties.

For reasons best known to itself, BSA opted for an engine capacity of only 35cc (similar to a 32cc Cyclemaster) whereas most competitors were of the European-standard 49.9cc. Even 15cc extra capacity makes a difference at this level of engine size but nonetheless a respectable output of 1bhp was claimed. Bore and stroke were 36mm and 34mm; the cylinder was machined from an iron casting and lay horizontally below and in front of the rear wheel spindle. No attempt was made to enclose or protect the engine unit, overhung outside the rear fork. The Wico-Pacy flywheel magneto looked particularly vulnerable to damage from bicycles falling off stands to port, aided by the extra weight. On the other hand, ease of maintenance could not have been bettered and this was probably what BSA had in mind.

So far, so basic, simple and ordinary. Inboard of the engine itself however everything was a lot more technical. Design and execution of the hub unit containing clutch, transmission, final drive and brake indicated access to good draftsmen, some serious foundry capacity and a very competent and skilled machine shop. Compared to most clip-on cyclemotor units, BSA engineering was of a high order, only to be expected of a company which started life in 1861 as a small union of gunsmiths and went on to become one of Britain's important industrial groups.

The cycle wheel incorporating BSA's engine was 26"×1¾", laced via short, heavy-duty spokes to a 9½" diameter pressed-steel hub casing. Within this casing fitted the engine unit, which, to quote *The Motor Cycle*, 7th May 1953; *"the inner, or right-hand crankcase half is an integral part of a single, large casting which forms the shoe-plate of the brake as well as an enclosing shell to house the clutch and gear transmission mechanism."* The outer, left hand casting was much smaller and only required to carry a main crankshaft bearing and the standard-issue Wico-Pacy Migemag S90 magneto (with a lighting coil) outrigged on the end of the left-hand mainshaft.

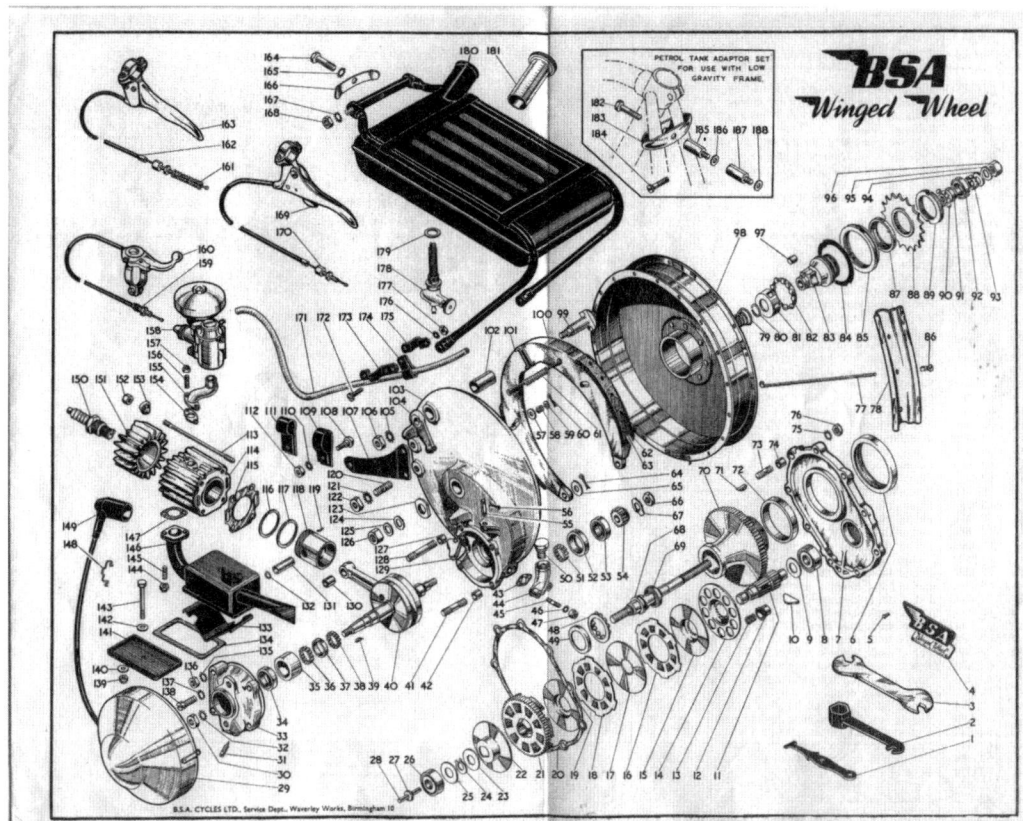

Within these two castings ran the crank; both mainshafts and their webs were of medium-carbon case-hardened steel, the crank-pin parallel ground and an interference fit in the webs, main bearings were one inch diameter rollers. Crank-pin big-end bearing was also by rollers; they ran inside the hardened and ground big-end eye of a case-hardened nickel-chrome steel con-rod of 50 tons tensile strength. On the other end of this con-rod was a slightly domed low-expansion silicon-alloy piston carrying two pegged compression rings and a fully-floating gudgeon-pin running in a phosphor bronze bush little-end, retained by circlips. The cylinder barrel was flanged onto the crankcase and topped by a hemispherical light-alloy cylinder head, this in turn spigoted onto the barrel, both of which were secured to the crankcase by four long studs.

These ran right up through radial cooling fins to the top of the head, where long nuts clamped ingenious saddle-washers bridging 4 adjacent pairs of fins.

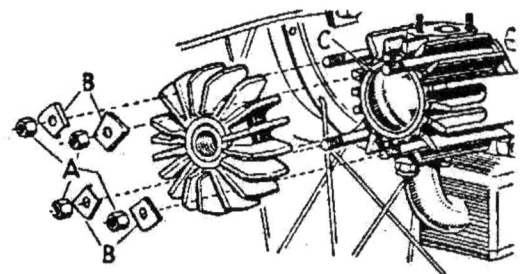

Fig. 6.—Cylinder head removed with the piston at T.D.C. The saddle washers, B, must be placed beneath the nuts, A.

Power transmission to the rear tyre was more complex, but one can well imagine BSA engineers resolutely refusing to consider any compromise. Bolting a roller to the end of their crankshaft and letting this rub a tyre to shreds or spin wildly in the wet was far, far too crude for them.

The right-hand end of the crankshaft was splined and carried a 17-tooth pinion. This in turn drove the 3-plate wet clutch via 66 teeth machined in the periphery. When the clutch was engaged, drive continued through to a small pinion behind the clutch drum, which meshed with the final drive gear riveted to the wheel hub. The effective ratio between mainshaft and wheel was 18.7:1. Cork inserts were used as friction material for the clutch and the entire gear train and clutch ran in an oil bath. Continuing its theme of better-than-average engineering, BSA had taken note of the bicycle freewheel failure saga and done away with this item completely. In its place there was a BSA Eadie coaster: a form of one-way roller clutch, silent and wear-resistant.

Finally, attached to the inner face of the transmission case, was a pair of substantial brake shoes 5¼" long by ⅝" wide. BSA was not taking any chances with inadequate bicycle stirrup brakes and it went on to offer the Winged Wheel as a complete machine, including a reinforced cycle frame manufactured by BSA Cycles Ltd.

This rare but rather poor photo shows the inside face of the right-hand transmission cover and those large, almost motor cycle-like rear brake shoes. Because of their position they were sometimes prone to oil contamination from the transmission.
(Power & Pedal)

Two other components also illustrated the care with which the Winged Wheel was conceived. Firstly, the carburettor: a specially designed miniature downdraft Amal (type 335/1) with an unusual feature.

In a quest to minimise the number of additional hand-controls festooned around a pair of handlebars, BSA had no doubt used their considerable leverage with Amal to order a special carburettor operated by a single control that not only moved the throttle slide but the choke as well.

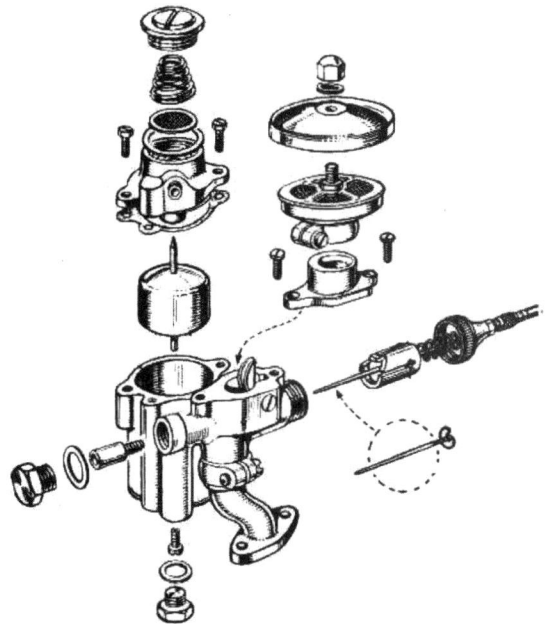

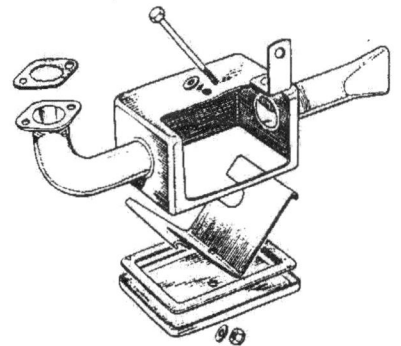

The throttle lever had a small ratchet which, when lifted, enabled the lever to be moved past the full-throttle position, where it then *"causes a blind groove in the end of the throttle slide to actuate a small tongue on the end of the pivoted strangler butterfly valve"*. In other words than those used by *The Motor Cycle*, the choke came on. Thought had also gone into preventing dirt from entering the float chamber, the lid of the float chamber was enlarged to form a well in which was located a filter, preventing particles of dirt blocking the tiny jets.

Though it may not be technically a very exciting part, the silencer also received some attention. It was designed to be taken apart for decarbonisation and comprised *"a box-section expansion chamber … containing a single baffle plate … and a short discharge pipe"*. Probably noisy then. A single through-bolt clamped the bottom plate in place. When this was removed the baffle plate could be taken out for cleaning and there was then plenty of space to give the silencer box a damn good riddling with a screwdriver.

This illustration, taken from BSA's very comprehensive owners manual, shows how a Winged Wheel should, in theory, slide between a cycle frame rear forks. The measurement between these was often different, depending on the frame manufacturer's criteria, so BSA recommended a time-honoured solution: *"the distance may be taken up with suitable packing-washers, always providing that there is enough length of spindle left at each side to allow for the proper fitting of chain tensioners, mudguard stays and wheel nuts"*.

On the subject of noisy two-stroke cyclemotor engines, 'Clip-on' (who was probably the editor, Frank L Farr) fulminated thus in the September 1955 issue of *Power & Pedal*:

"Go Quietly"

"It has always been taken for granted here that two-stroke power and two-stroke silence were mutual enemies, but I notice that the Continental machines nowadays are both more powerful and much quieter than they were a few years ago. The German manufacturers are taking this noise question very seriously for the very simple reason that public opinion is against noise and the popularity and freedom of the 50cc class depends on its not upsetting the non-riding public. The Italians don't seem to bother much but they do regard silence as a sign of quality and make their more expensive machines quiet to distinguish them from the rabble". Clip-on concludes: *"good machines are quiet, good riders are always quiet"*.

The theme of noisy 2-stroke clip-on units recurs in many magazines of the period and was obviously a common complaint, one owner reported of his Winged Wheel *"firstly, the normal engine noise is terrible. Whilst the silencing as such is fairly effective, the carburettor bark is most distracting ... the alloy transmission casing, too, actually seems to develop noise instead of reducing it".* *"The exhaust note, above 20mph, was rather sonorous"* noted *The Motor Cycle's* reporter with usual understatement.

It's free-wheel cycling when you ride a BSA Winged Wheel

BSA Cycles Ltd began building the Winged Wheel at the Waverley Works (the former New Hudson factory) on Coventry Road, Birmingham 10, production getting under way around August 1953. New Hudson autocycles were still being made there at the time and continued to be to be so until 1958, some 10,000 coming off the lines between those dates. First press road tests of the Winged Wheel appeared in late 1953, *The Motor Cycle* being the fastest off the line on 29th October. Amongst other details, it was revealed that BSA intended to sell their unit for £25 which, after all, did include the wheel and Dunlop Carrier tyre. Fuel tank capacity of half a gallon gave a claimed range of 100 miles and 200mpg was supposedly possible. As usual reality was rather different from the claim. *The Motor Cycle* managed 135mpg overall, *"under hard riding conditions"* during the road test and found *"speeds of between 20 and 25mph were well within the capabilities of the unit"*. This was quite good going for a small 35cc engine that, because it had a clutch and gear transmission, weighed in at a hefty 26½lbs. Overall gearing was also judged to be *"well suited to the engine characteristics"* and *"proved sufficiently high for there to be no indication of fuss at the highest possible cruising speed, yet low enough to provide excellent climb and easy starting"*. Also noted were *"favourable comments … received from motor cyclists and cyclists alike on the trim appearance and attractive beige enamel finish"*.

One has to remember that in the 1950s such things as magazine road tests were couched in excruciatingly polite terms, editors having no wish to upset regular advertisers and thus lose valued revenue. Nuances or shades of meaning were used to hint that, say, on a factory-supplied cycle and motor combination the brakes were perhaps *"less effective than might have been expected"*. In those days it was simply not done to say outright that said brakes were terrible, lethal, pathetic or useless and that the engineer responsible (as well as the bean-counter who limited his budget) should have their testicles nailed to a wall. Thus, an innocuous phrase such as *"vibration was virtually non-existent except at very high speeds"* in reality meant that anytime the rider wound his mount up to more than 20mph, everything attached to the handlebars was a blur, fingers would be nerveless within five minutes and high-frequency vibrations coming through the rock-hard leather saddle could put in doubt future fatherhood prospects unless speed was reduced. In its Winged Wheel road rest, *Power & Pedal* had the honesty to remark that *"when the revs must have been reaching some fancy figures, the engine could be felt through the pedals and bars and various bits and pieces on the machine worked loose during our test"*. The last part of that sentence has a familiar ring for regular users of 1950s cyclemotors today.

From introduction, the BSA Winged Wheel sold fairly well, though it should have been more popular, given the excellence of engineering compared to its competitors and the size of the company's long-established dealer network. The design of a Winged Wheel also proved to be something of a bonus when regular maintenance was required. Clutch, brake or carburettor adjustments and spark-plug cleaning could all be carried out outside the hub unit with the wheel still *in situ*.

(BSA)

Early on, a complete BSA cycle frame with Winged Wheel incorporated and a miniature Webb sprung front fork was advertised at £43.9s.6d plus tax. The Winged Wheel assembly could be installed in one of several cycle frames designed and produced by BSA specifically for its cyclemotor unit and, consequently, many were sold as complete machines. The gents cycle, Model 615 WW, was made of *"heavy gauge tubing to withstand the higher speeds and stresses imposed by Power cycling and a cranked top tube to give a lower riding position"*. Additional features included *"large mattress type saddle giving maximum comfort and control. Webb Spring Forks ... 26"×1½" Westwood wheel rims ... and ... a special lighting set, the Miller 6 T.M."*. The paint finish was either black or an attractive gunmetal *"with the usual B.S.A. super chromium plated bright parts"*. The same frame was available without the Winged Wheel at £17.14s.0d including PT or just the frame and forks at £7.10s. It could also be bought as badge-engineered Sunbeam or New Hudson marques and was also available as a lady's model: 635 WW.

Favourable press comments certainly helped sales initially, though one or two negative points were recognised. *"One of the disadvantages of the wheel unit is that the pure bicycle is 'lost' in the drag of the clutch and the constant mesh gears. The BSA was pretty good in this respect and there was no hard work in pedalling with the clutch out, although it could be felt and heard."* Another was, inevitably, noise. Power & Pedal on its hobby-horse again: *"Really this silence problem has got past being funny with cyclemotors but one is tempted to write that 'of course' the BSA is too noisy. Only about 50% of the racket seemed to come from the exhaust, as was evidenced by the fact that the rider's head had to be turned to check on four-stroking at times. Another 30% appeared to be inlet roar and the rest came from the gear drive amplified by the gears being encased in aluminium, a fine, resonating metal much used by jazz musicians to get more noise out of their banjos and guitars."*

I say, steady on chaps, that last sniffy reference to *jazz musicians* and *more noise* was a bit unnecessary. Perhaps Mr Road Tester had a particular dislike of jazz resulting from too much exposure to Acker Bilk or Chris Barber?

To compensate, the magazine found that: *"the built-in internal expanding rear brake, a super brake that is very powerful, very smooth and very sensitive to the control, a real brake in any weather and big and lightly loaded enough to last the lifetime of the unit"*. By contrast, in its test of 29th October 1953, *The Motor Cycle* opined that *"The hub brake on the test model lacked real power, though a slight improvement was apparent after 100 miles had been covered"*. However, some advantage was claimed when *"the bicycle was ridden in the rain. Whereas stirrup brakes lost power, the internal expanding brake retained its normal efficiency"*.

Webb SPRING FORK

Specially designed for **MOTOR-ASSISTED BICYCLES ★**

Here is the ideal Fork for machines with engine mounted IN or ABOVE the rear wheel or on the bottom bracket. Road shocks and vibration absorbed. Perfect comfort and control ensured.

British and Foreign Patents applied for

Also suitable for Tandems, Bicycles and Carrier Cycles

● Stress taken direct on compression spring in column tube

● Front Spindle and head positions maintained

● Perfect breaking with caliper, roller lever or hub brakes

Additional weight only 2¾lbs. approx.

Order from your Agent or write to us for Leaflet

H. C. WEBB & CO. LTD., TAME RD., WITTON, BIRMINGHAM 6

This advert shows the Webb spring fork fitted by BSA when a Winged Wheel was offered to the buying public as a mechanically sophisticated complete cyclemotor. It was intended to compete with a new generation of moped designs, many emanating from Europe, which were flooding into the UK. Too little and too late…

The 28th Earl's Court Cycle & Motor Cycle Show of 1953 took place between November 14 and 21 (admission 2/6d, "*A Show to Excite the Pulse of the Enthusiast*") and gave an excellent snapshot of the popularity still retained by motor cycles at that time. On Stand 25, BSA was showing 20 examples of every basic type of motor cycle it made from a total of no less than 39 different models: 125cc and 150cc two-strokes; 250cc side-valve and overhead valve (ohv); 350cc ohv; 500cc side-valve and ohv singles and ohv twins; a 600cc side-valve and 650cc twins. Special exhibits included a sectioned working model of the B32 348cc Gold Star, a sectioned 148cc Bantam Major D3 and a "*moving tableau featuring two 248cc side-valve C10L machines in 'work and pleasure' panoramas*". BSA had not been idle in the immediate post-war years. Such a broad range of offerings to the public must have kept its R & D department at full stretch, perhaps causing the delay in launching the Winged Wheel, which was not on display at this show.

By 1954 the price of a Winged Wheel had increased to £26.5s.0d; however, this was still slightly less than its most direct competitor, the Cyclemaster, at £27.10s.0d. Realistic production figures for the Winged Wheel are hard to come by and the suspicion can only be that BSA preferred not publish them (unlike Cyclemaster, who in December 1952 advertised proudly that it had already manufactured over 100,000 units) because sales were much lower than the company had expected. BSA had in truth misjudged the transitory nature of the clip-on cyclemotor market. It had taken too long to design and develop its motor-wheel and launched it too late to attract more than a small share of a market where competing products were already well established and had loyal followings. By then the market was changing, this was confirmed by the lugubrious sub-heading attached to *The Motor Cycle* magazine's Earl's Court Show report of 18th November 1954 which reported "*Motorized Cycles and Cyclemotors, Eleven Makes Exhibited at Earl's Court: Clip-Ons Outnumbered by Complete, Specially Designed Machines*".

In service the Winged Wheel nevertheless proved to be reliable and provided power-assistance in abundance, albeit with rather low gearing that meant hills were easily climbed but which induced correspondingly high revs at cruising speed. *Motor Cycle & Cycle Trader* magazine of the period issued Servicing Data Sheets based on BSA Cycles Ltd Service Department information and upgrades. The factory also issued its own Service Sheets, beginning with No W1 dated January 1954. This described a modification carried out by the factory, starting with engine BW 2700, which was provision of a drilling to release pressure inside the drive casing when the engine was hot. Presumably BSA's engineers had done too good a job sealing in the transmission lubrication, which appears to have been forced out past various seals by increased air-pressure within. A diagram showed where pre-BW 2700 engines should be drilled to alleviate this problem.

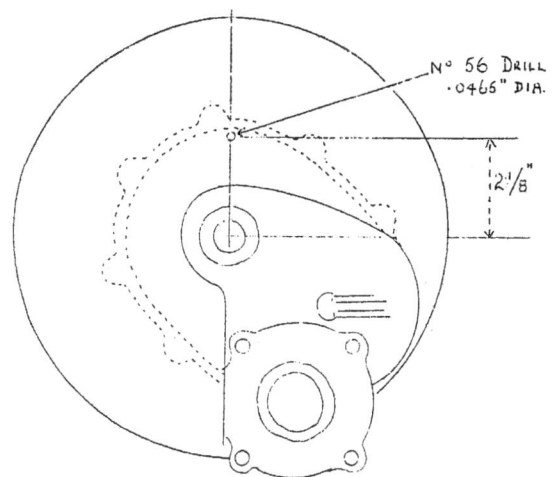

Other improvements for 1954 included a ¼ inch longer wheel hub spindle to enable a hub locknut (part 62-385) to be fitted. A different ball cage assembly (62-452) with external claws for the new spindle superseded ball cage 14-1872 (internal claws). The new ball cage would fit either length of spindle but *"on no account should the old 14-1872 ball cage assembly be fitted on the new pattern spindle"*.

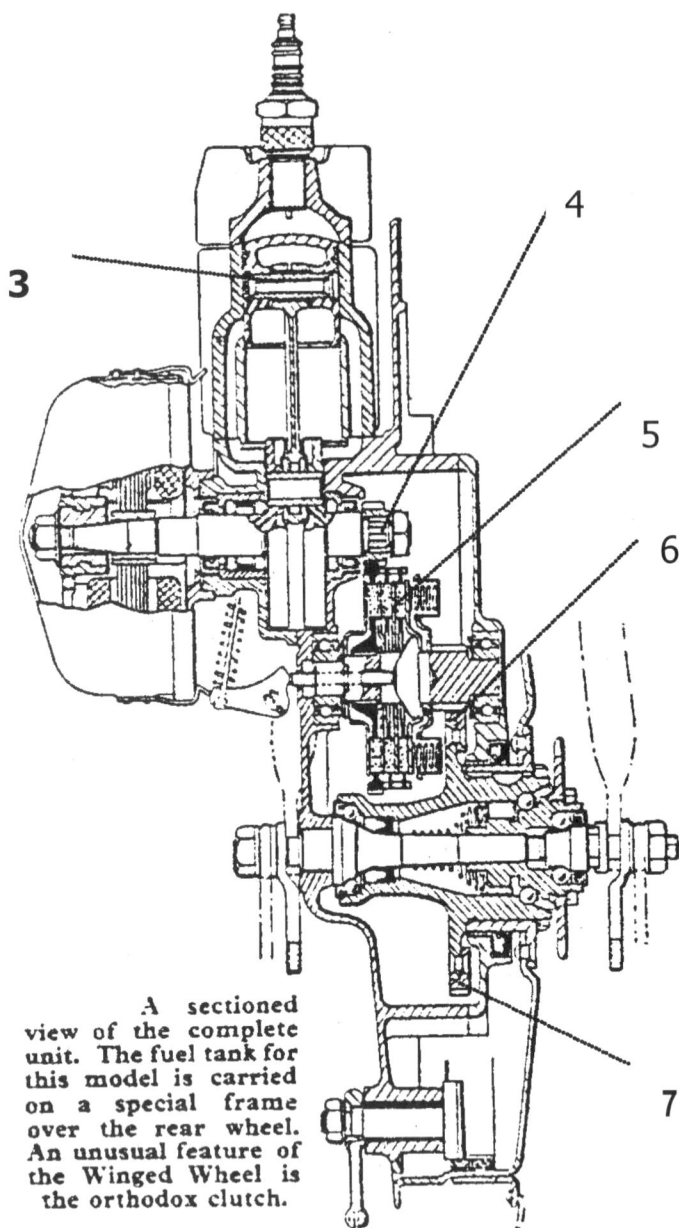

Sectional drawing (left) is a view from above the unit and gives a very good idea of the 'cascade' gearing that leads from the crank output gear **4** meshing with teeth machined around the clutch drum periphery **5**. Pinion **6** is driven from the clutch output side and engages with the final drive reduction gear **7** which is attached to the pressed-steel wheel centre. Number **3** is the piston.

Given the amount of engineering packed into a small space as indicated by this drawing, it is a surprise that BSA felt it could still make money with the Winged Wheel being sold retail for £26.5s.

A sectioned view of the complete unit. The fuel tank for this model is carried on a special frame over the rear wheel. An unusual feature of the Winged Wheel is the orthodox clutch.

Winged Wheel Service Sheet W2 detailed a set of fittings (part no.62-378, price 3/3d retail) to enable the petrol tank to be fitted to low gravity frames and W.3 an instruction on hub-lock ring adjustment. Apparently this was necessary in many cases after a machine had got beyond the running-in period and manifested itself by excessive play at the wheel rim, which *"can be mistakenly attributed to a slack wheel bearing adjusting cone"*. Tightening the cone further only resulted in the collapse of the wheel bearings, leaving the wheel play still in evidence. The fuel tank problem came about because the fuel outlet and tap were at the back of the tank. When the carrier and tank were fitted to a low or small frame the tank tipped down at the front so only a couple of pints of fuel were accessible.

BSA also offered a set of extra-long cables, clutch 62-391, brake 62-394 and throttle 62-397, for use when fitting a Winged Wheel to a tandem frame.

Motor Cycle & Cycle Trader printed a useful Winged Wheel tyre pressure chart in May 1955, based on a rider's weight:

Tyre pressure (lbs/sq.in)	40	43	46	49	52	55
Rider's weight (stones)	7	8	9	10	11	12

Remarkably few long-term tests of BSA's little power-wheel seem to have been published (perhaps because it wasn't around for very long) but *Power & Pedal* were sufficiently committed to the cyclemotor world to print an anonymous reader's experience of a Winged Wheel in September 1954, extracts of this article follow and begin…

"When the time came for my choice, I contacted Power & Pedal *by phone, explained my interest in the BSA and asked for comment. With their usual friendly interest the publishers … gave me the road test of the* Winged Wheel. *Obviously they were not impressed with this unit. So I bought one … and fitted it myself. Before running I found the petrol float had been inserted upside down and the contact breaker gap measured approximately ½" (normal gap would be 0.018"), the feed lead from the lighting coil had not been soldered to the terminal and the inlet nipple of the carburettor petrol feed was incapable of taking the flexible pipe … petrol fairly gushed out."*

A careful Pre-Delivery-Inspection had obviously been carried out, then. One cannot help but wonder if Mr Anonymous had had prior unpleasant experiences of BSA products, which had led him to perform major overhaul procedures on his Winged Wheel before even firing it up. He continues:

"After running I found that the free-wheel assembly had been maladjusted before leaving the works, had seized and blown up … indicative I think of very loose inspection at the sub and main assembly stages of production. Life settled down after this and my other complaints are directed mainly at the designers.'

His main gripe was aimed at the high overall noise level, both from the carburettor and gear train whine amplified, as previously recorded, by the large alloy crankcase casting. The ignition system was regarded with suspicion as being the probable cause of a four-stroking problem. The ubiquitous Wipac Migemag S90 magneto was not thought capable of supplying reliable sparks at over 6,000rpm (most clip-on units peak revs were much lower than a Winged Wheel), this suspicion deepened by the early factory substitution of a Miller BS19 flywheel magneto.

Despite all of the above, Mr Anonymous found the unit to be an *"attractive, reliable and soundly-engineered unit at a reasonable price … and good enough to hold its own against all, including its type competitor".*

By late 1955 the competition to BSA's Winged Wheel Model W1 was ever more fierce, with most manufacturers of clip-on cyclemotor units now going for the Euro-standard engine capacity of 49cc. Power outputs were rising, particularly amongst mopeds, as engineers developed their designs and fuel quality improved dramatically. Cruising speeds heading for the magic 30mph, leaving smaller capacity machines struggling in their wake.

At Earl's Court in November 1955, BSA displayed two sectioned working models of the Winged Wheel for public inspection on stand 148, which generated a certain amount of interest. According to *The Motor Cycle*, *"one gentleman … studied every component from every angle, watched the engine work as he turned the handle and generally appeared an experienced, technically-minded enthusiast. At length, he spoke to his patient wife in an awed tone: 'So that's how it gets me to work' he said."* However, no improvements or additions to the current model were listed. It might have encouraged more sales if the company had made some effort, for instance, to increase engine capacity to 49cc (hardly a difficult or costly task) and at the same time change final drive gearing to something less deafening. But sadly the Winged Wheel had become an abandoned orphan within the BSA motor cycle range, left to fend for itself in an increasingly hostile environment. Other more profitable models were taking precedence in the Sales Department, as confirmed by the company's display at Earl's Court. This featured amongst a total of 20 machines the more traditional Gold Star, Shooting Star and 650cc Road Rocket motor cycles, not to mention the ever-popular Bantam, plus two very significant new models, both scooters; the Beeza and Dandy 70. It was very clear that the Winged Wheel had been left out in the cold.

Scooters were in the ascendant, mopeds were taking great chunks out of the traditional clip-on and motor-wheel cyclemotor market, the poor Winged Wheel had nowhere to go except into oblivion. It exited the scene at the end of 1955, by then priced at £32.4s.0d as a result of the imposition of 25% Purchase Tax by Chancellor 'Rab' Butler in April of that year. An estimated 29,000 Winged Wheels were built over a nearly three year production period, far too few to make any real profit for BSA. This was a respectable figure nonetheless and, on a more positive note their survival rate is excellent compared to many contemporary, perhaps cruder, cyclemotor units, proof indeed of BSA's engineering excellence.

The Winged Wheel story does not quite end there however. In 1993 a company rejoicing in the name of Power Mobiles Private Ltd, Plot No.4 Mugalivakkam Road, Porur, Madras 600 116, India, produced a leaflet advertising *"a Cycle that works like a Moped"*. Lo and behold, the Winged Wheel *redux…*

Power Mobiles Pvt. Ltd., in technical collaboration with BSA Company Ltd. UK, had adapted a great deal of the Winged Wheel concept to produce an updated version which, while the layout was instantly familiar, looked much more modern.

"Low Cost

Gives your leg the winged wheel advantage to indulge in flights of fancy. Say goodbye to bus-stops … as you swish by on your wonder wheel with only an investment of around 2,000 Rupees and running cost comparable with public transport.

Easy Maintenance

…it doesn't require a mechanic as you house guest. So from the beginning you and we are hassle free.'

Strong and Durable

For all seasons this sturdy stud is as fit as a fiddle for a family on the move. The high torque engine … will make the ride simply smooth, exhilarating, delightful and particularly relaxing."'

If only BSA had adopted such an optimistic tone in the UK things might have turned out differently…

There is considerable doubt that Power Mobile's version of the good old Winged Wheel for the 1990s ever made it beyond a few prototypes and a brochure and we cannot determine if any were ever seen on the road. Perhaps in a future edition of this book we can stand corrected.

Sinclair Goddard and Co Ltd of 162 Queensway, Bayswater, London W2 were amongst the early arrivals on the clip-on cyclemotor scene, introducing their Power Pak to the press in April 1950. It was an original, all British design for a change and was not a descendant or version of any Continental machine. Sinclair Goddard engineers had designed a cyclemotor engine with a number of differences to the mainstream units of the time but above all with a quality product in mind. They had realised that, nice though a clutch and gear or chain final-drive may be, they were not strictly necessary for a minimalist 49cc clip-on and added weight, complication and cost to a unit.

(The Motor Cycle,
May 1950 ©
Morton's
Motorcycle Media
Ltd.)

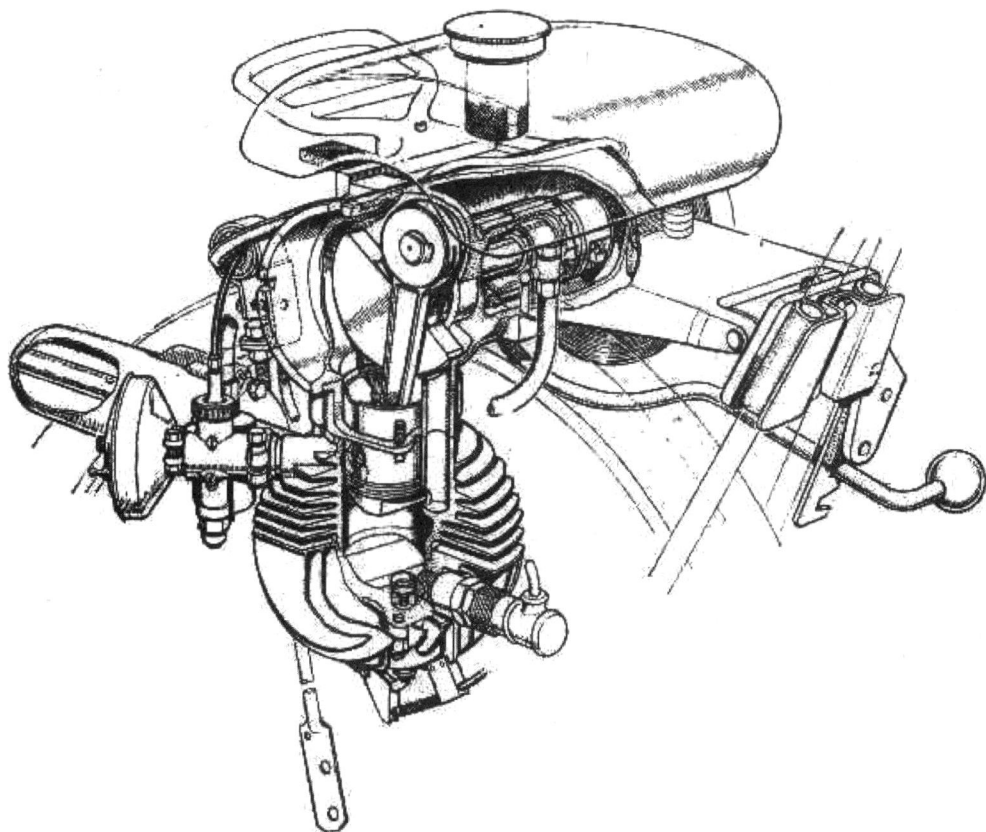

Durability and high-quality construction were of paramount importance for Sinclair-Goddard. The proof that this philosophy was correct can be found in Stone & Cox's factual listings of Motor Cycle Power Units from the 1950s and '60s (an early version of Glass's Guide for the motor trade). The Power Pak was still shown as being available new in 1961, eleven years after it had been introduced and long after nearly all other competitors had disappeared into oblivion, with the exception of the Itom and Cyclemaster.

The Power Pak, like its most similar rival the Mini-Motor, was a simple roller-drive unit fitted above the rear wheel but from there onward their differences were manifold. Firstly and most visibly, Sinclair Goddard had inverted its cylinder so it hung downwards beneath the crankcase. This was in the interest of superior cooling as there was a better chance a rider's thighs would not impede airflow quite so much as if it were horizontal and hidden behind a substantial bottom. This position also brought the weight slightly lower down, something of a consideration when a clip-on engine unit weighed 22lbs, often more than the bicycle it was propelling. Inside this cylinder however lurked some retrograde technology in the form of a deflector-top piston. Debate has extended over many years as to the merits or disadvantages of deflector pistons, which look as though they should do a better job of managing gas flow inside a two-stroke cylinder than a simple flat-top or domed piston.

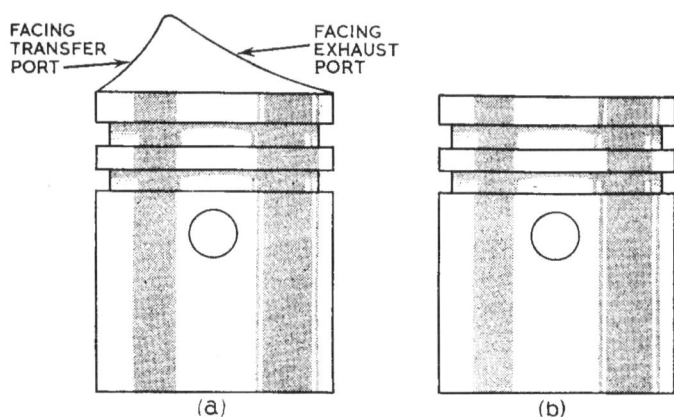

TYPES OF PISTON USED IN TWO-STROKE ENGINES.
(a) Deflector-type piston.
(b) Flat-top piston.

The theory was that an incoming fresh fuel charge, coming through a transfer passage, was deflected upward by the ramp into the cylinder head. Then it swept around and down the slope on the other side, scavenging burnt exhaust gases on the way and sweeping these out the exhaust port. This was supposed to prevent residual exhaust gases remaining in the cylinder and diluting the fresh unburnt mixture, creating conditions favourable to four-stroking. Any advantage gained with gas flow was probably nullified by the extra weight and inertia of the deflector piston and the patchy combustion caused by the irregular cylinder head shape. The flat-top design uses the angle of the ports to direct the gas flow, achieving the same results without the disadvantages of a big lump of metal on top of the piston.

VéloSoleX was a case in point; for many years the company stood by its deflector-piston engine design, of which several millions were built, only abruptly to abandon this and go over to a flat-top (well, slightly convex) piston, of which it made many more millions. It has to be said that a deflector-piston, clutch-less, 45cc VéloSoleX had a steam-engine's ability to pull away smoothly from practically zero revs whereas the later 49cc flat-top engine does not take so kindly to this sort of treatment, but other factors may be of influence. At any rate, nowadays only a few massive marine two-stroke diesels still use a deflector piston.

The Motor Cycle magazine, in its Earl's Court Show review of 15th November 1951, pointed out that emphasis was placed on the *"precision hand-built nature"* of a Power Pak unit by Sinclair-Goddard, and that *"ball and roller bearings are employed throughout, except for the small end of the connecting rod, which is bronze-bushed … a lively two-stroke of 49cc capacity … drive is direct on to the tyre by a new type of friction roller claimed to have a very long life"*. One unusual feature of the Power Pak, which contributed to a very compact unit, was the simple, overhung crankpin and counter-weight. This was supported on the inboard side by a substantial ball-bearing, not unlike the highly successful French VéloSoleX already mentioned. Indeed other similarities in design are also evident if one mentally turns a Power Pak downside-up, with the cylinder at the top and places it on a cycle front wheel.

According to the factory Data Sheet, salient characteristics of a Power Pak were as follows; bore and stroke were 39mm × 41mm, normal revs were 3,000rpm but no power output was quoted. The archaic deflector piston may have been a limiting factor of power output, hence a certain coyness about the facts. As usual with clip-on cyclemotor units, petrol consumption was claimed to be *"200mpg at Cruising Speed"*. Road test reports would give a slightly different story.

FIG. 1.

The above factory brochure illustration, viewed from the off-side, shows how neatly a Power Pak fitted over a cycle rear wheel. This picture is of a later version (from engine no 6751), the crankcase blanking plate 'O', giving access to the big-end bearing, is held down by three studs and nuts. In the first versions this plate took the form of a large screw-in cap. Inside the crankcase was to be found a steel crankshaft supported by two large ball races, extending across to the out-rigged magneto on the opposite, near-side, with a ribbed drive-roller sitting on the tyre in the middle. The substantial alloy mounting arm, part of the crankcase, can also be seen.

Fig. 3.

J

Z

K L Q X

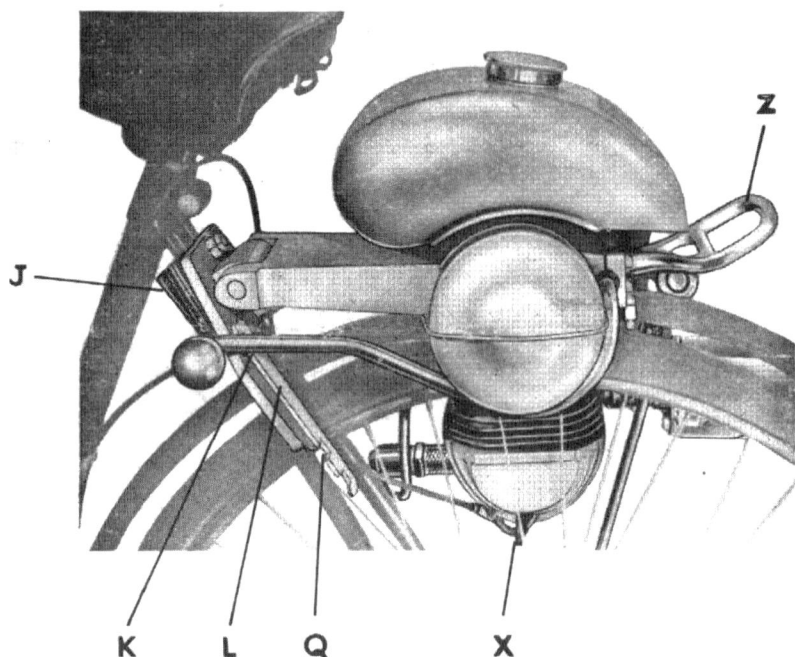

Another unusual feature could be found inside the crankcase: an aluminium-alloy con-rod (though some later Power Paks were fitted with steel con-rods, together with a modified crankshaft to suit. Con-rods are not interchangeable unless the corresponding crank is also substituted) supporting an aluminium piston with two rings. Petroil mixture to a ratio of 16 to 1 was supplied by an Amal 259/001D carburettor to a KLG WF50 14mm spark-plug energised by the inevitable Wico-Pacy Bantamag. This KLG plug, because it lived somewhat exposed to rainwater thrown up by the rear wheel, was waterproofed via an extended gland-nut that surrounded the porcelain insulator and a plug cap that fitted over the nut, providing a complete seal. The magneto rotated clockwise, contact breaker gap was 0.015" and ignition advance 33°. Thankfully, a decompressor was fitted as standard, unlike early Mini Motors, a Power Pak's most direct competitor, which did without.

Starting Instructions printed in the owner's Instruction Book went as follows: *"It is up to the individual driver to find the best method for easy starting, using either the Choke or the Carburettor Plunger, or a combination of the two, bearing in mind that more choking is required in colder weather".*

"Mount the bicycle, place the Control Lever in the 'Decompressor' position (right hand direction). In this position the Decompressor Valve (located at the underside of the Cylinder Head) opens … Note.- a loud hissing noise is heard when the Decompressor Valve is in use. Still holding the Control Lever in the Decompressor position, pedal the bicycle until speed has been gathered, a matter of a few yards. Move the Control Lever to the 'Half Throttle' position (left-hand direction). The Motor will Commence Running. CONTINUE TO PEDAL BRISKLY until you are SURE that the Motor is running smoothly. When the motor is warm this should only need one or two BRISK revolutions".

These instructions continue in a similar vein for another page, leading one to surmise that a Power Pak might not have always the easiest machine to start.

Engagement of the drive was effected by operating a near-side hand lever positioned below the saddle. This had three positions: disengaged, engaged normally and *"engaged for an under-inflated tyre"*, via notches in a plate attached to the forward mounting of the seat stays. Predictably, the third position was somewhat abused by many riders who used it to compensate for lack of traction due to bald or wet tyres, resulting in a quick and explosive death for what was left of the unfortunate rear tyre. *"A two-way lever on the handlebar controls the throttle and also the compression-release valve"*.

The Power Pak was advertised at £26.5s.0d and it was claimed that fitting the unit would only take 20 minutes work. Sinclair-Goddard did take some steps in its design to improve quality of life for its customers; the Power Pak engine was rubber-mounted at three points in an attempt to damp out those annoying vibrations. Two rubber tubes were slipped over the cycle frame rear forks and were clamped by the forward mounting, the other was a Silentbloc bush attached to the stay rod. This was clamped in place by the right hand wheel spindle nut. Another feature specified in Power Pak's brochure was a one-half gallon petrol tank, complete with a tank filler cap with a capacity of one ounce of two-stroke oil (5 caps per tank-full of petrol) having a shape which *"promotes a reserve level which can be brought to the front of the tank by tipping"*. The cross-section of this tank was kidney-shaped as it was wrapped around the cylindrical profile of the crankcase beneath.

R

N

E

T

V

S

F

D

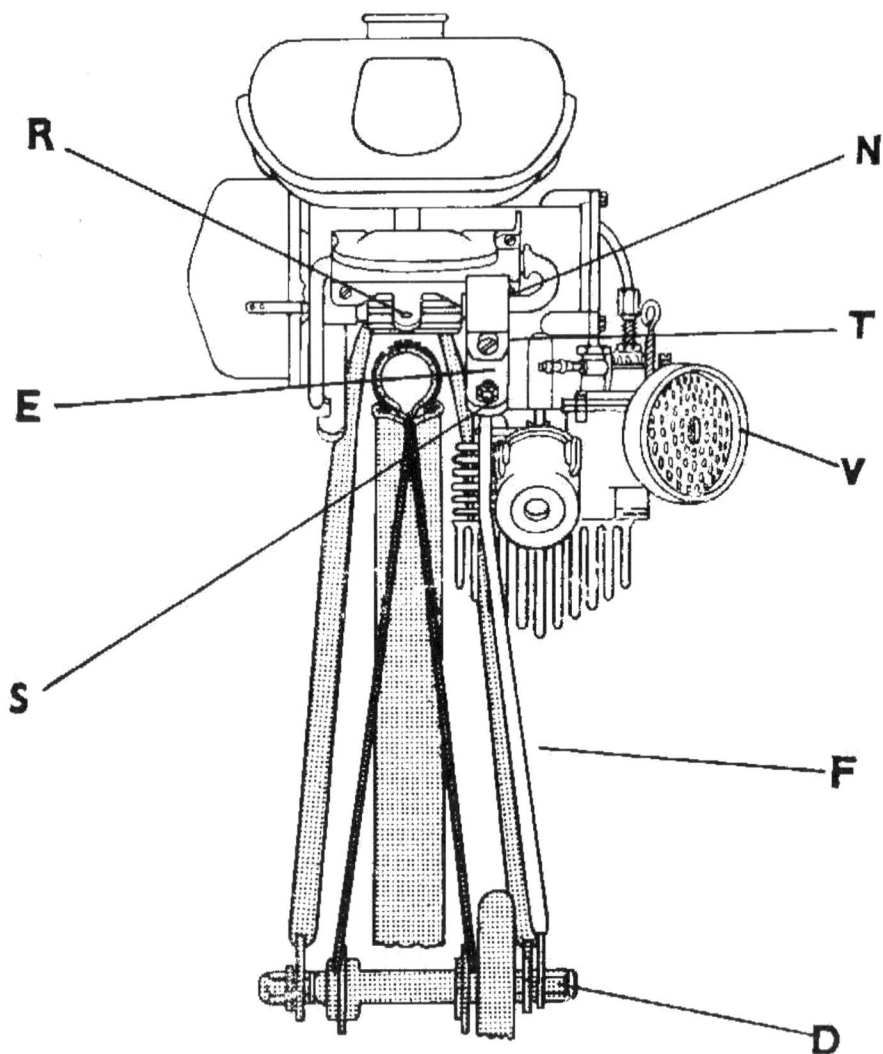

The above illustration, taken from the fourth edition Instruction Book (applicable to engines from number 2700), shows a motor *in situ* but fitted with an alternative carburettor from the Bletchley Engineering Co Ltd rather than the miniature Amal 259/001D originally used, which can be seen in Fig 1 of the same book. The BEC carburettor was designed to avoid leakage problems endemic in carburettors assembled from various components which had numerous seals and washers attempting to keep petrol in, while constant engine vibrations were working to ensure early disassembly of the carburettor and ensuing pong of disgusting Pool petrol. Though not a thing of great beauty or style, the BEC was of monobloc design, had minimal leakage points and probably did the job just as well as the more traditional Amal.

Amongst the parts indicated in the illustration, A was the Mixing Chamber Top, E the fuel feed banjo, H the Mixture Adjusting Screw, J the Flooding Control.

The BEC carb was a 'non-flood' carburettor, said to *"function perfectly over the most uneven road-surfaces ever likely to be encountered"*. It was fitted to standard Power Paks, the later Synchromatic clip-on unit always had an Amal.

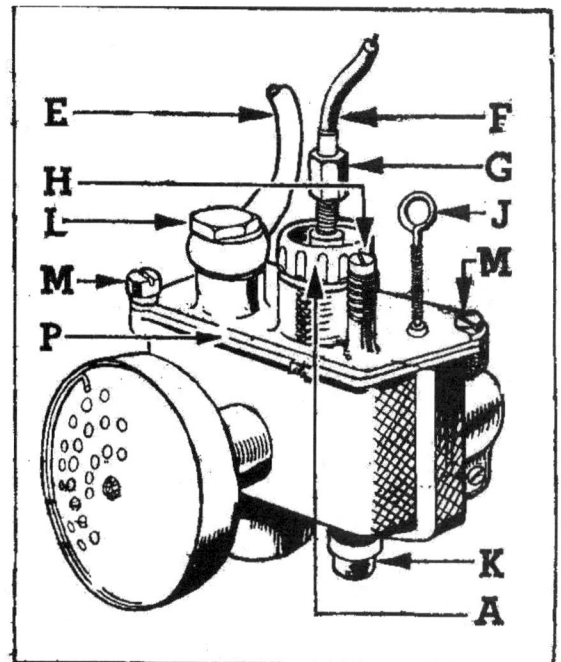

One of the earliest magazine Road-Tests carried out on the Power Pak was published in *The Motor Cycle* on 8th March 1951 under the heading *"Buzzing Around Box Hill, The Tale of a Gathering of the Micromotor Clan in Surrey"*. The article was a 4-page mass road test of no fewer than eleven MACs (motor-assisted cycles) carried out by five magazine staff-members on machines supplied by the manufacturers themselves. The test took place on February 20th beneath leaden skies and a traditional day-long English winter downpour. The eleven machines present covered virtually the entire industry and comprised, in alphabetical order; Bantamoto, Cucciolo, Cyclaid, Cyclemaster, Cymota, GYS Motamite, Mini-Motor, Mosquito, Power Pak, VAP and VéloSoleX. Quite naturally, and in the interest of journalistic objectivity and physical well-being, proceedings were centred around a local hostelry, the Burford Bridge Hotel, where Fleet Street's Finest were observed *"drinking coffee in the lounge"* … at least to begin with. Apparently the rain was *"sheeting down"* all morning so participants were forced to remain in the Snug, chewing the fat on cyclemotors until after lunch, when, miraculously, the weather brightened.

The proposition was that *"power-propelled cycles are nowadays common on British roads"* so *"why not ask the manufacturers to join us in a gossip on powered cycles and to bring with them at least one of their models for members of the Staff to gallop round the lanes"*. The Motor Cycle's article makes fascinating reading (one nugget of information relates *"Statistics indicate that about 60% of purchasers of micromotors are completely unfamiliar with any form of internal combustion engine. Instances were given of owners who had called for help when a plug lead became detached"*) and it is tempting to quote all four pages verbatim but we must concentrate on the subject in hand.

The Motor Cycle's test circuit comprised a section of the Dorking-Leatherhead by-pass, round the islands (*"to get the feel of low-speed pulling and manoeuvrability"*) and up Box Hill's zig-zag road with gradients ranging from 1 in 25 to 1 in 8 *"to see how much pedalling ... would be necessary"*.

Another interesting fact emerged from this test: *"Do drive rollers slip on wet tyres? The answer is 'no' so far as my* (Harry Louis - the article's writer) *experience showed. I tried every roller-drive attachment and never once obtained slip, even when I endeavoured to provoke it"*.

The Power Pak was one of these and included in some of the conclusions arrived at by *The Motor Cycle's* testers, namely it was *"supremely happy pulling hard at low revs"* and probably would be suitable for *"a middle-aged lady who wanted shopping transport"* (an extreme example) and who would require *"a simple and docile unit"* compared to others *"the hardened motor cyclist"*, who would probably choose 'a *"peppy"* job (Cucciolo anyone?)

By the Earl's Court Show time of November 1951, a few minor modifications had been made to the Power Pak unit in the light of users' experiences. The insignificant nature of these bore out the rightness of Sinclair Goddard's original design and its *"precision, hand-built"* construction. The first modification concerned the large, originally screw-threaded, crankcase blanking plate or door, which, because it was relatively easy to cross-thread, could result in a ruined crankcase casting. A much simple plate (already illustrated on page 97) fixed by three studs and nuts was substituted from engine number 6751.

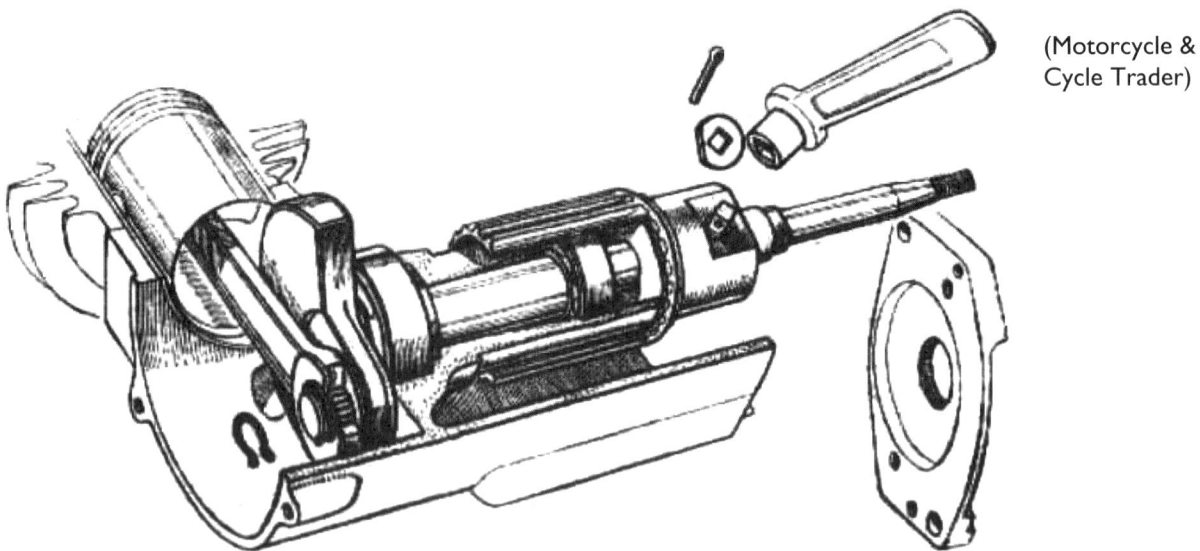

(Motorcycle & Cycle Trader)

The second modification was rather more serious, involving the circlip which held the big-end in place and which, if incorrectly fitted after an overhaul, could drop off. The ensuing mayhem was caused by the said circlip falling into the transfer port, where it would jam and severely damage both piston and cylinder.

The above illustration shows the later, heavier circlip which was designed so that, if it became dislodged, it would *"seize against the crankcase door, stopping the engine before anything more serious happened"*. The illustration also gives a very good view of the great simplicity inherent in a Power Pak engine and how well protected the mainshaft bearings were. Wear to the needle-roller big-end bearings was easily rectified by fitting a new set of 25 rollers, supplied as a service kit at the princely sum of three shillings and sixpence. Of the two ball-bearings supporting the mainshaft, the larger one directly behind the crank was lubricated by oil-mist, the smaller one behind the magneto flywheel was packed with grease via a nipple, two shots every 5,000 miles. Only one special tool was needed to overhaul a Power Pak, known in the trade as 'the bed spanner' and is shown above. This had a ¼" square bore and was used to undo or tighten the roller locking bolt onto the crankshaft. The name comes from a similar-looking spanner used to dismantle early 20th-century steel bed-frames.

F·E·S·T·I·V·A·L

The Power Pak was honoured twice in 1951; the recently-established Council for Industrial Design had chosen a beautifully-sectioned Power Pak motor mounted on a rear cycle wheel as part of its stand for the Festival of Britain. This was displayed at both at the South Bank Exhibition and as part of the Festival's Land Travelling Exhibition.

Users of Power Paks were not slow in writing to Sinclair Goddard, lauding their exploits with the machine; an example from 'T.G.B.' follows.

Dear Sirs,

I would like to report that, with a Power Pak motor fitted to my tandem, I have travelled approximately 10,000 miles, 1,500 miles with my wife on the back and daughter in the sidecar, and have experienced no mechanical troubles whatsoever. The motor has never let me down. I have not experienced any oiling plugs or starting trouble. I have had no extra maintenance costs or repairs, either to the motor or my tandem, since fitting the motor … I find the tyre wear to be very satisfactory indeed, as I have just done 1,500 miles on one tyre and the tread is hardly worn.

The power available from this little motor is amazing, and is ample to pull my family and myself quite comfortably on the flat WITHOUT TURNING THE PEDALS, whilst with some assistance, we are able to get up every hill under all conditions without experiencing any roller slip.

Yours faithfully…

Sinclair Goddard's dealers and agents were also more than satisfied with the product:

Letterhead:

TEL. 2702. ESTABLISHED 1863.

BENSONS FOR BIKES
BENSONS FOR PRAMS

Factors of:—
CYCLES. TYRES and ACCESSORIES.
PLATING. ENAMELLING.

31 & 33 LOWTHER STREET. YORK.
and 45 GOODRAMGATE

TELEGRAMS- "BENSONS BIKES, YORK."

District Agents for :—
SUNBEAM,
RALEIGH, HOPPER,
ROYAL ENFIELD,
HUMBER, B.S.A.,
HERCULES AND
PEERLESS CYCLES.

OUR REF.
YOUR REF. JB/TC.

Messrs. Sinclair, Goddard & Co. Ltd.,
162, Queensway,
Bayswater,
LONDON, W.2.   9th. October 1961.

Dear Sirs,

With reference to your letter of the 4th. inst.
ref: LEF/TT.

It gives me great pleasure to give you my
unbiased opinion of the Power Pak. Having now sold approx. 100
of these motors we have not a single dissatisfied customer, and
sales are increasing owing to their 100% reliability and performance - which is second to none !

I can personally vouch for this as I have tried
most makes, and there is nothing to equal the Power Pak - for
power, vibrationless running and reliability, and it is truly an
amazing little motor. I may add that when we have had these
motors in for decarbonizing - some two and three times, having
run approximately eight to ten thousand miles - we have not fitted
a single replacement part, and every motor is running perfectly.

Furthermore, it is surprising the tyre mileage
our clients are getting, anything up to five and six thousand
miles. While on other makes of motor some are not getting even
half that mileage. We have made a friend and a satisfied client
with every Power Pak we have sold.

In conclusion, may we congratulate you for having
produced such a perfect trouble free little motor which is such a
pleasure to handle, and is undoubtedly the 'Rolls Royce' of cycle
motors - the definition we always apply when selling or alluding
to Power Pak cycle motors. Assuring you of our closest co-
operation at all times,

We are,

Yours faithfully,

BENSONS for BIKES

104

A further endorsement of a Power Pak's abilities was printed in The Motor Cycle & Cycle Trader magazine:

No Oiling Troubles

A MOST SEVERE TEST

'It has, until now, been generally accepted that a two-stroke engine always suffers from 'oiling plugs', usually caused by too much oil reaching the cylinder head. To prove how successfully the Power Pak Decompressor Valve ejects surplus oil, the Silencer was removed and the Piston placed at the top of its stroke. A tablespoonful of neat engine oil was poured into the Cylinder Barrel and allowed to drain and settle inside the cylinder head, filling it and completely covering the sparking plug. The silencer was replaced, the bicycle mounted, and the Power Pak sprang into life after only six yards of pedalling'.

Come the early months of 1952, some more important improvements were made to the engine unit, which was effectively then offered as a new Standard model, also known as the Series B model. Firstly, the Wico-Pacy magneto now incorporated lighting coils. The Power Pak instruction sheet remarked that the new magneto with lighting coils would *"supply you with ample power for both head and tail lamps"*. Recommended bulbs were:

- Headlamp: 6 volt, 6 watt, 1.0amp
  (Bayonet or screw-type fitting)

- Tail Lamp: 6 volt, 3 watt, 0.5amp
  (Screw type fitting only)

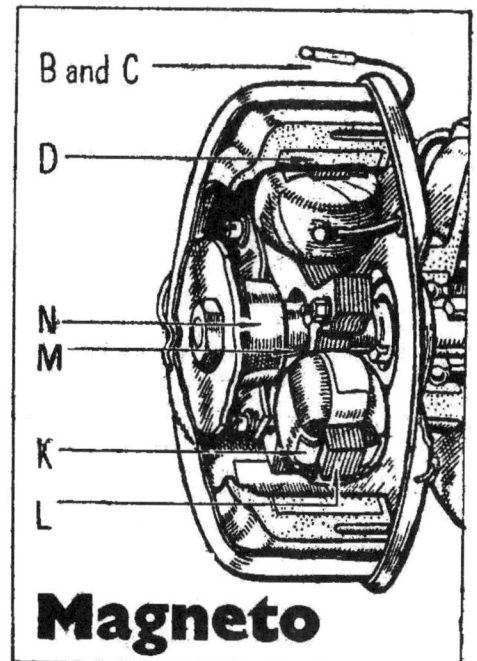

Next in line were a new, larger petrol tank, holding over half a gallon (though still of the same rather attractive shape) and the new BEC "non-flood" carburettor described previously. The drive roller was also substituted: a new, patented *EVERLAST* ribbed drive roller was fitted;

NEW PATENTED
'EVERLAST'
DRIVING ROLLER
which should outlive any roller yet produced.

One further modification was included in the 1952 program of improvements, the deletion of Power Pak's third emergency notch on the drive engagement lever. As previously noted, this had been used by many impecunious riders as a means of overcoming roller-slip on bald tyres. But the factory was discovering that, when used with a fully inflated tyre (the third slot had originally been intended solely as an emergency get you home measure for a soft rear tyre) this could damage the engine main bearings.

However, the biggest change concerned introduction of a new, second model Power Pak, the *Synchromatic Drive*, to be sold alongside the existing Standard model.

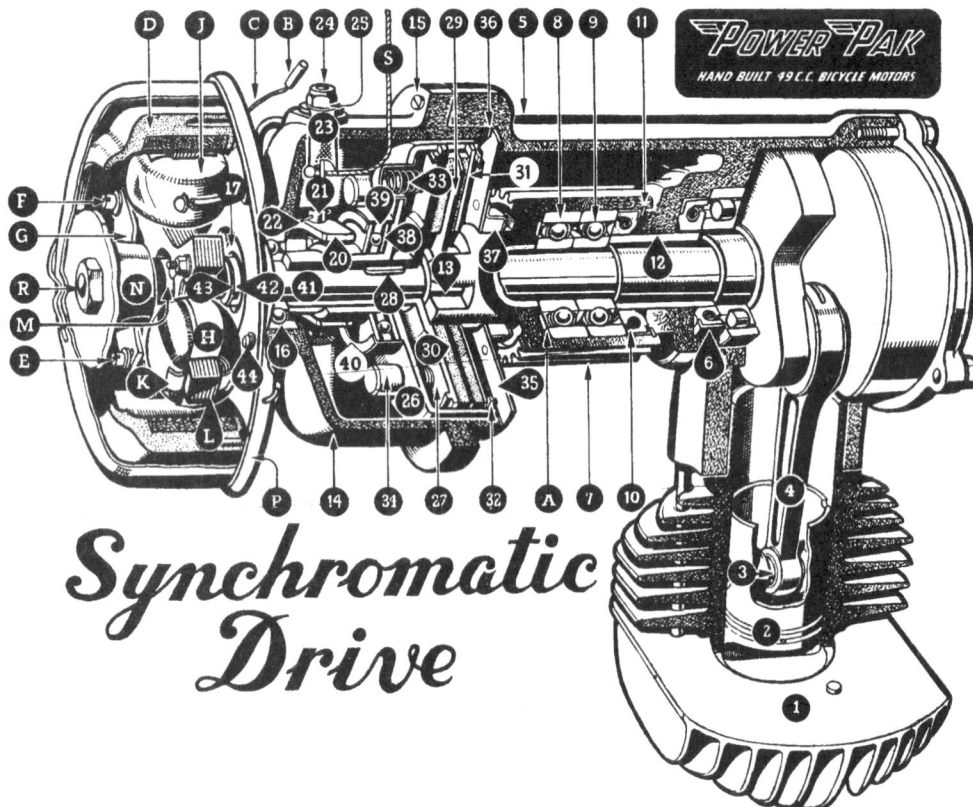

As can be seen in the above cut-away drawing, a single-plate friction-disc clutch had been mounted on the engine main-shaft, between the magneto and drive roller, entailing a major redesign and a new crankcase, bearings, crankshaft and control system. Power from the crankshaft was transmitted along a slimmer main-shaft to the magneto-flywheel on the other side of the crankcase while the clutch housing and drive-roller assembly were concentric to this. Engaging the clutch had the effect of locking the entire assembly together as one rotating unit and driving the rear wheel.

The Synchromatic Drive clutch was operated by a new handlebar twist-grip. This combined two operations in one: throttle and clutch engagement could both be operated from this single control, the decompressor valve of the Standard model being no longer needed, it was not fitted. To start a Synchromatic Drive Power Pak the twist-grip was turned clockwise to the *"Auto-Clutch"* position (clutch disengaged), the cycle pedalled a few yards to gain speed and the control turned to *"Power"* (clutch engaged). *"The Motor will commence running. Continue to pedal BRISKLY until you are sure the Motor is running smoothly"* according to the instruction manual amendment pertaining to a Synchromatic drive model. Closing the throttle hence had the effect of disengaging the clutch whilst opening it would engage drive to the rear tyre, the rider having first pedalled a little to help the clutch, a rather small unit that would not take kindly to slipping. All very simple and effective though stopping the motor, in the absence of a decompressor, required a different technique now: *"**To cut out Motor.** With the bicycle stationary, place the control in the 'Auto-Clutch' position and, with the brakes applied, gently and slowly turn the Control to 'Power' … thus stalling the engine."*

Synchromatic Drive

Introducing the New 49 c.c. Synchromatic Drive. Incorporating a self-engaging synchronized drive plus a fully automatic clutching system. 6 Star Motoring ★Fully automatic Clutch ★clutch "slip" "snatch" or "drag" virtually impossible. ★Fully automatic synchronized drive. ★Transmission "judder" virtually impossible. ★Automatic pre-set tickover. ★Motor "revving" virtually impossible. Designed for everybody young or old. Completely **effortless** automatic and foolproof with no pedal resistance. No thinking—no calculating—no worrying. Gives superb control, traffic manœuvrability and a standard of riding not yet dreamed of. Starting—stopping—accelerating—decelerating and clutching all automatically done for you by turning ONE CONTROL ONLY. No bicycle motor, motorcycle or even motor car has ever achieved this.

Every Power Pak is now supplied complete with New Dunlop Motorette Tyre, Magneto with Lighting Coil, Anti-Splash Guards, Complete Guage Set, Power Pak Cycle Pennant ALL INCLUDED IN THE PRICE

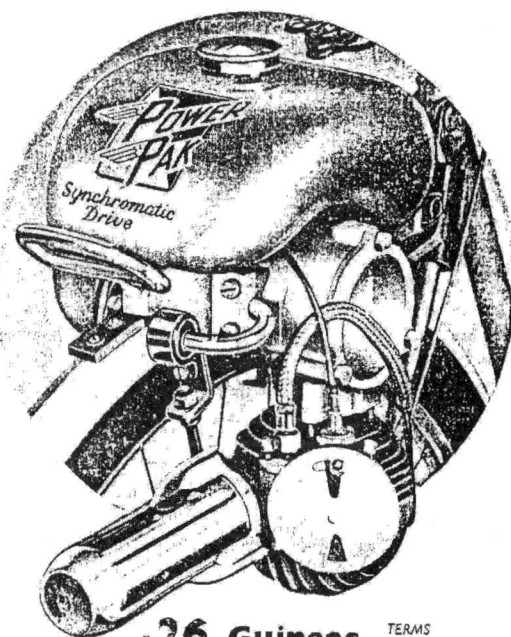

26 Guineas TERMS AVAILABLE

THE BICYCLE MOTOR WITH A BRAIN OF ITS OWN

A Power Pak Standard model (without clutch) remained on offer to the public at the new price of £25.4s.0d, a slight reduction on the previous price of £26.5s.0d current in 1951. A Synchromatic Drive Power Pak was for sale at just £27.6s.0d, a very reasonable 42 shillings (two pounds, two shillings - or even two guineas, if you like) more than the Standard model. Included in this price were a Dunlop Motorette roller-drive tyre, a tool-kit and even a Power Pak cycle pennant for attaching to the handlebars. Paint finish for the Synchromatic was a new, attractive, polychromatic copper colour.

Power & Pedal magazine published its assessment of the new model in the November 1953 edition with the following comments on Sinclair-Goddard's latest creation.

"Persistent demands from our readers for test report and service contributions … had already convinced us that the 'Synchromatic' Power Pak was a cyclemotor with a rather special appeal even before we had tested one. Closer examination immediately demands notice for the very high finish of all parts and this characteristic is notable throughout the assembly. The whole unit is a beautifully finished engineering job and the designer has given attention to quality in the smallest details."

Sinclair-Goddard's claims in advertisements that its unit was *"British Engineering at it's Very Best"* and *"The Hand Built Bicycle Motor with a Double Guarantee"* were vindicated. *Power & Pedal* continued: *"A major issue has been made of the damping of vibration and the claim of the makers that the steel roller driving on a pneumatic tyre is the finest shock-absorbing drive available is backed up by the provision of rubber vibration damping mountings for both the main securing clamp and the engaging lever gate … on the rear locating stay. This means that the entire assembly is rubber mounted at all points of contact with the cycle and the benefits of this system can definitely be appreciated in the riding comfort of the machine."*

As to the new clutch of a Synchromatic: *"It engages smoothly and disengages cleanly, drag being negligible and unfelt when standing at a tick-over. The interesting part of the idea lies in the methods of operation, which is by twist-grip, the same twist-grip that operates the throttle control. When the grip is in the "closed" position the clutch is withdrawn and the engine is free to tick over with the machine at a standstill."*

This was probably true of a nice new works supplied unit but less so with a few thousand miles under the roller. Amongst Power Pak users of that period interviewed for this book, one commented that *"the main problem was to get it to tick-over against the drag of the clutch"* and, as regards moving off under power, *"it was almost impossible to pull away using the clutch anything other than downhill"*. Hence all those exhortations in the manuals about pedalling BRISKLY off from a standstill. The Synchromatic clutch was effective if nursed but was of very small size, having been crammed into the slim cylinder that was a Power Pak crankcase and in cities *"with lots of stop-start it could easily get hot and bothered"*.

The Road Test Report continued: *"Maximum speed on the flat appeared to be just under 28mph but the slightest favourable grade or tail wind could put this up to somewhere around 35mph and the interesting thing was that this over-revving caused no distress to the engine nor any excessive noise or vibration to create alarm and despondency in the mind of the rider"*.

It was also noted (a particular *Power & Pedal* hobby-horse, this) that: *"The exhaust noise was a bit more than we think desirable, especially at night, but better than most contemporary machines. The note moreover was so 'clean' as to be really pleasant to an ear tuned to and interested in things mechanical."*

Power & Pedal also effectively confirmed some of the claims made by Sinclair Goddard for its Power Pak (*British Engineering at its Very Best … detailed design is unique and should not be confused with any other motor*) by noting: *"There was no mechanical noise from the unit at all and we give full marks for this very desirable achievement. We have never met a unit better in this respect in our whole testing experience. Another endearing feature was that the engine hardly ever four-stroked. Even on a mere whiff of gas it purred like a cream-filled pussy cat."*

I say, steady on chaps.

The magazine also more or less vindicated Sinclair Goddard's claim that its roller drive was *"unaffected by rain and functions perfectly in all weathers, even snow"* by commenting: *"The makers' claim that their specially designed and well finished roller never slips was justified for all practicable purposes although in fact we did manage to make it slip in wet weather by ham-handling the throttle at low road speeds and also when starting with a dead engine."*

Overall average fuel consumption was found to be 174.2mpg, a little short of the 200mpg claimed by Sinclair Goddard.

Nonetheless, certain criticisms were levelled at the Power Pak, despite general adulation from the testers. *"It is a stupid nuisance that the [Amal] choke control is out of safe reach of the saddle, necessitating a stop to open it after a cold start ... the standard complaint against over-the-rear-wheel roller drives that they throw mud and grit at the free-wheel ... is unhappily borne out on this unit, the makers have produced a neat little free-wheel guard for 5 shillings. This however is starting at the wrong end, we see no reason why the roller should not be effectively screened where the mud-slinging starts. It is not a light unit at 25lbs dry, so that with a full tank and the neat chrome-plated carrier which the makers fit (wrongly, in our opinion), it is near enough 30lbs and this is too far back ... the weight is felt when man-handling and riding with the engine disengaged. There is no apparent reason why the whole unit should not come several inches forward to bring the weight within the wheelbase."*

Another comment concerned the acquired reputation that a Power Pak ran hot. This was in fact a result of owners using higher octane fuel than the much-despised low octane Pool petrol for which the Power Pak had been designed. The same subject arose in a factory Service Bulletin, dealers were advised to tell their customers to continue to use low-octane fuel as no advantage was to be had from running on higher octane rating petrol and yes, there had been cases of higher than normal running temperatures.

A contributor to the correspondence columns of *Power & Pedal* in February 1954, Mr Harold Stripe from New Malden, provided a user's view of this problem. *"Regarding Power Pak engines overheating, I must insist, after exhaustive enquiry and personal experience, that this is sheer imagination, unless of course the poor wee thing is coked up solid. I've tried flogging mine unmercifully for 30 miles full-bore, including 40-plus down hills, without difficulty; it gets warm of course, but overheated, certainly not. This is with best quality petrol, Esso Extra included. After some 28 years experience with two-stroke engines I've found that 100 octane aviation spirit is the last word in fuel."* Mr Stripe also added a little extra for Power Pak owners. *"I bought a flywheel-mag removing tool, drew off the mag, drilled a small hole in the backplate, soldered one end of a length of HT cable to condenser wire of contact breaker and passed it through the drilled hole, fixing the other end to a chrome horn button on the handlebars, thus enabling me to stop [the] engine without wearing [the] clutch lining or jarring [the] engine."*

Power & Pedal concluded: *"The Power Pak is a first class motor, one of the very best, and approaches the ideal for comfortable, fussless riding, ease of handling ... and long, reliable service."*

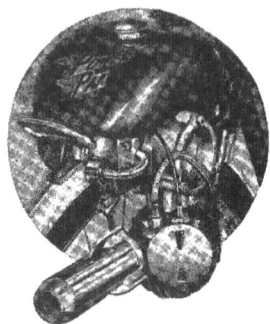

"The Bicycle Motor with a Brain of its Own" is pushing credibility just a little.

Curiously, for a manufacturer solely dedicated to the production of a cyclemotor clip-on unit, the Sinclair-Goddard company appears to have eschewed almost all forms of advertising in the motor cycle press. Magazines such as *The Motor Cycle, Motor Cycling, Power & Pedal* and other similar publications that carried much advertising for other makes of cyclemotor, had almost none for the Power Pak. One wonders if the Sales Dept at Sinclair Goddard were not indeed right in their decision. After all, the average potential Power Pak customer probably knew next to nothing about the inner workings of an engine and cared even less, his or her criteria being to get from A to B with minimal effort and cost and ride something which had the decency to start easily and not break down, that was all. Such people were far more likely to visit their local cycle shop in the hope of being well advised as to which clip-on unit was best, so Sinclair-Goddard put most of their efforts and publicity budget into training and encouraging local dealers, rather than throwing money at expensive national press advertising campaigns of dubious effect.

Published by SINCLAIR GODDARD & CO., LTD.   Vol. 163, 1952

NATIONWIDE OPINION!

THOUSANDS OF OWNERS SAY THAT POWER PAK IS THE BEST MOTOR

The public are continuously being told by manufacturers how good their products are. In order to find out just what the many thousands of owners think of the Power Pak Bicycle Motor it was decided to ask them frankly. As the makers do not come into direct contact with the user, they approached a number of leading recognised dealers throughout the country, who between them have sold and are responsible for maintaining thousands of Power Paks and who also sell other makes of bicycle motors.

They were asked to give their candid opinion. The replies must surely be the finest set of references ever held by any manufacturer.

● Every letter contained only the highest possible praise and we must state that we were overwhelmed by the complete satisfaction that the Power Pak bicycle motor has given.

We have not rested on our laurels however, and have studied in every detail how we can add to this amazing success and as a result we proudly present the 1952 model.

> Shown here is a letter from a cycle agent established in 1853, giving his unbiased opinion.

● AGENTS' LETTERS CONTINUED OVERLEAF

Above is unfortunately a very poor reproduction of the front page from a copy of Power Pak News, published by the factory and circulated throughout their dealer network for dealers and their customers. Such newsletters were fairly common at that time, Cyclemaster producing a similar house magazine entitled *The Magic Wheel*. Content of Power Pak News was breezy, upbeat and informative; articles ranged from ...

AGENTS LETTERS (THE ORIGINAL LETTERS MAY BE EXAMINED BY ANYONE)

Hornchurch and Romford District Agent; *"Performance is definitely satisfactory with solo cycles, even with sidecars carrying window-cleaners ladders etc. and tandems with sidecars attached, in all weathers and over cobblestoned roads- performance is as perfect in torrential rain as in dry conditions, with no 'slip' on the tyre- does not produce undue tyre wear- could have sold double this quantity".*

Edinburgh District Agent: *"Performance is excellent- trouble free service- no evidence of undue tyre wear".*

111

Newquay, Cornwall District Agent: *"Our appreciation of the design and performance - proved to be the ideal, especially in wet weather- the 'Everlast' drive causes no undue tyre wear and is constant in all weathers- customers report it is most reliable and trouble-free- we could have sold many more Power Paks".*

Bromley, Kent District Agent; *"Our satisfaction with the good condition of motors when they arrive and the excellent performance they give right from the start- all proved very reliable- service work is negligible- outstanding feature is very few spares needed by owners- impressed by smooth power and almost complete lack of vibration- general appearance excellent- only hope you will be able to let us have as many as we want".*

... to others along the lines of ...

371 MILES RUN COST 4/-! Wishaw Man Did 250 Miles to the Gallon

This weekend Mr.Robert MacIntyre, Russel Street, Wishaw (near Glasgow), sets out on his return journey to Baldock, some 40 miles from London. A Wishaw man, who was formerly employed at the cement plant, he has been working in the South for two years.

UNDER 24 HOURS

Recently he purchased a *Power Pak* for his Raleigh roadster cycle. On this machine he set out from Baldock to travel to Wishaw on holiday and accomplished the journey which registered 371 miles, in under 24 hours. This time includes stoppages on the road for meals. His machine ran magnificently...the run to Wishaw cost roughly about 4/- for petrol and with a similar outlay for the return run, Mr.MacIntyre's trek to Scotland and back will cost well under the 10/- mark. Two or three similar runs, he estimates, will fully repay him for his outlay on the *Power Pak*. Without it, Mr.MacIntyre, who holds a disability pension from World War II could not have undertaken such a long journey.

(Wishaw Press & Advertiser, 11th August 1950)

Sinclair Goddard also issued Power Pak Service Bulletins to dealers, detailing modifications and production changes as these were introduced. A Service Station, where defective units could be returned for repair, had been installed at 1-3 Shrewsbury Mews, Chepstow Road, Bayswater. One long-drawn-out subject covered in page after page of many Service Bulletins concerned *"Returning Empties"*. The company had had made special *"stout wooden containers"* with internal bracketry which were used to despatch complete Power Pak units to dealers. The containers remained company property and were supposed to be sent back empty once they had delivered a unit. The dealers however had found these boxes to be very useful indeed for other purposes ... as did the railways, whose task it was to transport empties. Dealers were plaintively requested to *"unpack the containers as soon as you receive them and return them to us immediately, consigning them as GOODS, not EMPTIES".*

Other items printed originated from dealers keen to promote Sinclair Goddard's product and, no doubt, ingratiate themselves with the company at the same time in the hope of increasing their quota of units.

4 UP ON A POWER PAK

REPRINTED FROM

The Motor Cycle and Cycle

𝕋ℝ𝔸𝔻𝔼ℝ

W. R. Walker, proprietor of the Hub Cycle Company of Kilmarnock Road, Newlands, Glasgow (seen steering the quad) who fitted the unit, claims 18 m.p.h. on the level with the machine as illustrated.

No story of the Power Pak would be complete without mentioning the exploits of Peter Lee-Warner. He fitted a tradesman's bicycle with a Power Pak Synchromatic unit, a great deal of travel equipment and set off on 20th March 1953 to ride to Australia and back. I cannot better the brief resumé written for the NACC web-page on Peter Lee-Warner's trip and quote it below:

"The intended route was outwards via France, Italy and the Balkans, Syria, Transjordan, Iraq, India, Burma, Siam and Malaya. The return journey was to pass through Egypt, North Africa and Spain. The cycle was fitted with a 2-gallon auxiliary fuel tank in the frame triangle and a tank of drinking water below the front carrier. By the middle of May he had reached Baghdad where he recorded an account of his experiences so far for the BBC Midland Region programme "What Goes On" which was broadcast on 28th May. It was while in Iraq that Peter changed his plans and decided to make his journey a trip around the world. September saw Peter on his return journey, flying to San Francisco on board a "Clipper" airliner. Then there was just the 3,000 mile journey to New York to complete before boarding the 'Queen Elizabeth' ocean liner for the voyage back to Britain. At midday on 20th October 1953, Peter Rode up to Australia House in London, the starting point of his journey, where he was greeted by Vivian Blaine, star of the musical 'Guys & Dolls'. The four-figure mileometer on the Power Pak read 5,501 miles- on the second time around. The Power Pak had suffered no mechanical trouble on the journey and had averaged 200 miles to the gallon. Part of the reason behind Peter Lee-Warner's journey was that he intended to emigrate to Australia and wanted to 'look the place over first'. He went to Australia for good in 1954."

(Power & Pedal,
May 1953)

Two heroes, one a 49c.c. cyclemotor and the other 33 year old Peter Lee-Warner, Ex P.O.W. and Chindit, holder of the Military Medal, left Australia House to commence a 23,00 mile bicycle trip to Australia and back on March 20th. They will pass through France, Italy, Yugoslavia, Greece, Turkey Syria, Transjordan, Iraq, India, Burma, Siam, and Malaya.

Lee-Warner is using an ordinary tradesmen's bicycle fitted with a standard production model, sychromatic drive, "Power-Pak" engine. Amongst the 195 lbs. of kit that he will carry will be a tent, sleeping bag, food suppties, emergency water rations and a cine camera. The Editor and staff of Power and Pedal wish to convey their sincere sympathy to the cycle and engine concerned.

Peter Lee-Warner found that, with his 2-gallon auxiliary tank, he had a range of about 600 miles, enabling him to tackle isolated desert crossings such as those to be found in Syria. The original spark-plug was still in use, he simply cleaned it regularly, the engine was decarbonised ever 1,500 miles or so, the average speed maintained where possible was 20-25mph and nothing broke or went wrong. This exploit amply vindicated the Sinclair Goddard philosophy of quality construction and materials.

Motor-assisted Cycle Trial

Few Competitors Fail to Gain First-class Awards
in Second A.C.U. Demonstration Event

The 30th April 1953 edition of *The Motor Cycle* magazine carried an informative report, headed as above, of the premier cyclemotor testing event organised by the Auto-Cycle Union (ACU). Such trials were popular in the 1950s as a form of low-cost motor sport and a means of challenging a man and his machine. The entry for 26th April 1953 consisted of 67 riders aboard a variety of cyclemotors including Power Pak (14 entries), Cucciolo (16), Cyclemasters (15) and Mini-Motors (8), plus a few relative unknowns such as Itom Tourist (3), Tailwind (3), Mosquito (5), VAP (1) and one *really* rare machine. This was the Jet, entered and ridden by Eric Lauritzen of The Jet Cyclemotor Co from Grønlandsveg 5, Slagelse, Denmark.

Indeed, the importance of success in an ACU trial for cyclemotor manufacturers can be judged by the number of works entries listed in the official programme; Sinclair Goddard had no less than six entries, including number 1. Others were Britax Ltd (Cucciolo), who entered four machines, one for the lovely Miss N Garlick; Cyclemaster entered three, Motor Imports Co Ltd (importers of Mobylette machines, who also entered a solitary Berini, no.44) with one machine and Mini-Motor who had four entries.

AUTO - CYCLE UNION.

MOTOR-ASSISTED CYCLE DEMONSTRATION TRIAL

SUNDAY, 26TH APRIL, 1953.

12 noon.

START and FINISH AT THE OLYMPIC WAY CAR PARK,
WEMBLEY STADIUM.
(By kind permission of Sir Arthur Elvin, M.B.E)

A Special Restricted Competition Promoted
by the Auto-Cycle Union assisted by the British
Two-Stroke Club.

OFFICIALS OF THE MEETING.

Stewards

Mr. A. C. Woollard   (A.C.U.)
Mr. R. S. G. Cawse   (B.T.S.C.)
Mr. F. L. Farr

Chief Marshal

Mr. J. C. Lowe   (A.C.U.)

Clerk of the Course.

Mr. E. G. Oxenham   (B.T.S.C.)

Scrutineer.

Mr. J. R. Jeary   (B.T.S.C.)

Timekeeper.

Mr. G. R. Evans
(A.C.U. Certified, Grade "A").

SPECIAL TESTS.

Audiometric Tests by Professor A. M. Low, A.C.G.I., D.Sc.
Brake Test - Mr. A. W. Day (in charge).

Secretary of the Meeting.

Mr. S. T. Huggott
Secretary, Auto-Cycle Union, 83, Pall Mall, London,S.W.1.

A.C.U. STAFF.

Messrs. H. Cornwell, V. Hows and K. Shierson.

ACKNOWLEDGMENTS.

Our thanks are due to ESSO PETROLEUM LIMITED
for the fuel and services they have provided
to-day, and to members of the British Two
Stroke Club for their kind assistance as
Marshals, etcetera.

Both the ACU and the British Two-Stroke Club are very much alive and active in 2004, over fifty years from the date of their trial in 1953.

Under the heading *"SPECIAL TESTS"* on the official programme cover reproduced above appears the mysterious reference *"Audiometric Test, Professor A.M.Low"*. Part of the ACU trial, amongst other activities such as starting tests, braking tests, hill-climbing ability and observed road sections was the Silence Test. Cost prohibits reproducing the photo from *The Motor Cycle* of this test, however it depicts a figure clad in a duffel-coat and woolly hat, hunched over a wallpaper-pasting table and with what appears to be two traffic cones, one in each ear. The caption reads *"Professor A.M.Low peeps at his phonery as J.Smith (Power Pak) rides by"*. He looks rather as if he has died of boredom. *"Those who made the least noise lost no marks, those in Grade 2 lost five, those in Grade 3, ten."* A special award was made for the quietest machine, in this instance a 25cc Cyclemaster ridden by A K Brimmer.

The upshot of all this archæology is that Power Paks featured at the top of the First-class Certificated list, taking the first three places, followed by a Cucciolo and two Cyclemasters. Sinclair Goddard either had the best riders at the event or the best machines, or a combination of both.

The British designed and manufactured Power Pak was the ONLY entrant with 100 marks"- Daily Herald, April 1953.

Further detail improvements were made to the two Power Pak models in late 1953. A fingertip tick-over adjuster was introduced on the Synchromatic, fitted to a new twist grip. Setting the carburettor to give a reliable idle on early Synchromatics often resulted in a too-rich mixture and consequent four-stroking at normal speeds, the tick-over adjuster allowed idle speed to be adjusted without enriching the mixture. The clutchless model became known as the New Standard and benefited from revised porting to improve engine efficiency and a twist-grip engine control. The price was revised and advertised at 19 guineas (the guinea was an old British gold coin worth twenty one shillings, taken out of public circulation in 1813). Why 1950s' prices were still being quoted in a currency unit that had ceased to exist one hundred and forty years previously is a mystery but was probably something to do with **tradition.**

The Synchromatic price was also revised, to 26 guineas.

Our Masterpiece — Synchromatic Drive

Sales of Sinclair Goddard's *"Masterpiece"* gradually began to slide, in common with many other clip-on cyclemotor manufacturers, as increased prosperity enabled customers to contemplate less primitive means of getting about. The company did what it could to hold on to its market by promoting an unlikely premise, that riding a Power Pak was actually cheaper than walking. This rested on the assumption that everybody wore comparable footwear to Army boots, these having a proven life of around 300 miles before needing re-soling at a cost of 12/6d. According to Sinclair Goddard, 300 miles by bus would cost 37/6d, 300 miles in Army boots 12/6d but *"300 miles of effortless Power Pak riding costs 11/3d, including everything"*.

It was a good try, but unfortunately even this imaginative price comparison could not change an irreversible trend that would wipe out all but a few Continental cyclemotor manufacturers by the turn of the decade.

49 c.c. Power Pak
Budget

★THE TOTAL COST OF RUNNING A POWER PAK—CALCULATED IN FARTHINGS!

PETROL AND OIL		1 FARTHING PER MILE
TAX-INSURANCE DRIVING LICENCE (on the basis of 100 miles per week)		½ FARTHING PER MILE
DECARBONISING If done by you 5d. for a Gasket every 1,000 miles If done by your dealer add one-fifth of a farthing per mile		⅕ FARTHING PER MILE
TYRE WEAR The average life of an approved tyre with the series "B" Driving Roller is 4,000 to 6,000 miles. For the Budget, however, we will place it as low as 2,000 miles of which you are guaranteed.		⅕ FARTHING PER MILE
REPLACEMENTS The Power Pak has no troublesome chains, belts, gears, pinions or sprockets. 'One moving assembly'		*NIL (The Power Pak is hand built and is the only motor that is guaranteed for twelve months.)*

AN AMAZING FACT—

RIDING THE LUXURIOUS

POWER PAK IS CHEAPER

THAN WALKING

CAN YOU AFFORD TO BE WITHOUT

THE POWER PAK ?

PROOF

300 miles on the bus   37/6

300 miles of walking   12/6
(At a recent Army test it was found that a pair of boots needed repairing after approximately 300 miles)

300 MILES OF EFFORTLESS

POWER PAK RIDING

COSTS 11/3d, INCLUDING EVERYTHING

THE TOTAL

COST IS

LESS THAN

1D / 2 PER MILE

These are facts - not slogans !

A number of Power Pak accessories were developed and sold through dealers though there was a limit to what could actually be done to a clip-on unit. Nevertheless, some useful items were on offer:

CYCLE PENNANT

PRICE 1/6 EACH
complete with fittings

This attractive pennant is weatherproof and enhances the appearance of your bicycle. It is supplied with a handle-bar clip, but if preferred, the front mudguard may be drilled and secured with the two nuts which are supplied.

● THIS ACCESSORY IS SUPPLIED FREE WITH ALL 1953 MODELS

FREEWHEEL GUARD [pat. applied]

Where a chain guard is not fitted this accessory has been designed to protect the free-wheel against mud and dirt.

PRICE: 5/- EACH

FITTING INSTRUCTIONS —
Slacken off the wheel spindle nut A. Push the guard fully home on to the spindle, preferably behind the Motor Stay Rod (as illustrated). If preferred, the guard can be fitted on the outside of the Motor Stay Rod. True the rear wheel and tighten the spindle nut.

49 c.c. POWER PAK 'STANDARD' — 24 GUINEAS
49 c.c. POWER PAK 'SYNCHROMATIC' DRIVE — 26 Gns.
Both models are now suplied FREE OF CHARGE with
**MAGNETO LIGHTING — A GAUGE SET
ANTI-SPLASH GUARDS — CYCLE PENNANT**
And a new DUNLOP MOTORETTE TYRE
which finally settles the tyre wear question!

ACCESSORIES

The following accessories with the exception of the Rear carrier and the Freewheel guard are supplied free as standard equipment with all 1953 motors.
These accessories and all spares are obtainable from your local dealer. If you should have any difficulties please contact us.

SINCLAIR GODDARD & CO. LTD., 162 QUEENSWAY, BAYSWATER
LONDON, W.2.   Telephone : Bayswater 6257 and 2828.

REAR CARRIER (Regd.)

PRICE : CHROME 19/6

This handsome carrier, fitted in minutes, fills a great need. You can now fit a Power Pak Bicycle Motor and have your rear carrier.

ANTI-SPLASH GUARDS [pat. applied]

PRICE 3/- PER SET

These guards are designed to protect the rider's legs from spray in wet weather. When fitted they must be butting against the side of the crankcase as illustrated. Note : There should be no gap between the front half of the mudguard and the underside of the crankcase.
● THIS ACCESSORY IS SUPPLIED FREE WITH ALL 1953 MODELS

POWER PAK
HAND BUILT 49 C.C. BICYCLE MOTORS

Sales of Power Pak units continued to decline through the mid-1950s before being discontinued, according to *The Motor Cycle*, in November 1955, but they recanted in January 1956: *"It is emphasised by the distributors, Sinclair Goddard & Co Ltd., that production of Power Pak cyclemotors is continuing and that full spares and servicing facilities are available"*.

Stone and Cox were still listing Power Pak as being available new in 1961 at a price of £31.17s.6d for a Synchromatic and £26.19s.6d for the Standard. This was a better survival date, if it was true, than most of Sinclair Goddard's competitors and proved once again the wisdom of manufacturing a reliable, quality product at a competitive price. Some 65,000 units had been made between 1950 and 1961, a very impressive total for a small company active in a fiercely competitive market. Into the late 1950s a small but faithful clientele, still convinced of the Power Pak's virtues, were continuing to buy new units. Appreciation indeed.

Sinclair Goddard did attempt one more way of reversing its declining sales graph; in common with a number of other clip-on manufacturers it joined the rush to offer customers an autocycle or moped, hopefully competitive with European imports.

"The Power Pak Mo-ped … a new powered cycle … is fitted with a 49cc two-stroke engine mounted on the bottom bracket … For ease of control clutchless transmission has been adopted. The rear wheel is roller-driven and the gear ration is 14.85:1" according to *The Motor Cycle* in a brief report dated 27th October 1955. The new frame was unusual: a large diameter oval tube, extending from the steering head to bottom bracket and fabricated from steel pressings also functioned as the fuel tank. *Power &*

Pedal disagreed on the material however and stated the *"light alloy frame includes integral tank in oval down tube; girder forks and 26"×2" tyres look after comfort ...the machine is light, simple and good looking. Very complete electrical equipment [is included], indicators, built-in speedo and panniers are featured in De Luxe models. Prices: Mo-ped £56-12s-6d and £66-10s-6d, Standard [clip-on] £28-7s-10d, Synchro £33-11s-0d."*

The factory photo reproduced above is of poor quality but clear enough to show the main frame & fuel tank and girder fork clearly, a strange combination of *avant garde* frame and antediluvian front suspension. There is little really new in this world however, the Mo-ped frame design is very reminiscent of the Italian-made BMG frame dating from 1952, which usually had a Mosquito unit fixed beneath the bottom bracket. The photograph also reveals that the engine, although still roller drive, is not a mere adaptation of the old Power Pak cyclemotor engine, but something completely different. In fact, the engine bears a striking resemblance to the Itom Tourist cyclemotor unit. The Mo-ped was a clean, integrated-looking machine and deserved to succeed, unlike some other rather badly conceived mopeds.

To remind ourselves of what every British and many Continental manufacturers were up against, the illustration below of NSU's renowned Quickly serves as a reminder of how far moped design had progressed.

Sensational NEW

Safe — Cheap — Simple
Autocycle
PRICE **£49 . 18 . 4** plus Purchase Tax **£9 . 19 . 0**
or Easy Terms

The Quickly price of £59.17s.4d including PT undercut Power Pak's Mo-ped De Luxe of comparable specification by over six pounds, a tidy sum in 1955.

The Motor Cycle magazine identified the growing gap between clip-on cyclemotors and mopeds in its report of 24th November 1955.

"True clip-ons have fallen on evil days. The purchase tax to which they are subject has made the total price of a motorised bicycle almost as great as the price of a moped proper; and now that mopeds have stopped being autocycles, the mass of tubes and cables which characterises the conventional pedal cycle has become the wallflower of the motor-cycle world. A few makers continue the old policy; certainly it makes for cheapness if not for charm ... there are several true ... clip-ons still being made. But the small price gap between them and the mopeds makes it seem unlikely that the clip-on type will continue much longer." They clung on for a while though; on 28th November 1957 the same magazine listed the following makes as still available: Cyclemaster, Power Pak, Itom Tourist, Vincent Firefly, Mosquito and Teagle. A Standard Power

121

Pak cost £28.7s.10d, the Synchromatic £33.11s.0d. By the 17th November 1960 there were only three left, listed in *The Motor Cycle's* Show Issue as Cyclemaster, Power Pak and Itom. A lot had changed in five years.

No records seem to have survived that give us any idea of how many Power Pak Mo-peds were made and, more importantly, how many were sold. Survivors are extremely rare so sadly our conclusion must be: not many.

"And now for something completely different" in the immortal words of the Monty Python team. The Ducati company thrives to this day, though owners of present-day Ducati superbikes might find it difficult to accept that the manufacturer of their ultra-high performance machines only began producing motor cycles in 1950 with clip-on cyclemotor engine units, albeit of radical design and very high quality.

(Motociclismo 1949)

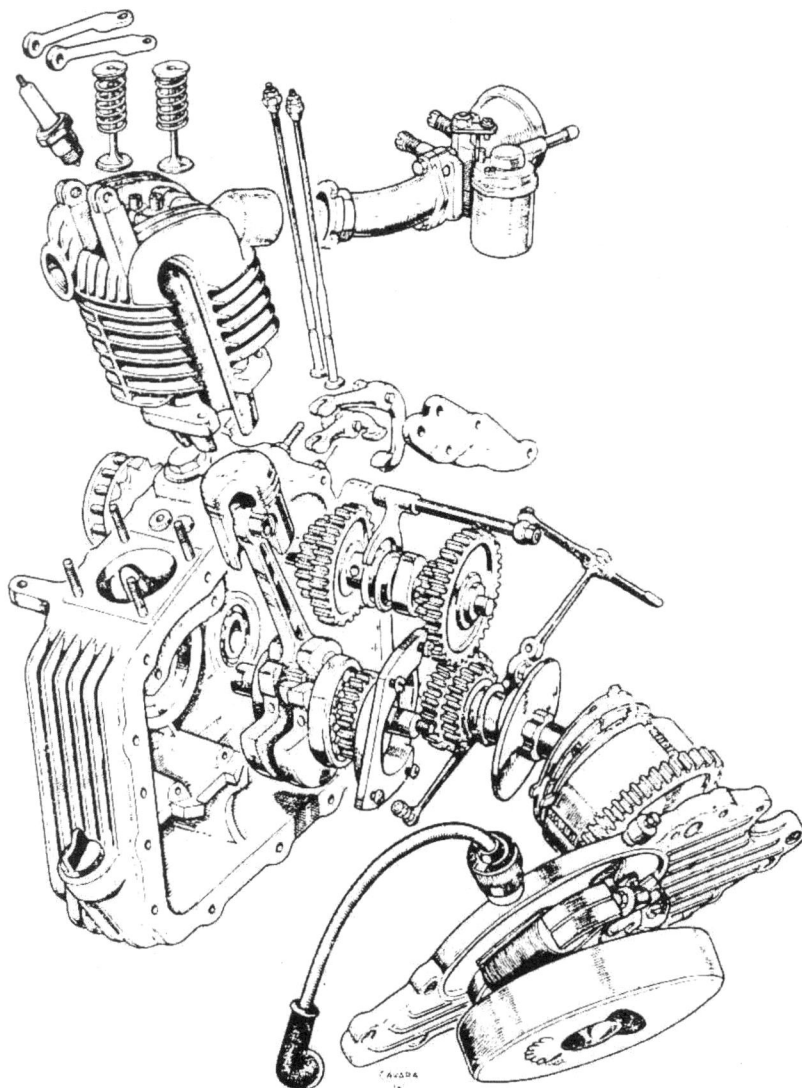

123

As can immediately be seen from the cut-away drawing, the Ducati Cucciolo (which translates as *Little Pup*) was created by original thinking married to outstanding engineering skills and true Italian passion for anything to do with an engine. To begin with, this motor was a four-stroke, unlike nearly all of the competition at that time (the contemporary and equally unconventional 4-stroke Motom, made in Italy but of Swiss design, being an honourable exception. Another was the 48cc 4-stroke Italian Pegaso moped, built between 1956 and 1964 by the SIM [Societá Italiana Motori] company, which employed many ex-Motom staff.) Ducati could have taken the easy route, saved considerably on manufacturing costs and stuck to the tried-and-tested, mundane but simple and cheap to make two-stroke formula. No. This was going to be Alfa Romeo 8C 2300-class engineering in a sea of Fiat Topolinos (not to denigrate Fiat in any way, they produced an excellent range of technically interesting cars in the early 1950s, encompassing the *Topolino* at one end, the *Otto Vu* at the other). Ducati's almost obsessive engineering excellence was to become the cornerstone of the company's post-war ethos and the foundation of its success right through to the present day.

Secondly, the Cucciolo, even for a tiny, 50cc engine, had overhead valves at a time when, in both car and motor cycle engineering worlds, inefficient and asthmatic side-valve engines were still very common. Then there was Ducati's clever construction of a gasket-less fixed-head cylinder, which avoided all the sealing and clamping problems associated with detachable cylinder heads, though at a cost - difficult access to valves for grinding or seating purposes. The cylinder and head assembly was cast in light alloy and had a shrunk-in cast-iron liner. Other advantages over two-stroke engines included avoiding the messy and inaccurate mixing of oil with petrol, the accompanying cloud of oil-smoke and frequent decoke-ing to remove resultant carbon deposits. A four-stroke engine also usually has more low-down torque and is better suited to hilly or mountainous terrain such as is frequently found in Italy.

Unconventional and advanced features abounded in the *Little Pup*; one such was the inclusion of an integral clutch coupled to a two-speed preselector gearbox, which in turn was connected to the original cycle pedal-chain. This meant that in theory almost any number of gears became available. For instance, a bicycle equipped with a Sturmey-Archer 3-speed hub or a derailleur could offer a mechanically sympathetic and experienced rider at least six gears when coupled to a Cucciolo. Although it looked like a miniature motor cycle engine, the Cucciolo was a genuine clip-on unit. Technically, it was vastly superior to any number of crude two-stroke, tyre-shredding, roller-drive contemporary competitors.

Such advanced engineering had many benefits: a power output that rose splendidly to 1.58bhp at a high 5,200rpm, thus enabling foolhardy cyclemotor riders to explore the rarified and frightening heights of 40mph speeds on a lowly push-bike. Even a Cucciolo's potential cruising speed of 30mph or so was higher than the average two-stroke cyclemotor's breathless maximum speed. Upgrading to drum-brakes was an absolute necessity for survival. Ducati recommended a maximum speed of 20-25mph, anything above this figure was *"strongly deprecated by the makers"*. Higher speeds could however be easily obtained by a little ingenious tinkering.

All of this excess velocity was compounded by the free wheel on the cycle hub, which meant that, like certain versions of the Saab car, shutting the throttle produced no engine braking whatsoever. This made for exciting travel, particularly in the wet, and required a great deal of forward thinking in order to avoid unseemly collisions with solid objects.

The background to the Little Pup's birth is typically Italian in that passion ruled over calculation and the boring bean-counters and yet somehow it seemed to make money. Like most European countries, the aftermath of WW2 meant to Italy a bombed and ruined infrastructure, an industrial base pillaged and expropriated by the Nazis for the Fatherland (despite Mussolini's Italy supposedly being Hitler's principal ally in the Axis) and an economy reduced again to a simple agrarian, 19th-century peasant level.

Amongst the sufferers was *Società Scientifica Radiobrevetti Ducati*, a small company founded in 1926 in Borgo Panigale, a suburb of Bologna, by Adriano, Bruno and Marcello Ducati. The three brothers each brought important talents to their business: Bruno trained as an architect (he would personally design Ducati's main factory building) and concentrated on management, Adriano was an innovative engineer, while Marcello organised manufacturing processes. Bologna is the capital of the northern region of Emilia-Romagna, an area steeped in history, art and culture from well before medieval times and which was greatly influential during the Renaissance. Bologna is still recognised as one of the great gastronic centres of Italy and remains to this day a powerful industrial and commercial centre. It was and is a working city. Unlike many neighbours such as Florence which have become vast tourist destinations, Bologna is a major road and rail hub and has been wedded to the motorcar and, above all, the motor cycle, since early in the 20th century.

The entire Catholic culture of northern Italy, including Emilia-Romagna, was quite alien to our Northern European, British and generally Protestant vision of life. Whereas 1940s engineers from Birmingham and Coventry might regard a pie and chips at the local pub and wearing a houndstooth jacket and cravat as relatively dashing, denizens of Bologna saw smart clothes, fresh *pasta*, voluptuous women and money as essentials of a good life. Many an evening they would

125

indulge in their excellent regional wines as an accompaniment to such delicious local dishes as *rumi formichino alla formaggio e fungi*.

Società Scientifica Radiobrevetti Ducati followed in the footsteps of one of Bologna's most illustrious sons, Guglielmo Marconi, initially manufacturing Manens condensers and other radiophonic items to feed the 1930s' boom in wireless sets. The company expanded mightily during this period, Benito Mussolini's priority of getting a radio into every home throughout Italy in order to spread his Fascist message helping considerably. Logically, Ducati soon became a maker of complete radio sets, claiming that their *"styling was always in the* 'avanguardia' *of the day"*, to quote Bruno Ducati. Other products were developed: an electric razor (*Il raselet*), an inter-office communications system called the Duofono, cinema projectors and a mechanical calculator named the Duconta.

This 1930s advert for a Ducati radio set reads as follows:

"For musical joy in your own home".

Judging by the *déshabille* of the model and her expression, she was hoping listening to the wireless was not going to be a solitary pleasure.

Il Duce's rantings could then be heard clearly throughout the land and so it was that by 1939 the Ducati company employed over 7,000 workers, Bruno had been given the honourific title of *Cavalieri del lavoro* by Mussolini and Ducati had opened branch offices in London, New York, Sydney and Paris. Mussolini's formation of the Axis alliance with his friend and idol Adolf Hitler in 1936 had the consequence of an ever-closer modelling of the Italian state on that of Hitler's Germany, including a similarly massive rearmament programme followed by unprovoked invasion of one's weaker neighbours. By 1940 Ducati had created a vast factory at *Borgo Panigale* and had become major suppliers of field radios, gun sights and optical artillery components to the Italian military.

Many other new products began to stream forth from the factory as *fratelli Ducati* explored new boundaries.

One such was the revolutionary Micro-camera, made possible by Ducati's precision machining and optical lens manufacturing capability. It was far in advance of its time, predating Kodak's similar camera by almost a decade.

Following the *débacle* of Italy's surrender to the Allies on 8th September 1943, British and American forces fought their way north, pushing Hitler's armies before them. Unfortunately for Ducati, on the 12th October 1944 American Flying Fortress bombers dropped an estimated one hundred tons of high-explosive ordnance onto *Borgo Panigale* during an air-raid, in the process completely flattening Ducati's factory and destroying the entire contents.

After the armistice negotiated by Marshal Badoglio with the Allies had been signed in September 1943, many engineers were immediately occupied by thoughts about what on earth they were going to do to make a living. One such was the remarkable *Avvocato* Aldo Farinelli, a lawyer, engineer and writer who was associated with the small engineering firm SIATA, an acronym for *Società Italiana per Applicazione Tecniche Auto-aviatorie*. Before the War, SIATA had specialised in, amongst other things, the manufacture of tuning-kits for sundry Fiat motorcars and had subsequently carried out much secret engineering work on behalf of occupying German forces during the conflict.

Farinelli and his associates at SIATA knew that post-war Italy would be back in the ox-cart era and that there would be a desperate need for some form of simple, inexpensive personal transport, preferably based on a pedal-cycle, which most people possessed. A small, low-compression four-stroke auxiliary engine of some kind would fit the bill, something that would run on more or less any fuel (unlike a fussier two-stroke), including distilled wine alcohol. Working in secret after the Armistice of 1943 (such activities were in direct conflict with dictates issued by Mussolini's Republican government, not to mention the occupying German forces), Farinelli started producing drawings of his idea: a *micromotore* that would assist a cyclist in going about his business. Raw materials to build a prototype were next to impossible to find. Farinelli diverted small quantities of war-related commodities for his own use (at great risk) but eventually had a working engine fitted to a bicycle and running around the streets of Turin by late 1944. Legend has it that the short stub of an exhaust (a non-essential silencer would have used up precious steel) produced a sharp yapping sound, which suggested an affectionate name for his creation: *Cucciolo* - a little puppy dog.

Italy after 1945 was utterly destitute. In 1943, the retreating Germans had taken with them the country's entire gold reserves but, although these were eventually recovered by the Allies, only a small proportion was returned, most being retained as war reparations. Thus, the only remaining internal source of capital was the Vatican, whose vast wealth had miraculously managed to survive the war almost intact. In conjunction with a government redevelopment organisation, IRI, the Vatican agreed to assuage its guilt and help fund post-war reconstruction; a number of industries in dire need of help were identified, including Ducati. Demand for field radios and artillery gun sights was understandably not high post-war and with over 9,000 workers to employ somehow, Ducati could not be allowed to fail. Moreover, a ready and ravenous market existed for a *micromotore* unit to power bicycles so IRI bent to its task. A deal was struck with SIATA and Ducati was granted a licence to manufacture the Cucciolo, though SIATA retained the rights to sell the unit.

This reproduction of early Ducati Cucciolo artwork (used as a flyer for the splendid Ducati Museum) looks even better in the original colour version. *"Vi porterà ovunque"* translates as "It will carry you everywhere". The engine illustration is what was usually called an artist's interpretation and only approximates to the actual design. It is nevertheless accurate enough to reveal the method by which a Cucciolo was attached to a cycle bottom bracket via the two open clamps shown behind the cylinder.

The choice of an efficient four-stroke design was amply justified; right from the beginning, one brake horsepower was available at 4,500rpm even using available awful fuels, more could therefore easily be obtained in the future. Farinelli chose to use the original bicycle drive chain as the means to transmit power to a cycle rear wheel rather than a roller-to-tyre drive or separate chain and sprocket. The engine clamped to the front downtube via a clamp and two half-moon clips attached to the rear of the engine. These swung over the bottom-bracket housing, clamping the unit firmly to the stongest place on the cycle frame. It needed to be. A Cucciolo-equipped cycle became a lightweight motor cycle rather than a motorized cycle and looked all the better for this.

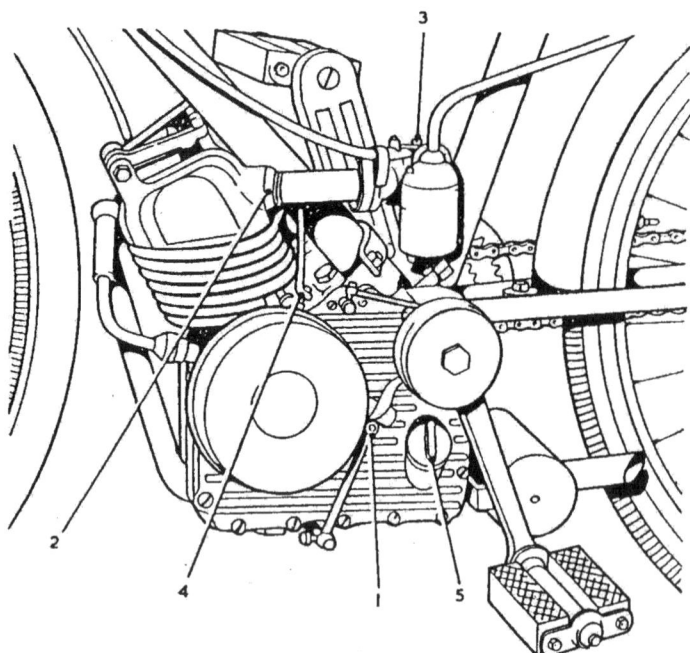

FIG. 20. THE DUCATI "CUCCIOLO"

1. Clutch adjuster.
2. Carburettor lock-ring.
3. Throttle cable lock-screw.
4. Headlamp terminal.
5. Oil filler.

Special attention should be paid to these points during assembly.

Both pedal cranks & chain wheel of the cycle were set aside and replaced by the Ducati components described below. Additionally a special extended bottom-bracket spindle substituted the standard item. The replacement for the right-hand pedal and chain wheel assembly, of cast aluminium, was internally toothed and fulfilled another role which will be described later. A replacement left-hand pedal crank had an offset to clear the engine. The existing cycle chain was then attached to and driven by an output drive sprocket fitted to the Cucciolo engine unit. This was good in theory while power remained at 1bhp or less but as output increased with better fuels and correspondingly usable higher compression ratios, the limitations of standard bicycle rear sprockets and spokes became all too apparent. One such was the propensity of a Cucciolo engine, when married to a fixed rear sprocket (no free-wheel) in order to take advantage of engine-braking, to unscrew said sprocket from the hub on overrun with unpleasant consequences for the rider.

The Ducati Cucciolo (also known as the type T1) was an immediate, huge success in Italy. 15,000 were already on the road by 1946, 25,000 by the end of 1947 plus several thousand more being exported to other penurious European countries. Production was running at 245 engines per 8-hour shift by 1948. Ducati soon found the initial agreement established with SIATA too restrictive and negotiated to take over sales as well as manufacturing. The upshot was that SIATA and Aldo Farinelli each became a beneficiary of a royalty payment from Ducati for every Cucciolo made and sold.

Bore and stroke were an almost square, 39mm × 40mm, giving a capacity of 48cc, the compression-ratio a reasonably high (for the time) 6.24-1, giving a power output of 1¼bhp. An exhaust-valve lifter was fitted to reduce compression for starting. Max revs quoted were high at 5,200. As usual, fuel consumption was reckoned to be of crucial importance to prospective buyers, Ducati claiming that *"provided the recommended speed-range is observed"* (unlikely) *"a petrol consumption of 250-300 mpg will be obtained"*. Note the *"will"*, indicating a firm conviction that

Cucciolo riders would scrupulously stay below the recommended 25 mph maximum speed in order to achieve good fuel economy. Really.

Early versions of the Cucciolo all-aluminium crankcase were split horizontally at approximately the crankshaft axis. The cylinder was cast integrally with this part of the engine block, but it proved to be difficult to machine correctly and the valves were virtually inaccessable, disadvantages outweighed advantages so a simpler, improved variant was quickly introduced.

The crankcase was now a one-piece die casting, while both the left-hand side-plate and cylinder became detachable items. Other changes included a relocated exhaust port, now facing forward, and repositioning the oil-filler to the left side of the engine rather than at the front.

Cucciolo valve-gear merits closer inspection, partly because of the novelty of having valves at all in such a tiny engine when almost every other competitor opted for the simpler two-stroke design, but also because a unique design was used. The illustration below shows the earliest Cucciolo engine layout, with both inlet and exhaust pipes facing backward. Steel rockers, pivoted from cast-in lugs at the front of the aluminium cylinder head, were drawn downward by the two pull-rods, not pushed up, as in a conventional push-rod arrangement common to overhead-valve four-stroke engines. Valves were opened by a pad that bore on the valve-stem toward the back of each rocker. Note that in this version the top end of each pull-rod is formed as an eye, hooked over the curved end of each rocker. An original design feature that worked well in practice but unfortunately allowed no adjusting of valve-stem clearances, short of grinding metal off the valve-stem, to compensate for temperature variations and receding valve-seats.

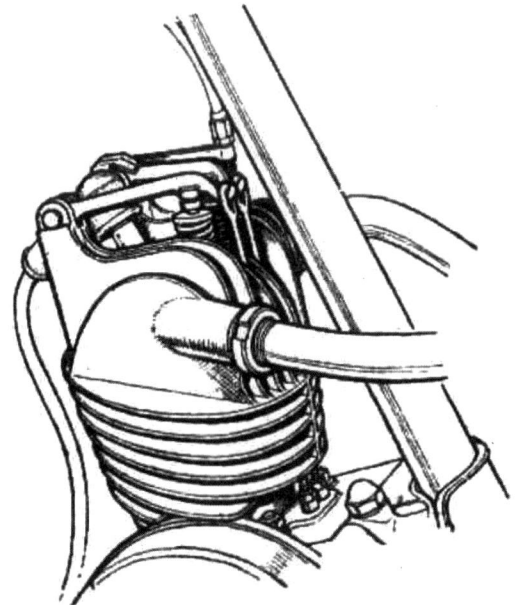

Wishbone levers inside the crankcase actuated both pull-rods, where another Ducati novelty was evident. Both inlet and exhaust levers were positioned in such a way that they could be actuated by a single cam-lobe, thus economising on machining and case-hardening costs. Though excellent in theory, this unusual layout meant that the single cam profile, being asked to perform two tasks (inlet and exhaust valve dwell angles are normally quite different), did neither especially well.

The two pads indicated ran on the same cam

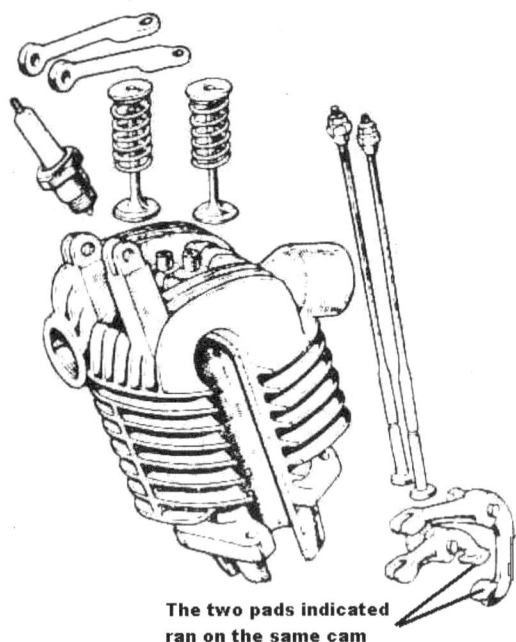

Later production versions (above) changed things around considerably; the exhaust now faced forward, to the right of the head, whilst the inlet move slightly inboard. Rockers and pull-rods were of a more sophisticated design; angular deflections were now taken care of by tiny balljoints at the top of each pull-rod, held in place by adjuster nuts and lock-nuts. Notice how slim these pull-rods are, not being required to resist bending whilst pushing against a strong valve-return spring. The advantages of this layout are that both rockers and pull-rods work in tension and so can be thin and light, thus cutting down on high-speed inertia loadings and allowing the engine to rev freely. Because of the light loadings involved (a Cucciolo's valve gear really is tiny and lightweight) Farinelli did not see the necessity of providing any pressurised oil supply, instead, periodic attention with an oilcan was deemed sufficient. Recommended valve-clearances were; inlet 0.006" exhaust 0.008", both with the engine cold.

The unusual though not original idea of using a single cam was superseded by 1950 when individual cams for each valve were fitted, with the consequence that power output and flexibility improved. Another minor improvement was made to the free-wheel device situated in the pedalling crank.

No cover was provided to keep out dust and grime, a Cucciolo's valve gear could be seen doing its job naked and unashamed, something *The Book of the Cyclemotor* was not entirely happy with, noting that *"it is rather a pity the makers have left the valve-gear exposed, since it must inevitably get very dirty. A pressed-aluminium cover held by a clip would be quite sufficient to protect and neaten the job"*. Evidently the editors of this book had forgotten some of the more splendid 1930s creations emanating from J A Prestwich & Co (better known as the proprietary engine-maker JAP) which adorned the front of many a Morgan 3-wheeler and were equally naked and unashamed about their valve-gear. A cover would appear in future years.

Sparks were provided for a Cucciolo by a Ducati-manufactured exposed flywheel magneto which also incorporated lighting coils; these produced 12 watts power at 6 volts *"enough for a bright headlight and rear light"*. Contact breaker gap was unusually small at 0.010" and was set just before top-dead-centre, so not much ignition advance there then. Recommended spark plug was a

Champion L 10 with 14mm threads and a gap of 0.018". A 2-jet 14mm Weber carburettor provided mixture though many a Cucciolo had a Dell'orto equivalent fitted.

Power from the crankshaft was transmitted to another rarity for average cyclemotors: a clutch. This mechanism originally consisted of a series of nineteen thin metal discs, ten driven & nine drive. The drive discs were usually bronze, although some were also of steel. Initially, the clutch had no friction linings; these appeared later in some versions. Ducati's clutch was designed to allow a small amount of slip, cushioning engagement of drive, and to be virtually wear-free. The unit shared the engine's oil, which was fine in the 1950s, when a simple monograde SAE 30 mineral oil was universally used but it has proved to be intolerant of modern multigrades. Their low-friction formulations allow a lot more slip at inconvenient moments for a Cucciolo rider. Sump capacity was just over half a litre, the oil being shared between the crankcase, clutch and transmission, so recommended change intervals were frequent at between 500 and 700 miles, depending on use. Viscosity ranged from SAE 40/50 in summer to SAE 30 in winter.

As for a concise description of the inner workings of a Cucciolo 2-speed pre-selector gearbox, I cannot better the following from Philippa Wheeler:

"The earlier Cucciolo gearboxes were built in unit with the motor and the limited space available was used with an elegance of function. It is unusual in that the output shaft is in fact the layshaft receiving the selector fork whereas the 'mainshaft' is the clutch assembly with associated pinions supported at each end by uncaged quarter inch rollers in hardened pressed in tracks. The output/ layshaft, splined on the drive side projects to the exterior and carries the external slip sprocket and drive chain. This shaft is supported by a substantial bearing at the drive end and the ubiquitous rollers at the timing end. It also supports the camshaft as a bearing surface for the camshaft's long needle rollers.

The first time visitor to a Cucciolo interior is confronted by an array of straight cut gears. First to be lifted out is the camwheel driven by the crankshaft pinion. On its underside is a small pinion that drives the clutch and its associated gearwheels now fully revealed. This in turn lifts out to show the two fixed gearwheels at the inner end. Now you are left with the two output/layshaft sliding gears and their selector fork of which more later. The two gears are each kept in or out of rotation with the output / layshaft by three ball bearings nestling in holes in the shaft to locate and drive (or not) each gear wheel. As the selector fork slides the cogs to and fro in and out of engagement with the small fixed cogs on the clutch, the balls engage with detents in the gear wheels where they bear on the shafts, providing the drive. Difficult to describe but amazingly compact simple and trouble free in operation. The movement of the selector fork to achieve this wizardry is provided by its (adjustable) location to a spindle. This runs along the upper rear interior of the crankcase and projects to the exterior through a hole just behind the top rear of the magneto flywheel. The spindle has three detents which engage with a spring loaded ball. Fully in moves the selector fork to the low gear position, the centre to a neutral position where the sliding gears freewheel and outwards gives you top gear. This multiplicity of straight cut gears gives the Cucciolo its characteristic wailing and gnashing of teeth, music to the ears of the cognoscenti coupled with the sharp bark of its four stroke exhaust."

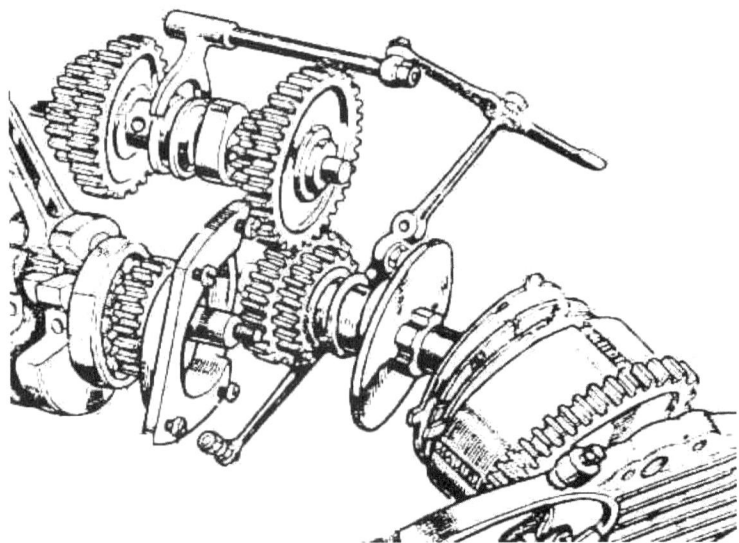

Gear pre-selection was arranged via the cycle pedals incorporated with the Cucciolo engine unit; left pedal forward selected low gear, right pedal forward for high gear, engagement of either gear was simply a matter of operating the clutch lever once. On release of this lever, the appropriate gear engaged forthwith followed by the clutch taking up drive. Very simple and effective.

Distinctive sounds appear almost to have been a Ducati company obsession, to mark the successful launch of their Little Pup they commissioned a renowned composer, *Maestro Olivero*, to write a song lauding the qualities of their cyclemotor engine.

Nowadays almost anything is possible with publicity, however, in 1946 to have a great musician write what we now know as a jingle was unheard of.

FORSE UN BEL SOGNO TU PORTI IN CUOR SOGNI CHE TI REGALI L'OTTO CILINDRI COLOR MARRON MA IO MILIONARIO

NON SONO ANCOR E PER ACCONTENTARTI TESORO BELLO SAI CHE FARO SE VUOI VENIR CON ME TI

PORTERÒ SUL CUCCIOLO IL MOTORINO È PICCOLO MA BATTE COME IL MIO CUOR PER

MONTI E PER CITTÀ ANDREMO VELOCISSIMI UNITI E FELICISSIMI

DOVE CI PORTA L'AMOR E COL MOTOR NOI CANTEREMO QUESTA BELLA CANZON CHI

CI VEDRÀ C'INVIDIERÀ E UN CUCCIOLO POI CANTERÀ SE VUOI VENIR CON ME TI

PORTERÒ SUL CUCCIOLO IL MOTORINO È PICCOLO E BATTE COME IL MIO CUOR

SAI CHE UN BEL SOGNO IO PORTO IN CUOR SOGNO CHE TI REGALO L'OTTO CILINDRI COLOR MARRON UN MILIONARIO

NON SON ANCOR MA PER ACCONTENTARTI TESORO BELLO SAI CHE FARÒ MI PORTERAI CON TE ANDREMO

INSIEM SUL CUCCIOLO IL MOTORINO È PICCOLO E BATTE COI NOSTRI CUOR PER

MONTI E PER CITÀ ANDREMO VELOCISSIMI UNITI E FELICISSIMI DOVE CI PORTA L'AMOR

E COL MOTOR NOI CANTEREMO INSIEM QUESTA BELLA CANZON

SE VUOI VENIR CON ME ANDREMO INSIEM SUL CUCCIOLO

IL MOTORINO È BATTE COI NOSTRI CUOR E BATTE COI NOSTRI CUOR

XXIII

135

A rough and ready translation of the highlights reads as follows:

"Perhaps you carry a dream in your heart, you dream you make yourself a present of that eight cylinder car…but you are not a millionaire…do you know what I will do, if you'd like to come with me? I will carry you with the Pup…the engine is small but beats like my heart. Through mountains and cities, we will go very fast, united and happy, it brings us love and, with the engine, we will sing this beautiful song. People who see us will envy us…and the Pup will then sing. If you want to come with me, I will carry you with the Pup…the engine is small but beats like my heart. You know, I carry a beautiful dream in my heart, I dream that I give you the eight-cylinder car but to satisfy you, beautiful treasure, do you know what I will do? I will ride with you. We will go together on the Pup. The engine is small and beats with our hearts. Through mountains and cities (and so on…) …the engine beats with our hearts and beats with our hearts".

The music is reputed to be based on *"Vola Colomba"* by Gian Franco Vené.

In Britain commercial success also came easily to the Cucciolo, it was first introduced in 1950 under the auspices of Britax (London) Ltd of 115-129 Carlton Vale, London NW6. Britax nowadays is a high-tech aerospace company but its origins post-WW2 were more humble and lay in the manufacture of nylon webbing seat-belts, a development of its war-time business making crew harnesses for RAF fighter and bomber crews.

Initially Britax offered the Ducati Cucciolo to the purchasing public as a *"Cycle Auxiliary Motor* (that*) is making cycling news in all parts of the world because it incorporates absolutely new and sensational features never before embodied in so small a motor unit … A miracle of compact precision engineering, weighing only 17½ lbs. Moreover, its cunning positioning between front and rear wheels makes for perfect balance and stability".*

Just for once, such claims were largely true for the Cucciolo, unlike many manufacturers' rather desperate forays into the furthermost reaches of advertising hyperbole, searching for the killer sales pitch. Retail price in 1950, including Purchase Tax, was £40, rather a lot of money when compared to other clip-ons but there then it was no contest in terms of quality and performance, the Cucciolo was streets ahead of anything else.

The Motor Cycle magazine, in its road-test dated 31ˢᵗ January 1952, concurred wholeheartedly. In its opinion, *"certainly the engine is as lively as any small canine could be ... it would hardly be accurate to describe the Cucciolo as a motor-assisted bicycle - rather it is a power-bicycle. For at no time during the test was it necessary to use pedal assistance once the motor was running. Hill-climbing abilities of the diminutive engine were exceptional. Shooters Hill West ... is over half a mile long, with an average gradient of 1 in 17 and a maximum gradient of 1 in 6. With a light following breeze and an approach speed of 30mph, the Cucciolo climbed the full length of the hill in top gear; the speed never dropped below 20mph."*

Exceptional indeed. Few, if any, other clip-on units were capable of such a feat without varying amounts of LPA (light pedal assistance - one of the great euphemisms of our time) from the rider to help a struggling two-stroke.

The Motor Cycle continued: *"On another run, a stop and re-start was made on the steepest part of the hill. The machine (in this test, the cycle to which the unit was attached was a Phillips lightweight roadster with hub-brakes and a fixed rear sprocket) pulled away in bottom gear without the use of pedals and without the rider resorting to an abnormal amount of clutch-slipping"*. Average petroil consumption for the test was a realistic 140mpg, rather less, as expected, than Ducati's optimistic figure of 250-300mpg. As regards *Power & Pedal* magazine's hobby-horse, engine noise, *The Motor Cycle* was less inclined to roundly condemn cyclemotor engines as intolerably noisy. It reported that *"the exhaust was fairly well silenced ... (and) sounded distinctly 'healthy' when full power was used ... rather like that of a distant lusty single at high revs"*. Quite loud then - but they seemed to actually enjoy the sound.

Performance was also exceptional, *"speed in excess of 40mph. A cruising speed of 30-35mph was maintained quite easily for mile after mile. After running on full throttle for ten miles the engine showed no signs of overheating; indeed, it was possible casually to stroke the cylinder fins without burning one's fingers"*.

Such outstanding performance from a 48cc clip-on engine was not lost on sporting cyclemotorists. A Cucciolo quickly became the mount of choice for competitors, aided and abetted by Britax who entered many factory bikes in a variety of British events such as the ACU cyclemotor trial of April 1953. Abroad, the Cucciolo was already hugely successful. At the *Autodromo di Monza* in 1951, Ducati mounted a series of record attempts using a modified Cucciolo engine and established the following international records:

- 47.6 miles in one hour   (average 47.6mph)
- 229.6 miles in five hours   (average 45.9mph)
- 520 miles in 12 hours   (average. 43.3mph)
- 990 miles in 24 hours   (average 41.3mph)
- 1,885.5 miles in 48 hours   (average 39.3mph)

A similar record attempt was mounted in 1953 by Britax at Thruxton to prove the *"high standard of reliability and performance of the Ducati 48cc cyclemotor"* and to test the new Britax cycle frame, specially designed for a Cucciolo engine (more information on this development later in the chapter). The test was observed by the ACU and in 31 hours 2 minutes *"the machine covered 1,267.2 miles at an average speed of 39.7mph. This speed, astonishing as it is, might have been even higher but for such obstacles as fog, rabbits on the course at night and a ramp over a water-pipe which had to be taken at over 50mph and caused the machine to leap some 20 feet every lap. At the end, the Cucciolo was still lapping as well as ever at 44mph. The fastest speed obtained was over 59mph, yet the engine on being stripped was in excellent condition throughout"*.

Other competition and test successes included:

- First Class Awards at the ACU Trials of 1952 and 1953,
- covering a London to Paris run in 9 hours in February 1953,
- a London to Cardiff run under severe winter conditions,
- numerous local Trial events
- Cuccioli raced at Harringay, Wimbledon and Rayleigh Speedways, the only 50cc machines to do so.

All these achievements were apparently made *"WITHOUT MECHANICAL FAILURES"*, if Britax publicity is to be believed.

Such successes amply demonstrated not only the mechanical robustness of Aldo Farinelli, SIATA and Ducati's Little Pup design but the exceptional performance that could be extracted from 48 tiny cc. At the time, better torque from the Cucciolo's four-stroke engine regularly beat the unsophisticated 2-stroke competition, whereas nowadays the reverse is true, modern 2-strokes are capable of producing extraordinary outputs.

TRIAL BY CUCCIOLO

How Mr. Arnold W. Jones (Technical Department Britax Ltd.) followed " THE EXETER "

THE expressions, of surprise at check points and the remark that "A Special Medal ought to be given to me" were caused by the fact that my machine in the Exeter was none other than a 48 c.c. *Cucciolo* mounted on an ordinary bicycle fitted with the luxury of spring forks.

Certainly an unusual mount for such an event, but nevertheless it gave me the opportunity to follow this time-honoured trial and enjoy a most memorable week-end at the cost of a few shillings.

So many people have asked me "How did it go ?" that perhaps my experiences may be of interest to others and may encourage the more sporting cycle motor owners to "have a go" at main road trials.

The Exeter as most people are aware covers some 300 odd miles of main and secondary roads and includes some several not too severe Trial Hills with a few miles of "continental" going. Competitors start at 10 p.m. and ride through the night finishing at about 3.30 p.m. the following day. During this time an average speed of about 20 m.p.h. has to be maintained and as usual marks are lost for being early or late, and failure on the hills. On the night run no difficulty was experienced in maintaining the set average. The excellent *Cucciolo* lighting equipment proved entirely adequate except in the heaviest mist, and greatly assisted in maintaining the schedule. A hectic two wheeled slide on a patch of ice caused quite an exciting moment, but the lightness and natural stability due to the position of the motor unit ensured no loss of control.

Using a normal road gear the machine was quite capable with, bottom gear engaged of tackling all hills encountered except the actual trial's hills themselves; these had to be pushed up while the clutch was being slipped, but these drastic measures did not have any ill effects on the clutch which required no attention throughout the trip.

Motoring over rough tracks and through mud and water was revelled in by the little machine and the fact that no damage was suffered by the cycle frame tends to disprove any theories that cycle motors are too powerful and heavy for normal cycles.

The brakes which were of the normal internal expanding type were more than adequate even on the steepest descents which, in some cases, were of considerable length.

The normal size cycle tyres fitted proved adequate and due to the direct chain drive of the *Cucciolo* no excessive tyre wear was experienced.

Bournemouth was reached without real incident with the rider not unduly fatigued if a little saddle sore.

At no time did the engine give the slightest anxiety or appear any the worse for its journey. Just over one gallon of petrol was used and it would be difficult to find a cheaper and healthier form of entertainment.

Did somebody mention "The Land's End ?" ! ! !

Britax (London) Ltd was not slow to realise that it had acquired the concession to import and sell in Britain truly the best cyclemotor clip-on unit. Sales rocketed but it was becoming increasingly apparent that a power output of 1.25bhp was really too much for many cycle frames and definitely too much for standard cycle stirrup brakes. Consequently, Britax decided to negotiate the manufacture of a complete cycle specifically designed for the Cucciolo engine, from one of the oldest names in cycle-frame manufacturing, Royal Enfield.

The Britax cycle, introduced in 1954, was *"specially designed (for the Cucciolo) to to give the additional safety, strength, dependability and riding comfort which are absolutely essential to the enjoyment of cycle-motoring at its best."* Royal Enfield had come up with a desirable combination of low riding-position, drum brakes front and rear (*"ensure ample stopping power"*) and pressed-steel girder front forks with rubber suspension. Frame size was 19", bracket height 11¼", ground clearance 6". Wheels were of 26"×1¾", fitted with Dunlop Roadster Baloon tyres, a teardrop-shape 1¼ gallon fuel tank was supplied and the whole confection was finished in a very classy dark maroon enamel paint, perfectly set off by ample chrome plating. Price was quoted as eighteen guineas, plus £3.12s.9d Purchase Tax. All a purchaser had to do was fit his Cucciolo engine unit or, if he or she did not have one, a complete new cycle and engine combination could be bought for £61.8s.6d including Purchase Tax.

Production modifications to the Cucciolo kept pace with riders' experiences and expectations, Ducati introduced many minor improvements along the way. In October 1952 the carburettor choke diameter was slightly increased, to provide a *"sweeter-running engine"* it was claimed. This also gave the incidental benefit of increasing power output to a stirring 1.58bhp. To cope with this as well as the common problem of riders over-revving their Cuccioli, stronger valve-springs were fitted to prevent valve-bounce at over 5,200rpm. The clutch had acquired the reputation of being rather fierce, so work was carried out to improve smoothness and reduce drag.

Output from Ducati's magneto lighting coils was increased from 12 to 15 watts at 6 volts, the previous output being less than adequate for cycles capable of over 35mph.

One optional extra offered was a hand gear-change control, price one guinea, which brought the gear-change up to cross-bar level, for those still wedded to tank-mounted gear levers. In 1954, Britax also introduced a few improvements to its Royal Enfield-sourced cycle frame. A double-action twist-grip incorporated the exhaust-valve lifter, steering lock-stops were fitted as were heavier-duty mudguards and stays and four bolts now held the rear-wheel drive sprocket in place.

Production figures for Cuccioli made at the Ducati factory in Borgo Panigale were astronomical compared to British-produced clip-on units. By 1954 Ducati was making some forty thousand cyclemotor units a year (plus a further 30,000 motor cycles of capacities greater than 50cc). This also points out the vastly bigger cyclemotor market Ducati enjoyed in Italy in comparison with the legislation and prejudice-ridden British equivalent. Despite such a tremendous throughput, *"every engine unit is given a bench-test before it is passed through for assembly. We saw that shop - the noisiest place in Bologna! A dozen or so units were roaring away, the 48 and 65cc models for an hour, the 98cc versions for two hours"* to quote John Thorpe's article from *Motor Cycling*, dated December 16th 1954, which was written after he visited the factory. He also noted the fact that *"Ducati is unusual amongst Italian motor cycle concerns - the factory employs a considerable number of women. In fact the ladies comprise fully one third of the total labour force of one thousand. Their nimble fingers, it is found, are better than men's when it comes to assembling the intricate, almost watch-like small-capacity four-strokes which are Ducati's speciality".*

Britax in Britain was not alone in appreciating the qualities and commercial opportunity offered by the Cucciolo. In France, M Rocher had entered into a licensing agreement with Ducati and was making the complete unit at Cenon. In Europe the Cucciolo was also the clip-on unit of choice for the competition-minded *cyclomoteuriste*. Long-distance events were the Cucciolo's forte, such as Paris-Nice ("*8 Cuccioli in the first 11 places*") and Paris to Athens: "*3 Cucciolos at the start, 3 Cucciolos at the finish, roads in terrible condition, temperatures of up to 50°C, many mountain passes, 40kgs of equipment carried on each bike*".

Other competition successes listed included Cyclemotor Cross and the following World Records:

- 10kms at 72.756kph
- 50kms at 72.434kph
- 100kms at 72.000kph
- 500kms at 69.598kph

Motocycles magazine in its Paris Show issue of October 1, 1951 noted that: "*every user of a Cucciolo enthuses about its robustness and endurance, thus destroying the unfair reputation for fragility that this type of small 4-stroke engine had*".

Le Raid Athènes-Paris couronne le palmarès inégalable du

cucciolo

Saison 1950-51

CROSS CYCLOMOTEURS :

1er à St-Cucufa — 1re à Piscop — 2e à Sucy-en-Brie — 1er et 2e à Sablé-sur-Sarthe — 2e à Meaux — 1er, 2e, 4e au Critérium National — 1er et 2e à Beauvais — 1er et 2e à Niassles — 1er à Bayonne.

PISTE " LA MÉDAILLE " à BUFFALO :

1er de chaque épreuve, 1er et 2e en finale.

PARIS-NICE :

1er du classement individuel (8 Cucciolo dans les 11 premiers — Côte du Mont Agel : 1er, 2e, 3e, 4e 5e, 6e, 8e — Classement spécial Scooter : 1er Cucciolo.

RECORDS DU MONDE :

10 kms : 72 kmh. 756	100 kms : 72 kmh.
50 kms : 72 kmh. 434	500 kms : 69 kmh. 598

ATHÈNES-PARIS :

3 Cucciolo au départ, 3 Cucciolo à l'arrivée. Routes défoncées, température 50°, passages de cols, 40 kgs d'équipement individuel.

SALON : HALL DU CYCLE -- STAND 317

$48 cm^3$

MOTEUR AUXILIAIRE

cucciolo

M.ROCHER

USINES À CENON (Vienne)

CONSTRUCTEUR FRANCE

Serv. Comm. 36 bis, Av. de l Opéra, PARIS

143

Britax was well aware of the manifold commercial possibilities offered by such a potent and reliable engine unit as the Ducati Cucciolo and by 1954 was offering two more very different variants. First came a scooter, known as the Scooterette, powered by the standard Cucciolo 48cc 2-speed engine and then, rather surprisingly, the Hurricane racing motor cycle appeared, claimed to be *"the smallest racer on the British market"*

The Hurricane racer, complete with expensive and cumbersome alloy fairings.

The Britax Cucciolo and Scooterette both shared the same frame, though the scooter was fitted with smaller, 2.50"×20" wheels and Dunlop tyres. It was offered to the buying public for £99.18s.0d, making the Britax-Cucciolo look very reasonable at £61. For the same amount as the Scooterette aspiring competition riders could place an order for the Hurricane racer. Unfortunately, neither of these new versions achieved any great sales success. The Scooterette was never sold in viable numbers and the Hurricane was too far ahead of its time - British buyers in 1955 were not yet interested in sub-250cc racers. The Hurricane did have the distinction of being the first *"production racer offered for sale anywhere in the world"*, though the weight of the hand-beaten aluminium fairings negated any advantages gained by streamlining. They must have cost Britax a fortune to have made so the company were perhaps rather relieved that few were sold.

The Cucciolo "pup" cartoon was used in many places, including factory brochures and adverts and indicates the affection with which the "little pup" was held by Ducati, who never forgot where its bread-and-butter sales came from, no matter how advanced its other motor cycle models became.

THE NEW RACER (*R. D. Vaughan Williams up*)

WITH the appearance of the Britax-Ducati *Hurricane* it is safe to say that formal 50 c.c. racing has arrived. Informal 50 c.c. racing has been taking place for some months. Devotedly tuned clip-ons without their silencers have been reaching speeds well into the forties.

The new Britax is powered by the Ducati 4-stroke 48 c.c. engine already familiar under its model name of *Cucciolo*. But before taking to racing the *Ducati* has undergone a number of modifications. Austenitic valves and double coil valve springs have been fitted and the engine equipped with a special *Amal* carburettor. There is a trumpet exhaust.

The streamlines of the *Hurricane's* metal skin reveal a family likeness to the *Scooterette*, pictured in *Power and Pedal* last month. Wheels are 20 ins. x 2.5 ins. The machine weighs 97 lbs. and is priced at £99. 18s. 0d. including P.T. Special tuning is available for an extra £6.

To say that the *Hurricane* is exciting to ride is to put it mildly—particularly if one is unfamiliar with racing motor cycles. A run is needed to start the machine. The saddle is well back and the expert, provided that he is thin enough, can place his chin on the tank. Thus mounted he may roar along at over 50 m.p.h.—and to say " roar " is no poetic fancy. At first the steering seems extremely light, but this settles down as the speed increases.

It is worth while comparing the price and performance of the *Hurricane* with that of a 125 c.c. machine, the smallest to race hitherto. A 125 c.c. racing machine costs over £250 and has a top speed of 75 m.p.h. plus. The *Britax* costs under £100 and has a top speed of 50 m.p.h. plus. Economics alone would seem sufficient to assure the popularity of 50 c.c. racing. Two racing meetings for this class of machine have already been planned for 1955.

146

YOU CAN NOW FLY YOUR CYCLEMOTOR TO FRANCE BY SILVER CITY AIR FERRY FOR 5 /-

This advertisement appeared on the front cover of Power & Pedal magazine's April 1953 issue and depicts Mr.Martin Rendall of Reading who *"by the connivance of a friend in the right place, spent his twenty-second birthday on an enjoyable trip from his home to Paris at the cost of 49/6½d. This remarkable feat was accomplished by riding via London to Lympne Airport, flipping across the channel to Le Touquet by Silver City Airways ferry plane* [remember them? Deafening, rattly old Bristol Freighters, skimming along 500ft above the oggin for 20 minutes] *and then riding on to Paris to finish the trip with still a drop of petrol left from the gallon taken on* [note that extra petrol tank]." Costs were; 35/- passenger fare (Winter rate), 5/- cyclemotor ticket, 5/- Ministry of Aviation Tax and 4/6½d for the aforementioned gallon of top-grade petrol.

In June 1955, further improvements made to the Cucciolo unit, a new version known as the M55 filtered through to the British market. Most noticeably, an aluminium cover was now fitted to the cylinder head, protecting the valve-gear from road dirt and, incidentally, quietening down the customary thousand-grannies-knitting sound. Camshaft profile was altered to provide more low-speed torque, apparently at the expense of top speed, though this was barely noticeable. More apparent were major changes to the two-speed gearbox; the previous pedal-operated pre-selection system was abandoned in favour of a more modern instantaneous twist-grip gearchange. The drive-side pedal crank was also changed for steel rather than the damage-prone aluminium casting used thus far.

The Ducati 55E moped was introduced to the British market in August 1956, having been previously available in Europe. It was a handsome-looking homogenous machine that successfully camouflaged the clip-on origins of Cucciolo motive power. The lightweight pressed-steel backbone frame incorporated a full rear mudguard, rear suspension via coil-spring damper units was a definite bonus, leading-link front suspension and proper hub brakes all contributed to the 55E being very satisfying to ride.

By 1956 the Ducati factory in Italy was also producing a wide range of light motor cycles in a variety of capacities, selling almost as many as the company could make on the home market alone where sales had simply rocketed, such was the popularity of its machines. Ducati was also very aware of growing economic prosperity throughout Western Europe and was seeing a considerable decline in domestic Cucciolo sales. Serious inroads into the Cucciolo market were being made by new-fangled and fashionable scooters. Most of these were manufactured by two industrial colossi: Innocenti with its Lambretta and Piaggio with Vespa. The availability of small, reliable and increasingly cheap cars - such as the Fiat 500 or *Topolino* (Little Mouse), first introduced in 1936 but carried over after the war until 1955, when it was replaced by the new generation rear-engined 600 - also contributed to the decline. Rural Cucciolo users (the majority post-WW2) found a scooter (you could get the whole family plus a goat on one of those) or a Fiat tin box much more to their liking than a power-assisted bicycle. Of no help either had been a law passed in 1950, which limited the top speed of cyclemotors such as a Cucciolo & cycle combination to a top speed of 35kph, in a fruitless attempt to reduce road accidents. It's hard to believe that legislators in a speed-mad country such as Italy even attempted such a restriction. In your dreams, boys.

European accessory makers were quick off the mark in offering a range of practical "dress-up" extras for the Cucciolo. This advert dating from March 1952 illustrates items manufactured by AGF Accessories.

From left to right they are: polished aluminium rocker cover, gear-change lever and linkage (for all frames), centre stand (patented fixing) and a replacement left-hand pedal assembly incorporating a back-pedal or coaster brake mechanism for connecting to a rear drum brake.

Also of interest in this advert is the superb-looking AGF backbone frame, looking very much like it was designed for the Cucciolo, with hub brakes front and rear, girder front fork and fuel tank incorporated in the large-diameter main frame tube.

ACCESSOIRES
BREVETES SUR LE MOTEUR CUCCIOLO

CACHE-CULBUTEURS 1.400 frs

LEVIER de VITESSES pour tous cadres 660 frs

BEQUILLE fixation brevetée 1.060 frs

FREIN RÉTRO-PEDALAGE avec manivelle gauche 2.200 frs

Ets FAIZANT FILS et Cie
4, rue Hoche, COLOMBES (Seine) - CHA. 08-47

Britax must have also noticed this trend taking hold in the UK and began planning for the future. The company divested itself of the UK stock of Cucciolo spare parts, transferring them to KVP Motors, moped and scooter specialists of 3 South Parade, Gunnersbury Lane, Acton, London, in September 1956. Britax for a short time continued to sell the complete Cucciolo unit but its corporate sights were already set a lot higher and the Little Pup no longer figured as a major profit-earner. If the truth were known, Britax was by then probably making more money manufacturing car accessories and automotive and aeronautical seat-belts than it ever did with the Cucciolo and was on its way to becoming a large conglomerate. Britax must also have been aware that Ducati was moving on to greater things with a popular and highly successful range of sophisticated 4-stroke motor cycles, which the company had every intention of marketing via its own network in the UK. It was only a question of time before the Little Pup was put down.

The end for the Cucciolo in the UK came, laconically, with a single line commentary in Stone & Cox, page 344, under Motor Cycle Power Units: *Cucciolo (Italian)* and below the last specification entry for 1956, *"Manufacture discontinued"*. How sad; the Little Pup, raucous, clattery, quirky and fast, had frightened its last customer.

A typical English pub scene on a sunny summer's day: Cucciolo propped against the kerb, a glass of real ale in hand & good company. What else is there in life?

(Photo courtesy of Philippa Wheeler)

Vincent-HRD: *"hallowed be thy name, thy kingdom came, thy will was done..."*

That a company such as Vincent with the highest of reputations for engineering excellence should even consider putting its name to a clip-on cyclemotor engine unit was an indication of the dire straits it found itself in, post-WW2. Popular motor cycle manufacturer BSA may have gone in a similar direction with its Winged Wheel unit, but *Vincent...* This was like Bentley Motors deciding to make Bond Minicars under licence.

In 1928, Philip Vincent had bought the manufacturing rights to the HRD motor cycle from Howard R Davies, a well-known racing motor cyclist who founded the company in 1924. Davies produced Massey-designed machines of advanced design, equipped with 348cc and 490cc side-valve engines (plus some ohv JAP-powered models) and of a low and sporty appearance. He won the 1925 Senior TT on the Isle of Man on one of his own motor cycles; Freddy Dixon won the 1927 Junior TT similarly mounted. By 1928, the HRD company had been sold to Bill Humphries (related to OK-Supreme marque founder, Ernest Humphries) who subsequently sold it on again to Phil Vincent. Vincent then set up business as Vincent Engineers (Stevenage) Ltd at Stevenage, Hertfordshire.

HRD motorcycles were immediately improved with the addition of rear suspension, followed in 1935 by an entirely new 497cc high-camshaft ohv engine, the Meteor, both to Phil Vincent's designs. This 497cc unit in turn gave birth to what is probably the *ne plus ultra of* motor cycle engines.

Production of the Vincent 998cc, 47 degree V-twins started in 1936 and would continue for 20 years. It must surely be the most imposing and handsome of bike engines, all polished alloy and gleaming black enamel. Following the war, Phil Vincent manufactured variations of his engine and sold them as the Rapide, Black Shadow, Black Knight, Black Prince and, later, the extremely fast Black Lightning. This last was an 84mm bore x 90mm stroke racing version, giving 100bhp, and was used successfully by the likes of René Milhoux, George Brown and Roland Free for record-breaking. Roland Free reached 156.71mph, running on alcohol fuel.

Series C
Vincent Black
Shadow

Competition victories were many and included the Clubman's TT; a list of Vincent motor cycle racers reads like a who's who of top riders, with John Surtees, Phil Heath, Dennis Lashmar, Cliff Horn, Jock Daniels, Joe Davis and many others. In 1950 Vincent brought out another single, a 499cc adaptation of the V-twin without the rear cylinder, though it was probably more complicated than that. Vincent motor cycles of all types were built up to a high quality standard which ensured an equally high retail price, a problem that became evermore difficult for the company to live with as the 1950s progressed and motor cycle sales of all types plummeted. The situation worsened to the point that Vincent had to make something, anything, to improve its cash-flow. This is where the Firefly came in.

It was not even a Vincent design. The Firefly was reputedly drawn up by a Mr Polisky from Poland who was at the time working for H Miller & Co Ltd of Birmingham, purveyors of lighting equipment, switch gear, magnetos, coils and sundry electrical items to a multitude of motor-cycle manufacturers, including Vincent and Velocette. Miller saw its clip-on engine as an outlet for some of these electrical components, introducing it to the public in January 1952.

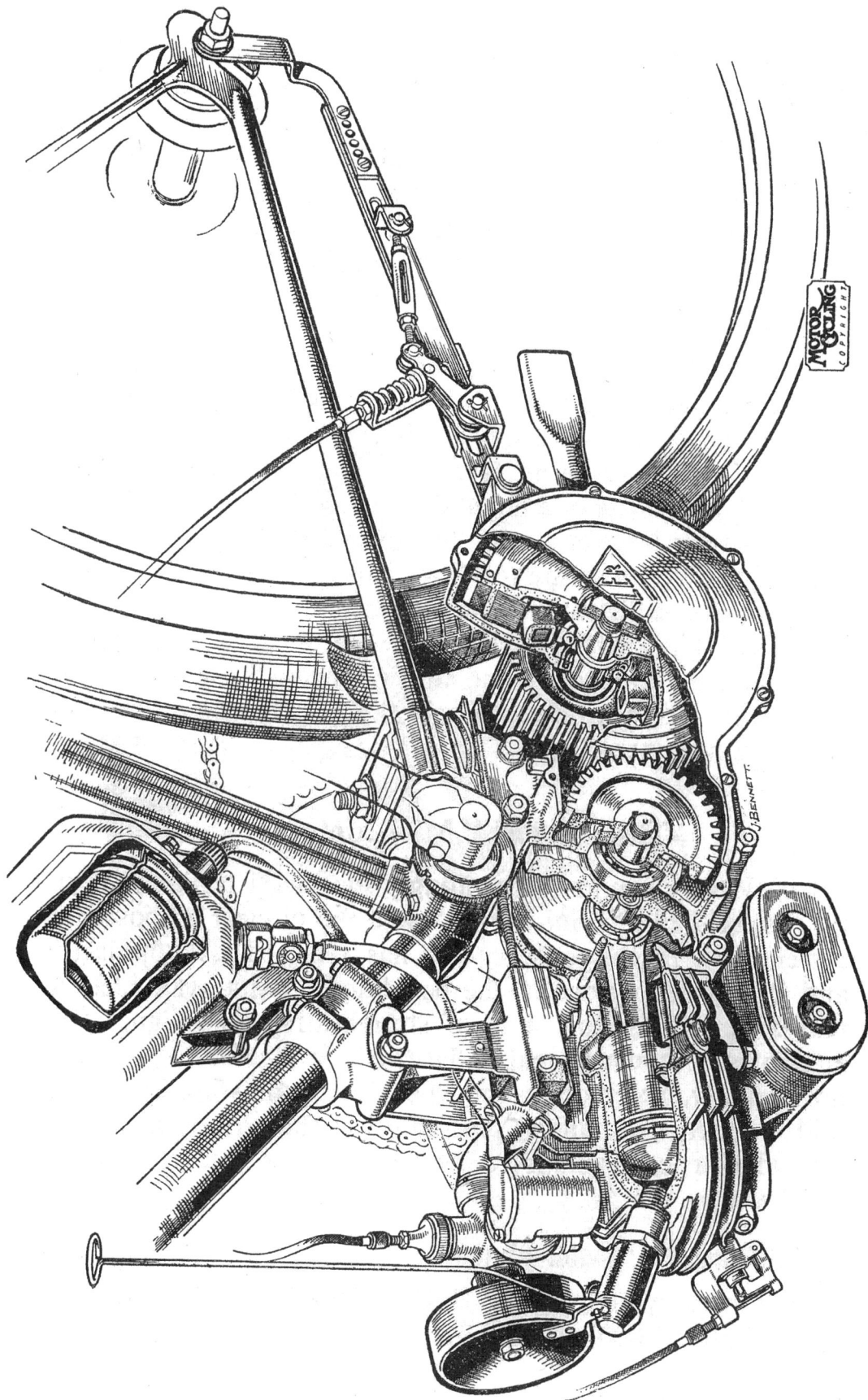

MILLER POWER UNIT AT BRUSSELS

Novel Engine Makes First Public Appearance .

This headline in *Motor Cycle and Cycle Trader* magazine of January 25 1952 heralded the arrival of the Miller clip-on unit at the Brussels Salon.

"First public appearance of the two-stroke lightweight engine unit developed by H.Miller & Co Ltd. is on the stand of their Belgian associates ... Development work on this has been carried out for some three years, although the secret has been a very well kept one, and prototype units have been given exhaustive tests both in this country and on the Continent." Unfortunately at that time *"no date for production can yet be given, as this depends so much on the supply position, particularly that of ball-bearings".*

So difficulties were still being experienced with precision-engineered items such as bearings, even though seven years had elapsed since the end of hostilities.

Miller's plan to increase its production volume by manufacturing this bottom-bracket-mounted engine was short-circuited by Phil Vincent 18 months later when he bought the design & tooling. Miller was perhaps secretly quite glad to be shot of it (the unit was simply known as *The Miller* until Vincent took over the design) as it was no doubt more complicated and costly to make and very likely much less profitable than light-bulbs, magnetos and lamps.

An early assessment of Miller's new unit was published in *Motor Cycling*, January 31ˢᵗ 1952, which concluded: *"With the unit on test in Birmingham, starting proved remarkably easy, the engine firing almost as soon as the pedals were turned and the decompressor lever released. A subsequent restart proved it possible to dispense with the decompressor. Plenty of power was available and an ability to two-stroke evenly at low speeds and with light load was revealed. Control, with but two levers, was simplicity itself. No price has been established, but whatever the final figure may be, the quality of material and the detail design is excellent".*

"Considerable interest was aroused in June (1953) when it was announced that Vincent's were to produce the Firefly cyclemotor ... intended for mounting to the bicycle bottom-bracket", as *The Motor Cycle* magazine of 19ᵗʰ November 1953 described it. Vincent was to join the ranks of bottom-bracket fitted units and were in good company with the likes of Cucciolo, Mosquito and Itom Tourist. The principal advantage of this layout was a low centre of gravity and hence directional stability, but

the principal disadvantage was having to make the engine narrow enough to fit between standard bicycle pedal cranks. This entailed using a primary drive and reduction gearing to bring the drive roller into the same space as the engine and was correspondingly more expensive to manufacture. It also placed the electrics directly in line with muck and water projected backwards by the front wheel, so, many British competitors remained loyal to fitment over the rear wheel for the sake of simplicity and cost.

The Vincent Firefly was a notably compact but otherwise fairly conventional two-stroke engine of 38mm bore × 42mm stroke, giving 47.6cc capacity and a claimed 1bhp at 4,200rpm. It weighed 24lbs, the 4-port cylinder barrel was cast-iron with cooling fins parallel to the ground, the sand-cast head and slightly domed piston (with three pegged rings) were of light alloy. The piston had two cut-aways in the skirt, giving a long transfer-port dwell which helped increase output. A decompressor was fitted. Ball-race main bearings, fitted with synthetic-rubber oil seals, support a crankshaft assembled from machined steel forgings bridged by a ground, hardened ½" diameter crank-pin pressed into the two halves. The crank pin on early versions is unusual in that it was internally bored with a taper at each end. Inserted in each taper were steel cones that were tightened by a countersunk bolt, expanding the crank-pin and thus assuring an immovable assembly. Later versions had a more simple press-fitted crank pin. Big-end roller bearings ran directly on the crank, housed within a forged steel connecting rod; a phosphor-bronze little end bush provided the gudgeon pin bearing.

Drive to the rear tyre was via a larger-than-average 82mm diameter steel roller, the reduction of 2:1 between crankshaft and final-drive being achieved by gears keyed onto tapers and running in an oil-bath. The smaller crank drive gear was forged from nickel-chrome steel; the driven gear was twice the size and a *"composite structure. [The] larger pinion is the drum of the 9-watt A.C. generator and carries the magnets and poles* [presumably of Miller manufacture] *within its periphery. It is mounted on a shaft which passes through the stator coils and is keyed to take the roller which drives on the rear wheel"*, (*Power & Pedal*, Sept 1953). This generator provided current to the coil for ignition and to lights and a horn. A neat, polished aluminium casing covered the driving pinions and electrics. The drive roller had been carefully considered and incorporated a flexible rubber liner bonded between the keyed inner member and external ribbed driving part that contacted the rear tyre. The *"combination of cushion drive, reduction gear and large diameter roller absorbs vibration and provides a large bearing area on the tyre, avoiding slip and improving the life of the tyre."*

Applying power to the rear wheel had been looked at closely, the designers coming up with a novel and ingenious solution to the perennial problems associated with roller drives. High pressure on a tyre in order to produce traction even under extremely wet conditions resulted in fast tread-wear rates, excessive power losses and eventually structural damage to said tyre. Light pressure on a tyre had other negative effects: notably unreliable traction in anything less than ideal, dry conditions. The resulting roller spin against a tyre tread quickly wore the surface into waves and scallops, to the detriment of tyre life, traction, rider comfort and the owner's bank account.

Vincent (or rather Miller) overcame these problems to a certain extent, its roller engagement mechanism was *"a toggle gear mounted below the near-side chain-stay of the cycle frame, the clutch-type lever on the handlebar being pulled in to draw the engine back on its slides and engage the roller with the tyre"*. The large diameter (82mm, around 3¼") also helped by distributing driving effort over a larger area of the sorely tried rear tyre tread than was usual. Recommended indentation of the tyre surface was between ⅛" and ¼" for a correct setting. A novel rear stay arrangement between the engine and rear wheel spindle took reactions from the roller on the tyre; it allowed pedal chain adjustment independent of roller position. The rear wheel could also be removed and replaced (to mend a puncture, for example) without disturbing the roller adjustment.

Unsurprisingly, *"special attention has been lavished on the electrical side of the design"* (*Power & Pedal*, September 1953), Miller not being prepared to sire a pup and sully its reputation in this respect. Further unusual design features abounded inside the low-tension generator: four stationary coils in square formation were fixed to the inside face of the alloy casing, while four magnets inside pole-pieces rotated around them. The contact breaker arm was triangular, *"the foot of which engages on an internal cam formed by a shaped sleeve that is pressed into the hollowed end of the mainshaft"*, (*Motor Cycling*, January 31st 1952). Ignition timing was 3mm before TDC, contact-breaker gap between .015" and .018" though this apparently was amended to .022" to .024" by late 1954. Another unusual feature was mounting the HT ignition coil within a housing situated inside the bottom of the fuel tank rather than incorporated within the magneto itself. It was thus well protected from the elements but perhaps uncomfortably close to five pints of inflammable two-stroke mix.

Stone & Cox listed the 48cc Vincent Firefly as commercially available at the retail price of £25.0s.0d. This was slightly more than 10% of the price of a 499cc Vincent Comet for slightly less than 10% of the cubic capacity.

What immediately became apparent to road-testers of the time was that the Firefly was something of a goer.

The VINCENT *"FIREFLY"*
A New British Unit

Power & Pedal rhapsodised about *"real acceleration from 10mph to a maximum of 28mph … but there seems to be no top limit to the ability of the engine to rev and it was still going smoothly when the maximum limit of safe control demanded the cutting back of the throttle"*. The Motor Cycle concurred in its review of 18th November 1954, stating *"one of the neatest and liveliest of British cyclemotors is the Vincent Firefly"*. A Firefly would, according to *Power & Pedal* *"accelerate without pedal assistance up grades of the order of 1 in 20 and [it] climbed most main road hills well … for real appreciation, however, the Firefly has to be cruised on open roads at about 22mph. This it did effortlessly on half-throttle with ample reserves in hand and an immediate response to a touch of the lever when a gradient or traffic conditions demanded. With this performance and the knowledge that the tank held enough for a hundred miles cruising range with unembarrassed refuelling if required, it was a pleasure to take the road on a fine day and feel that the whole of Britain was there for the taking"*.

Goodness me! Cynical, gnarled & warty cyclemotor testers writing for *Power & Pedal* were seldom this lavish with their praise; anticipating riding off in the general direction of a nation-wide sunset rather than buzzing home for tea ASAP was very unusual indeed. The Firefly was evidently something rather special: a high-performance clip-on unit.

FIGURE 1.

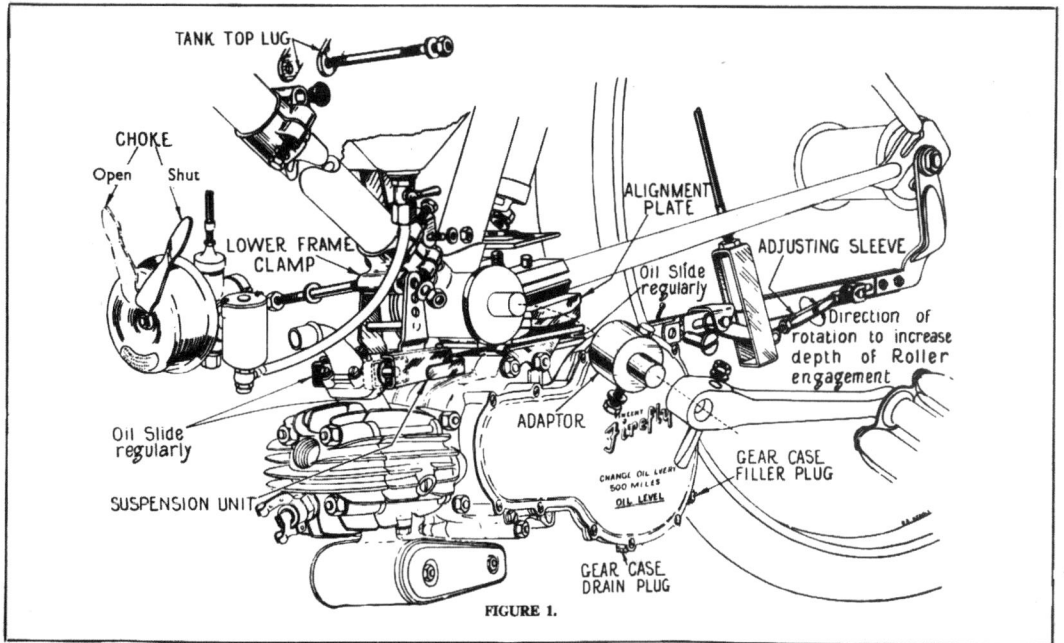

The drawing above, taken from the *"Instructions for Fitting and Maintenance of the Vincent Firefly All Weather Cycle Motor"* is particularly interesting since it shows clearly the method of attachment to a cycle frame plus the adjustable stay and toggle gear used to engage the drive roller with the rear tyre. Note that this is a different, third type of stay compared to two others previously illustrated. Especially noteworthy are the compact dimensions of the exhaust system and closeness to a cycle frame of the engine unit which, on average, gave four inches of ground clearance beneath the silencer. On cycle frames equipped with a bottom-bracket stirrup-brake mechanism, the operating rod, stirrup, etc. had to be removed, as it would foul the Firefly engine. Vincent recommended replacement with *"the Phillips cable rear brake set No.410"*.

Cycle Fitments — PHILLIPS

WESTWOOD CABLE BRAKES

These Brakes are designed for riders who prefer their wheels built with Westwood type rims, but at the same time, require their Brakes with Cable control.

Westwood Brakes are ideal for use with motorised bicycles and with this purpose in view they are available, to order, with large Stirrups suitable for 2" tyres.

No. 405. Westwood Front Brake. Complete with Waterproof Covered Cable, and **No. 11 Lever.** $\frac{7}{8}$" D Fork Clips supplied as standard, $\frac{3}{4}$" D or $\frac{3}{4}$" Round, supplied to order.

No. 410. Westwood Rear Brake, for Seat Stay Attachment. Complete with Waterproof Covered Cable, and **No. 11** Lever. $\frac{3}{4}$" D Stay Clips supplied as standard. $\frac{3}{4}$" or $\frac{5}{8}$" Round, supplied to order.

No. 444. Westwood Rear Brake. Complete with Waterproof Covered Cable, **No. 11** Lever and Model " E " Leg Clip Fastening. $\frac{7}{8}$" D Stay Clips supplied as standard. $\frac{3}{4}$" Round, to order.

On all Westwood Cable Brakes, the Cables are supplied Black as standard. Silver can be supplied to order.

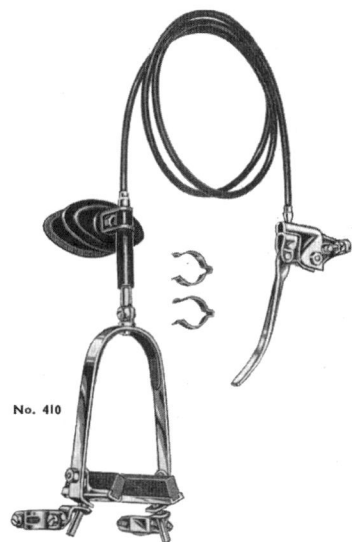

No. 410

The drawing below reveals the rather unusual Miller magneto and drive roller side of the engine, together with two supplementary handlebar controls for engaging and disengaging the roller and combined decompressor and throttle lever.

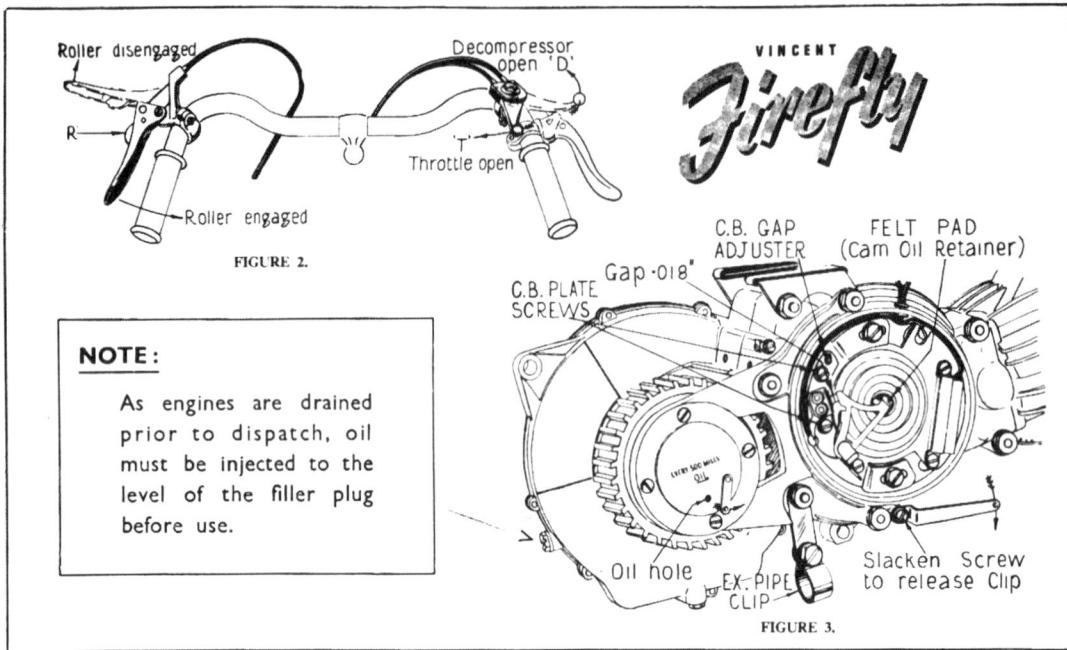

Roller disengaged

R

Roller engaged

FIGURE 2.

Decompressor open 'D'

'T'
Throttle open

VINCENT
Firefly

C.B. GAP ADJUSTER
Gap ·018"
C.B. PLATE SCREWS

FELT PAD (Cam Oil Retainer)

Oil hole
EX. PIPE CLIP

Slacken Screw to release Clip

FIGURE 3.

NOTE:

As engines are drained prior to dispatch, oil must be injected to the level of the filler plug before use.

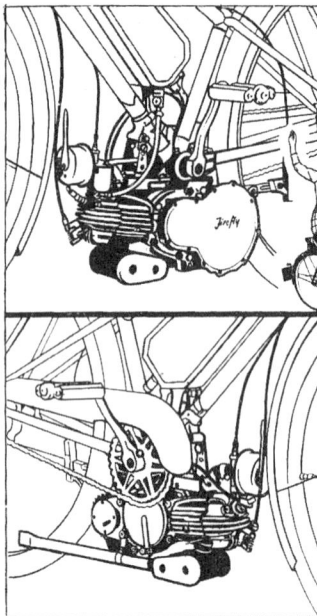
"Except for one serious defect, of which more anon, the Firefly lent itself equally well to the utility run to the local shop or pub and, except even more for that one serious defect, it was a handy mount for the daily trip to the office and back. In town the natural ability of a cycle to take advantage of every foot of road was backed by the lively acceleration and complete controllability of the unit and gave better average point-to-point times than any car. The engine has a notable ability to tick over- at modest constant revs - and this enabled stops and restarts to be made with the engaging lever used as a clutch as soon as the pedals had the machine moving. The good weight distribution of the low-hung, centrally disposed engine and the inclined 5-pints tank offer maximum stability under

all road conditions. Power came on exceptionally smoothly even when the engine was four-stroking at low speeds. There was some toe-tickling vibration at the pedals but none at the saddle and hardly any at the handlebars. Response to the handling of the throttle lever was delightfully positive and 'clean' feeling." Philip Vincent must have felt amply vindicated in his choice of clip-on design on reading such commendations.

However, there is always a downside to such good performance and in the case of the Firefly the serious defect alluded to above was, inevitably, noise. *"On the wrong side of the account"* harrumphed Power & Pedal, *"we must regretfully state ... the Firefly is the second noisiest unit we have yet tested and the sight of pedestrians a hundred yards in front turning their heads to see what was coming up behind shewed that it was not only the rider who heard the howl"*. Granted that excessive engine noise had always been something of an obsession with *Power & Pedal* magazine's editor, Frank L Farr, but in the case of the Vincent Firefly such criticism does seem to an extent justified.

"Why the Vincent Company should turn out a 50cc cyclemotor that makes more row than their Black Shadow of twenty times the capacity we do not know. When we visited the Works they talked of 'Two-Stroke Crackle' and seemed to think that it was laid on by the angels as an inevitable two-stroke sin!" quoth *Power & Pedal*. Not much co-operation from the factory then; probably Vincent's engineers regarded the Firefly as an imposed alien orphan, not remotely up to their usual engineering high standards, NIH (Not Invented Here) and all that. It was also far too small, a 20th the size of most Vincents.

Power & Pedal concluded its extended Road Test with the following: *"this high-performance British cyclemotor allied to the correctly designed cycle in which it was tested form an autocycle that can ... stand with the best ... and we confidently predict a long and successful future for this excellently designed and built unit. For the rider who wants to get there and back with ease, comfort, confidence and at a lively average speed the Vincent Firefly is definitely a Good Buy"*.

Fuel consumption was usually around 200mpg at 25mph though Ted Davis, Vincent's Chief Development Engineer, remembers one irate owner complaining he was only obtaining around 137mpg, *"the same as a Black Shadow at the same speed in top gear"*. No doubt said owner rode everywhere flat-out, a great temptation with a Firefly.

Vincent used a slightly unusual engine numbering system which requires a little explanation, for example its 1,000cc twins were numbered F10AB-1-*nnnnn*, F10AB-1B-, F10AB-2- etc, the 500cc singles F5AB-2A- but some were also F5AB-1-. The first production Firefly would probably have been numbered T05AB-1-50001 with sequential numbering thereafter. **T** means two-stroke, **05** indicates 50cc, **A** means aluminium engine cases, **B** is a two-wheeler but the significance of the hyphenated figure one is unknown. One could hazard a guess that it could have been changed to a **2** for a future 'Mark 2' Firefly. The earliest known surviving Firefly at the time of writing is number T05AB-1-50052, the latest T05AB-1-57176, all engine numbers being stamped across the join on top of the crankcase halves after assembly, indicating at least 7176 units were built altogether.

ROAD TEST REPORT

The VINCENT "FIREFLY"

Evidently *Power & Pedal* magazine was much taken by the Firefly because another road test report appeared in April 1955 opposite a full-page Firefly advert highlighted with red and blue ink (reproduced on page 151). The context for an article this time was: "*It has become increasingly difficult to make objective assessments of attachment engines [in] competition [with] built-in-one-piece light autocycles** which set high standards, not so much in performance, as in comfort, silence, appearance and ease of handling. This is particularly true of the high-performance types of which the Vincent Firefly is definitely one. The unit we have just tested has been improved since our last report was published eighteen months ago*".

"*The ability of the engine to maintain 25-30mph for long spells on undulating main roads remains its best feature … At about half-throttle a speed of around 22-25mph could be maintained indefinitely with ample power reserves in the engine and complete comfort on the part of the rider. At this speed the exhaust is not unduly loud and the note quite pleasant to the rider's ear*" (perhaps Vincent engineers had taken heed of *Power & Pedal's* previous acid comments regarding the "*serious defect*" of noise?), "*but at higher revs both exhaust and mechanical noises became obtrusive. Some at least of the latter seemed to be exaggerated by the resonance of the new-shaped fuel tank as it was noticeably worse when the tank was under half full.*"

The magazine was however more enthused by the qualities of a Firefly's roller drive and ignition: the "*geared roller with its integral 'cush-drive' grips the tyre cleanly and firmly without having to be squashed hard into the tread. In wet weather the slip was negligible and in dry there was none at all … Most interesting design feature … is the ignition system which embodies an AC generator in the roller drive gear. In terms of results this system pays off well, the low speed spark is a perfect beauty and it is this that guarantees a start within a few feet in any weather. The generator also affords ample lighting current over its full speed range with no blacking out on corners*". The Firefly was also given high marks for finish and appearance but "*the test unit leaked oil at several points*". A familiar failing, as all cyclemotorists know.

Power & Pedal concluded: "*To sum up, the Vincent Firefly is a very good example of the under-bracket attachment unit that is specially suitable for serious, mainroad travel. So long as there is a market for attachment engines* (a very telling little phrase) *this one will command a leading position for its good performance and interesting and practical design*".

---

* The term moped was not in current use in 1955, this is what *Power & Pedal* refers to.

161

The Firefly generated some interesting correspondence regarding wet ignition problems, something it appears to have been prone to.

Firefly Reply

Mr. J. Franklin of Northolt says that he has got over his wet weather ignition trouble by fitting a large splashguard to his front mudguard, this is not such a good idea as it sounds. I fitted a large motor cycle flap to my machine but found that it blanketed the engine too much and after climbing a long hill it was very hot indeed. I have now fitted a plastic dress guard to the front mudguard and fitted a further flap to the bottom of the existing one; even in the heaviest rain hardly a drop of mud is thrown on to the engine and no cooling air is cut off. What we want and cannot get are deeply valanced mudguards as were fitted as standard to Roadster cycles of the *Dreadnought* type.

The main trouble is caused by rain running down the tank on to the coil down the lead to the plug, I have taped up the joint at the coil and fitted a waterproof plug cover ; a *Champion* fitted with a screw so that it may be locked to point downwards; the clip-on types tend to point upwards owing to the pull of the lead so allowing rain to run in. I have also scrapped the suppressor, this caused me trouble on two or three occasions. My pet dealer tells me that these fittings are causing a lot of trouble on a popular unit that reached the 100,000 mark a long time ago, he scraps them as fast as they come into his workshop.

Regarding his query re plug gap, I always get satisfactory results by following the makers recommendation i.e. .022 to .024. The *Firefly* has coil ignition which requires a larger gap than that for a magneto, I also use a K.L.G. 5.50 plug instead of the F20 fitted as standard, I find it gives me just that extra punch.

Engine engagement control. A good deal of this heaviness is caused by the control cable being assembled dry, it pays to well oil this and regularly oil it, the action will be much sweeter, I have also followed your advice and let my tyre down from 60lbs. to 35lbs.

I have had further correspondence with Messrs. Vincent and the following facts may be of use to you.

(1) They are altering their petroil mixture from 16-1 to 24-1 so that in future the mixture will be two measures of oil to ½-gall instead of the present 3 measures. Not only will this be a saving in cost but the ordinary gallon can will just hold 1 gall of petrol and the necessary oil. With the heavier mixture this was not possible and it meant using two cans with a lot of messy measuring.

(2) A waterproof sparking plug cover with suppressor incorporated is to become a standard fitting.

(3) They are making arrangements to sound test the *Firefly* with the aid of modern sound testing equipment.

(4) *Roll engaging mechanism.* They say "We agree, however, that on many machines the operation of the unit falls far short of the possible standard and we are investigating the possibility of incorporating some detail improvements "

It seems worthwhile worrying the makers until they do something about it. I have now run just over 1,500 miles, petrol consumption to date 210 m.p.g., the makers claim 170 m.p.g. so I am quite satisfied with my riding methods.

T. WAYMOUTH PRINGLE
South Croydon.

162

The Pride & Clarke advert reproduced on page 162 dates from December 1954 and gives an inkling of things to come. One of the biggest London-based distributors of clip-ons, cyclemotors, motor cycles and three-wheelers was already offering a great number of different makes; one could hazard a guess from this fact that exclusive dealerships were less than profitable by then. The Shadow of the Angel of Death for many a clip-on manufacturer also features prominently: Motobécane's Mobylette De Luxe was offering vastly more comfort and performance than British-manufactured equivalents. At approximately double the price of a clip-on a customer bought a complete homogenous machine with proper brakes, a clutch, lights and a purpose-built frame with appropriate wheels and tyres, a machine built without compromise. Increasing prosperity meant a Mobylette was now affordable to many that were tempted by more sophisticated dynamics than those afforded by a push bike with crude little engine strapped on somewhere.

Phil Vincent was aware of this threat and acted accordingly; in early 1955 press adverts appeared to promote the…

This 'new' model was available in two configurations: Gentleman's or Universal (which French manufacturers would call *ecclésiastique*, access being easier over a lowered crossbar whether a skirt or cassock were worn, an important point in Catholic countries) and was offered at a very competitive on-the-road price, £38.19s.3d including sprung fork and purchase tax. In comparison, a Cyclemate sold for £48.19s.6d, a Mobylette £49.16s.0d and a Phillips Motorised Bicycle a princely £55.12s.0d, all including PT. So the Vincent Firefly Power Cycle was aimed at undercutting prices of most competing marques, without sacrificing the best qualities of the Firefly clip-on engine, those of outstanding performance with economy, if not silence.

The Vincent Firefly Power Cycle was in reality a special frame for the Firefly clip-on made either by the Sun Cycle Co or Phillips, these had been launched two years previously, in July 1953, being supplied to customers with the engine unit Vincent factory-fitted. Sun had offered its frame without the engine at £18.17s.3d including Purchase Tax. Vincent was selling the engine itself for £25.0s.0d. So the cost of these individual items combined would have been £43.17s.3d. By buying the Power Cycle complete at £38-19s-3d, customers saved nearly five pounds and got the sprung front fork thrown in free. Whether this resulted in a stampede of new buyers is not known, nevertheless the Firefly Power Cycle was a well-conceived amalgam of items from two quality manufacturers even though it did lack a certain one-ness when compared to Continental competition such as the Mobylette or the hugely successful NSU Quickly autocycle. It beat both of these on price however and deserved to be a success.

A further blow to Vincent's aspirations for the Firefly Power Cycle was struck by Messrs Fichtel & Sachs AG of Schweinfurt, West Germany, who introduced an all-new compact **integrated** engine and gearbox unit to the UK in February 1955. Of superb modern design and construction, the Sachs engine produced 1.25bhp at 4,100rpm from 47cc and featured lighting coils, a multi-plate clutch, two-speed gearbox and incorporated pedals with a clever back-pedal brake mechanism on the offside. Even the special little Bing carburettor was built in to the top surface of the main casing and rubber cushioned mountings were fitted to the cylinder head and top rear of the gearbox.

The Sachs unit instantly rendered obsolete most cyclemotor engine & transmission units available at that time and was obviously aimed at those who were creating and producing the new generation of mopeds. It must have also given many a British cyclemotor and clip-on manufacturer a sinking feeling; how on earth would they compete with such a sophisticated unit? Having such a compact unitary engine and transmission available on demand freed many small European moped manufacturers from the financial constraints of developing and making engines. Using the Sachs unit allowed them to design and build frames, buy-in proprietary wheels & brakes, lights, saddles etc- and produce very satisfactory mopeds at low cost. Millions of Sachs engines were made and sold all over the world.

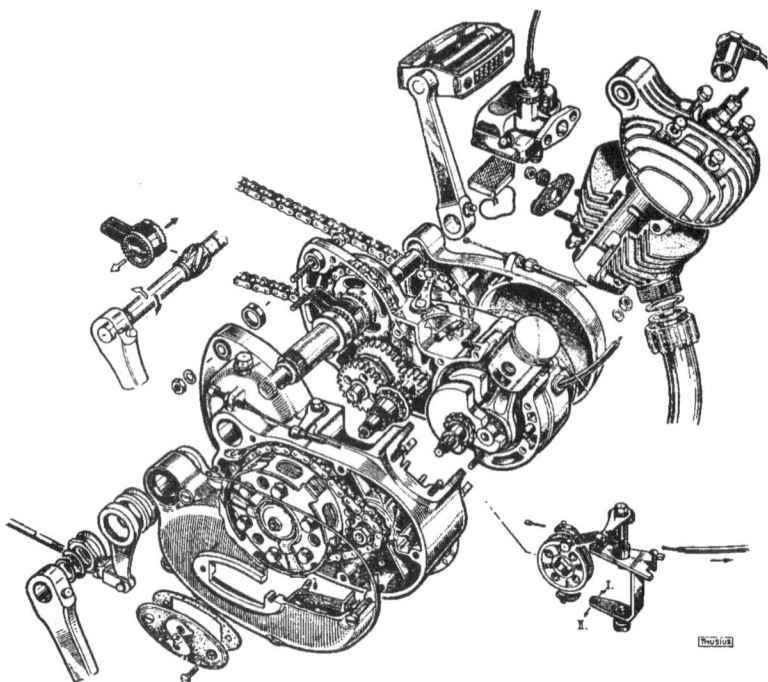

Such technological advances as these did little to help sales of the Firefly, which by early 1955 were flagging. There was nothing intrinsically wrong with it in fact, performance was rather better than the average, it was simply overtaken by progress, prosperity and more modern designs from rejuvenated European manufacturers. Changes to taxation didn't help either; the imposition of Purchase Tax in March 1955 at 25% pushed up prices, albeit marginally, the Firefly being advertised at £25.19s.8d in the same month.

Power & Pedal magazine published a report on the January 1955 Brussels Show which noted *"sad to say, that once more, Continental competitors have been astute enough to 'get cracking' ....on new products whilst their British counterparts seem to be dozing peacefully beside their out-dated models. If anyone wanted further proof of this, the Brussels salon would have given it. The bicycle with clip-on, still main product in this field at British factories, was not to be seen. But the autocycle has developed into its very own form, it has indeed become a beautiful, practical and safe vehicle of a design all its own"*. It has to be said in defence of British manufacturers that their market was tiny in comparison. Huge European factories turned out models designed for pan-European distribution, aided by compliant and simple legislation, whereas UK makers struggled against all manner of mule-like bureaucratic obstinacy and petty regulations. No wonder cyclemotors were so much more successful abroad than at home.

A generic European autocycle, or *moped* as they soon became known, featured some or all of the following: underslung engines at pedal level, final drive by chain, low and strong step-through pressed-steel frames, small diameter wheels with balloon tyres and drum brakes, comfortable saddles and fuel tanks as part of or mounted on the frame. Front suspension was commonplace, rear suspension increasingly so. A sub-genre was also manifesting itself: small-capacity light scooters as exemplified by Britax and its Cucciolo-based Scooterette, the German Victoria Nicky and others. *Power & Pedal* was quick off the mark too, sub-titling the magazine as *"incorporating THE SCOOTER"* from late 1954, thus nailing its colours firmly to the mast.

One of the first issues of *THE SCOOTER* carried a revealing article entitled *Cyclemotor to Scooter* by Mr F W Quigley who explains why he had just bought a second-hand Vespa.

"I had graduated to the scooter by way of five cyclemotors and one autocycle ... all the cyclemotors were purchased as new ... I calculate that in a matter of 4 years I must have spent about £150 in all, or the price of a second-hand car of doubtful reliability. In my pursuit of the ideal cyclemotor I was not slow to adopt refinements of spring frame, enlarged mudguards and so on, so that all that was left of my original pedal cycle, when I traded it in for the scooter, were the handlebars and pedals! The reason for my persistence was that I liked cyclemotoring but was unable to achieve my ideal of what a cyclemotor should give in service. [This] ideal was a cyclemotor of such mechanical reliability that I would not myself have to be a mechanic to keep it on the road. In practice I found they required frequent attention at inconvenient moments. Most of this was not serious engine trouble, but in the case of the friction drives - bad attachments to the cycle frame and snapping cables; as regards the built-in-the-wheel jobs, of which I owned two, weak spokes in one case and the constant whiskering of the plug in the other. My experience with the cyclemotors suggests that the successful cyclemotorist is a good natural mechanic - the kind of man whose eyes light up with interest whenever his engine shows signs of packing in - mine register a mixture of wrath and despair."

British clip-on and cyclemotor manufacturers were in the main still producing first-generation Continental hand-me-down machines which might have been perfectly adequate in the late 1940s or a year or two into the 1950s when expectations were lower and finances tighter but, five years or more on, were not what the paying public wanted. Life had moved on. Phil Vincent found himself in this trap with the Firefly, a decent enough machine when conceived but now outclassed. If truth were told he was probably not that interested in it anyway, the Firefly had been seen as a stopgap generating some revenue until something else came along. Nothing did: money was not available to develop a modern replacement; sales struggled on, as did the Vincent company itself, but the situation went from bad to worse. An attempted marriage of convenience with NSU in Germany to retail the NSU Fox lightweight motor cycle came to nought and the inevitable could not be staved off. Perhaps Phil Vincent had hoped the Firefly would be his saviour but sadly it was a case of too little too late, even at the introduction of the Miller in 1952 customers were aware of new, sophisticated machines available in Europe. It would only be a matter of time before these were sold in the UK. In all probability the few sales made after 1956 came from dealers' stocks and were very small, until none was left on the shelves.

This chapter would not be complete without at least a passing reference to one rather unlikely variant on the Vincent Firefly Power Cycle theme: the Gundle Handymotor carrier cycle. One final indignity was visited upon Phil Vincent's powerful little clip-on unit in the form of an adapted Gundle delivery cycle which could be bought with a massive standard front carrier and equally huge optional rear carrier, wicker baskets, small front wheel with stand and tradesmen's plate just waiting for some Gothic script declaiming

𝔍𝔣𝔬𝔯 𝔍𝔬𝔫𝔢𝔰 – 𝔥𝔦𝔤𝔥 ℭ𝔩𝔞𝔰𝔰 𝔐𝔢𝔞𝔱 & 𝔓𝔬𝔲𝔩𝔱𝔯𝔶

𝔇𝔢𝔩𝔦𝔳𝔢𝔯𝔢𝔡 𝔗𝔬 𝔜𝔬𝔲𝔯 𝔇𝔬𝔬𝔯 𝔞𝔱 𝔑𝔬 𝔈𝔵𝔱𝔯𝔞 ℭ𝔥𝔞𝔯𝔤𝔢.

𝔗𝔢𝔩𝔢𝔭𝔥𝔬𝔫𝔢: 𝔏𝔩𝔞𝔫𝔡𝔶𝔰𝔰𝔶𝔩 352

Note the low centre of gravity

YOUR DELIVERY PROBLEMS SOLVED

THE VINCENT "FIREFLY" ENGINE

2-STROKE ENGINE with a bore of 38 mm. and a stroke of 42 mm. giving a capacity of 48 c.c.

COMPRESSION RATIO : 5 : 1.

IGNITION : Ignition coil supplied by A.C. generator.

CONTACT BREAKER : Simple and accessible contact breaker of patented design.

LIGHTING : 9-watts from A.C. generator.

CARBURETTOR : Amal.

LUBRICATION : Petroil mixture 16 : 1.

PETROL TANK CAPACITY : 5/8 gallon. Approx. 165 m.p.g. (according to load).

DRIVE : Through resilient pulley of 82 mm. diameter.

WEIGHT : Engine and tank 24 lbs. (11 kilos). Carrier cycle complete with engine 3 qrs. 12 lbs. (42.7 Kilos).

THE GUNDLE "HANDYMOTOR" CARRIER CYCLE

FRAME : 20in. Heavy design to withstand all stresses. Engine lugs brazed to frame. Black finish

WHEELS : Front 20in. × 2in. with internal expanding brake hub. Rear 26in. × 1⅜in. × 1½in. motorette with Coaster brake hub.

SADDLE : All weather.

CARRIERS : Front 22¼in. × 16¾in. to take a basket 16in. deep. Rear 22¼in. × 16¾in. to take a basket 9in. deep.

LOAD : Up to 1 cwt. (51 Kilos).

(No. P. Tax) Price : £47?? Ex Works

Price and Specification ruling at time of despatch

Extras

	£	s.	d.
Front and Rear Lamps	1	5	0
Chain Guard		5	0
Rear Carrier	2	10	0
Pump and Clips, Tool Bag and Tools		13	6
Deep Wicker Basket	1	19	0
Shallow Wicker Basket	1	5	0

All–up weight of the substantial Gundle bicycle fitted with a Firefly motor was only 16lbs short of a hundredweight (which was 112lbs in old money) or, for those of a decimal persuasion (hopefully most of us these days), some 42.7 kilos. Payload was an equally substantial one hundredweight (51kgs).

At least Gundle had fitted some decent brakes: a good-sized front drum and rear coaster brake, hopefully powerful enough to arrest the headlong progress of Dai, the butcher's apprentice, whose head was turned by Megan the waitress at the Cozee Café down the High Street. Megan would lean provocatively over the counter by the window whenever she heard the loud buzz of Dai and his Handymotor coming down the road, laden with sausages and pies on their way to the Cefn Coch Inn half a mile away. Megan rather liked the look of Dai and Dai rather liked the look of Megan, but he would have been better off looking at the road in front as Mr Jenkins the haberdasher was in the habit of parking his Morris Minor just round the corner from the Cozee Café. Gundle no doubt bore such events in mind when specifying braking power.

The Motor Cycle Show Issue magazine of 28th November 1957 still showed the Vincent Firefly as available and according to Stone and Cox's listings of the British market, the Firefly was still sold as late as 1959, after which date *"manufacture discontinued"*.

Still, owning a Vincent had a certain cachet, even if the owner failed to tell a listener that his was not a Black Shadow.

British Salmson Cyclaid Limited was a post World War 2 offshoot of the venerable company British Salmson Aero Engines Ltd, created as a subsidiary of the French *Société des Moteurs Salmson* to make aero engines during the First World War and installed in Raynes Park, London SW20. Like many such enterprises after the Armistice, the French *Salmson* company owned two enormous but virtually work-free factories with huge overheads and corresponding staffing levels, the consequences of wartime expansion which had industrialists all over Europe searching for almost anything to make in order to keep their skilled workforce occupied and at least pay the overheads.

Société des Moteurs Salmson's founder, Emile Salmson, was born in 1859. His company was making civil engineering equipment by the turn of the 20th century, large machines for *travaux publics* being a speciality. Emile soon tired of work-a-day equipment and his dreams turned to flying, at that time the equivalent of space-travel in the 1960s, a new frontier to be crossed. He associated himself with a Monsieur Aimé in 1908 in order to construct a flying machine; apparently it was an early helicopter concept which sadly remained very much attached to *terra firma*.

The following year *Salmson* (the French company is written in *italics* to avoid confusion with the British Salmson company) provided financial support to two Swiss engineers, Georges Henri Marius Canton and Pierre Georges Unné, who had patented a novel seven-cylinder water-cooled radial aero engine.

A joint company was formed in 1912, *Société des Moteurs Salmson - Système Canton Unné,* to manufacture this promising engine in a new factory situated at *3 avenue des Moulineaux, Billancourt.* The patent engine departed from established radial design in one crucial respect. A conventional 7-cylinder radial uses one master con-rod with six other link rods pivoted from this, just above the single big-end. This results in a geometric imbalance since the master rod swings round the crank-pin with a different motion from the other, shorter, rods, but it all works after a fashion. *Canton-Unné* eliminated this imbalance by inventing a clever epicyclic gear system which held all seven rods in correct positions, doing away with the master rod & link rod layout and the inherent imbalance of this design.

SMS produced many thousands of this engine with various outputs and multiples of cylinders, from the 80bhp M7 in 1913 to the massive 500bhp Z18 of 1918. During the war, *Salmson* also manufactured a range of its own aeroplanes, the most successful being the Sal.2-A2 two-seat reconnaissance biplane, widely used by both French and American squadrons. By the end of hostilities the *Billancourt* factory covered 26,000 square metres and was capable of producing 700 engines, 200 Salmson aeroplanes and 1,500 magnetos a month with a 9,000-strong labour force.

Société des Moteurs Salmson's first business contact with Britain came about as a result of the post-war situation and an immediate need for cheap cyclecars, which *"provided the earliest form of motoring for the masses"* (to quote G N Georgano, editor, Encyclopedia of Motorcars). *Salmson* took out a manufacturing licence with the British company GN for its wooden framed, belt-drive V-twin cyclecar, designed and built by pioneers H R Godfrey and Archie Frazer Nash at the Etna Works, Hendon, from around 1910.

Initially GN (Godfrey & Nash) used 1,100cc air-cooled JAP engines but in 1911 progressed to building its own V-twin, using Peugeot cylinders but subsequently with 100% GN manufactured parts. Production volumes were very low, seldom exceeding two cars a week. After the war Godfrey and Frazer Nash negotiated a deal with The British Grégoire Agency Company whereby GN moved into the old British Grégoire factory at East Hill, Wandsworth and, able to expand production considerably, redesigned the car to incorporate a more robust steel chassis, a conventional steering box instead of wire & bobbin, and final drive by chains rather than belts.

Archie Frazer Nash at the wheel of a GN for the 200 Mile Race at Brooklands, 1921.

© Book Club Associates, Denis Jenkinson, Chain Drive to Turbocharger, 1985

As a result of all these changes the GN became an agile little car, *"roadholding was excellent … aided by high-geared steering … weight of just on 6 ½cwt … in conjunction with reasonable power and good low-speed torque …gave a sporting performance and attracted many sportsmen"* (Georgano again). Today, amongst VSCC members particularly, a good GN is still highly prized.

Three early GNs assemble for a cyclecar rally sometime in the 1920s, exact date and location are not known. Traffic in rural townships was still very sparse in those days and the prospect of meeting several spiritedly-driven GNs out for a rally doesn't bear thinking about. Note the complete lack of front-wheel brakes on all three cars.

This then was the model taken on by *Salmson* in Billancourt, where production began in 1919 and over 3,000 were made in the first two years, justifying the company's decision to go ahead. By 1921, *Salmson* had decided it could produce its own car and engaged the eminent engineer Emile Petit to design it. Not terribly successful at first, it was flimsy, had no differential and an odd, single push-rod per-cylinder 1,100cc four-cylinder engine. However, Emil Petit redeemed himself soon after by designing a jewel-like twin-overhead cam version for the Cyclecar Grand Prix, which then made it into production in an improved chassis. It was to sire an extensive and renowned range of small, sporting *voiturettes* that lasted until the late 1920s. By 1926, a *Salmson GP Spéciale* had front brakes (previously absent), a 4-speed gearbox and could be ordered with a Cozette supercharger bolted to the tiny 1,100cc motor, giving a top speed of over 70mph. The company would go on to greater things throughout the 1930s, lasting eventually into the 1950s and becoming one of the respected great French *marques de prestige*.

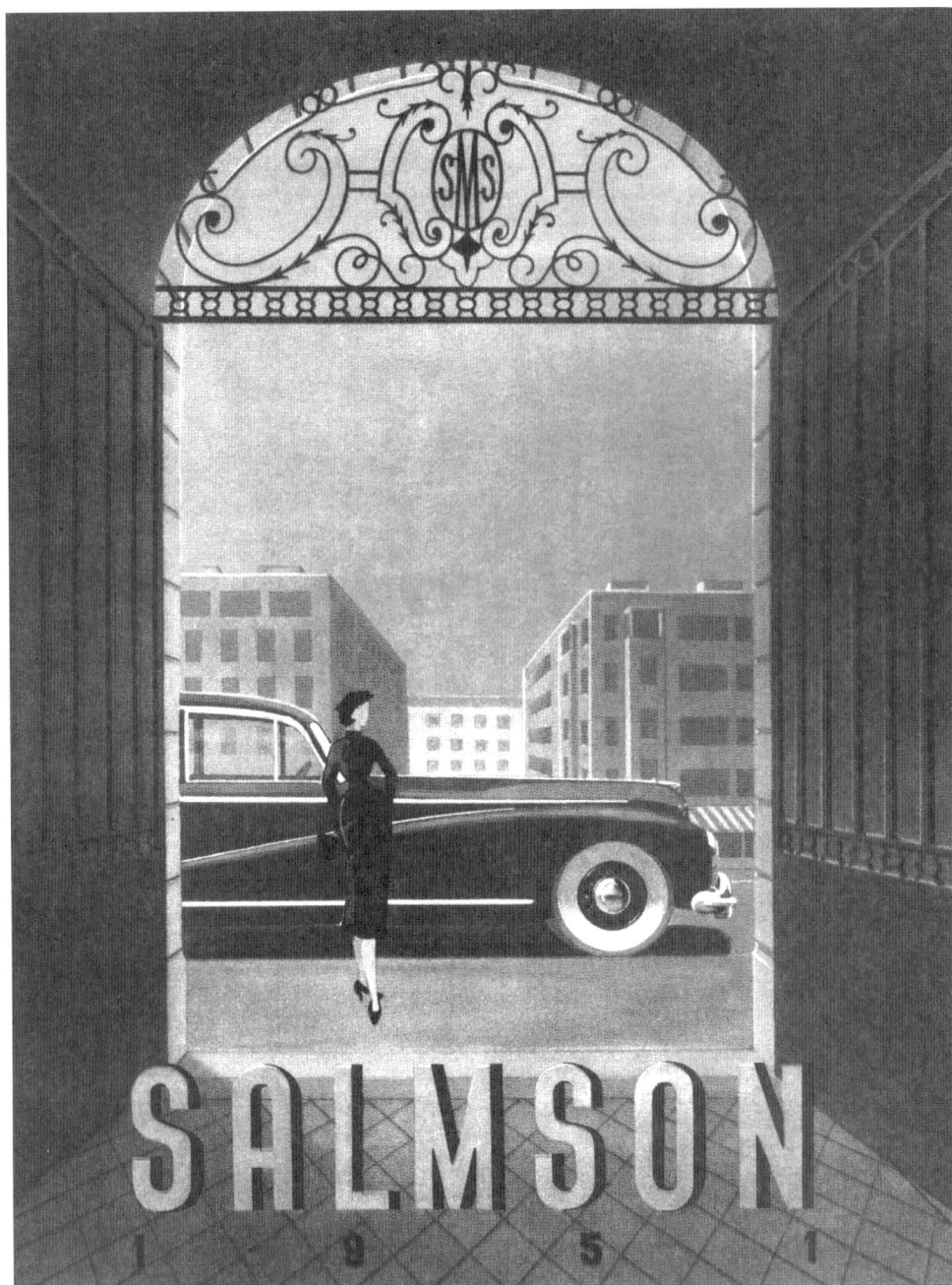

Meanwhile, back in Raynes Park SW20, things were also looking up. In a satisfyingly symmetrical move, British Salmson began production in 1934 of a modified version of the French *Salmson* S.4C model with 1½ litre 4-cylinder twin OHC engine, renowned as a fast, sporting tourer. Later models became inevitably larger and slower, culminating in the 20-90, which was an entirely British 2.6 litre twin-cam sportscar[*] with independent front suspension but was only made in small numbers. The British Salmson company continued to undertake aeronautical subcontract work whilst also acting as importers and distributors of French-made *Salmson* cars until 1939, so it was all very complicated and incestuous.

Found in the wreckage of WW2's aftermath was the rump of a once-great empire: the British Salmson company, bereft of work and about to go under. The factory was sold to fellow aero-

---

[*] It was called that but, being rather large and somewhat overweight, was hardly a sporting motorcar

174

engine manufacturers D Napier & Son in nearby Acton. Like many other such enterprises post WW1 and WW2, Salmson saw cheap and simple personal transport as a possible way to survive and settled on manufacturing a clip-on cyclemotor unit. British Salmson directors formed a new company, British Salmson Cyclaid Ltd, registered at 76 Victoria Street, London SW1, but they lacked both a design and a factory in which to produce the "Cyclaid". The first problem was remedied by purchasing a licence to manufacture the engine from Rex, a German-designed 31cc 0.75bhp cyclemotor attachment unit that was originally front-wheel mounted. Indeed the first 200 Cyclaid units had Bosch magnetos and "German-type" castings. The British Salmson company claimed that the Cyclaid was *"British designed and built throughout, to precision limits"*. It was certainly British-built throughout once production was under way but only the mountings and peripherals were British-designed throughout. Some poetic licence was allowable however in view of the quality of the end product.

The second problem was where to make the Cyclaid. Initially, this was solved by a rumoured sub-contract to Napier to manufacture a few units at British Salmson's old factory but all subsequent production took place on an industrial estate in Larkhall, Lanarkshire, Scotland. Some confusion exists as to whether this really was British Salmson Cyclaid's own factory though the company always quoted that as their factory address. In reality most Cyclaid parts were bought in and the Larkhall operation was largely one of assembly and machining. Original factory instruction sheets for the manufacturing processes were apparently in German with hand-written English translations alongside. Surviving paperwork indicates that an initial batch of 6,000 sets of components was ordered, with another 6,000 an option.

Whether by good luck or judgement, British Salmson Cyclaid had chosen a design to manufacture that corresponded closely with its own aero-engineering ethos and would have been something it might have created itself. For ease of installation and access, a rear-mounted unit was excellent, mainly because noise and incontinent oily emanations were kept behind the ears and trousers of a rider. The frequently bewhiskered and befouled spark-plug was also to hand for cleaning; this operation would not therefore involve kneeling and or reaching under dripping bottom-brackets, to the detriment of a rider's suiting. Primitive roller drives were rather *passé* for a company used to aero-engineering and refined sports-car standards. Uniquely, a long reinforced-rubber V-belt transmission *"which, as any old-time motorcyclist will confirm, is probably the smoothest of all positive drives" (The Cyclemotor Manual, 1952)* from engine to wheel was used as it was relatively unhindered by rain, had shock-absorbing qualities and, above all, was quiet. The large driven pulley was attached to rear wheel spokes via a series of peripheral bolts, thus the crudities of chains and rollers were bypassed, to the ultimate benefit of Cyclaid owners and riders.

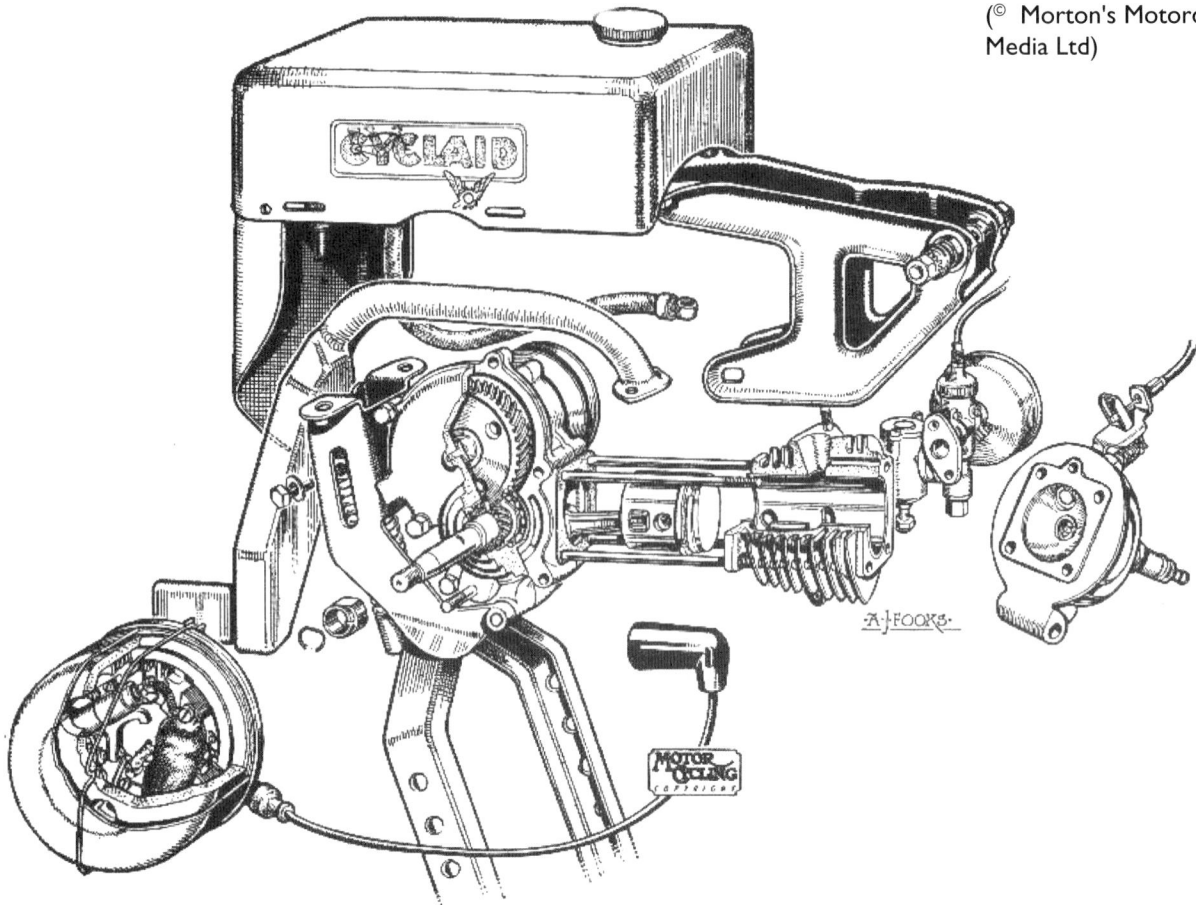

Coincidental with this plan for transmitting limited power to the rear wheel of a push-bike, the Cyclaid's designers had also decided to incorporate other slightly unconventional mechanical features in their clip-on engine unit. Cubic capacity, whether limited by bureaucrats or other considerations, was also a contentious issue, the European norm generally being 50cc or just under. In the Cyclaid case, designers followed the same route as those who created the Cyclemaster, BSA Winged Wheel and others in estimating that little more than 30cc would suffice, provided the engine was of an efficient design. The oversquare bore and stroke of 35mm×32mm gave a cylinder capacity of 31cc which, in conjunction with a low 5.6:1 compression ratio but good breathing, produced a respectable 0.7bhp at 3,550rpm, *pro-rata* much the same output per litre as a Cyclemaster engine of 25.7cc, which produced 0.6bhp.

Another aim was to produce a real lightweight clip-on unit, given that it would be mounted high up above the rear wheel. To this end an aluminium cylinder was used, with either an iron or steel liner, depending on whether you read *The Motor Cycle* (iron in this case, 14th December 1950) or *Power & Pedal* (steel, November 1952) and *Motor Cycling* (steel, 11th November 1954). As a general cyclemotor rule at the time, cylinder barrels were entirely of iron, with the obvious weight penalty. All surviving Cyclaids in the late 1990s seem to be fitted with steel liners, perhaps iron liners were fitted at one stage but wore out more quickly than steel ones? Most Cyclaid press adverts mention iron liners so we are not sure which is correct 50-odd years after the event. A hardened-steel connecting-rod ran on roller bearings, the little-end being a phosphor-bronze bush. A total of three ball races carried the crankshaft. From there drive was taken via spur reduction gears to the pulley countershaft, overall gearing being 18.5:1. The engine unit was mounted horizontally over the cycle rear wheel and supported by substantial pressed-steel plates front and rear, the front carrying *"Silentbloc bushes through which pass a specially strengthened saddle-pillar pinch-bolt"*, according to *The Motor Cycle*, 14th December 1950. An inverted

U-shaped member connected to the rear wheel spindle with special nuts provided a series of mounting holes, enabling the Cyclaid to be fitted to a variety of different size frames. Drive-belt tension was maintained by a spring-tensioner once the correct length of belt was fitted. The belts were available in a variety of sizes: Cyclaid spares requested *"state size of frame and wheel when ordering"*, the company unfortunately did not list all the sizes available. An unsympathetic owner, using a stretched or over-long belt, who tried to compensate by jacking up the unit using the mounting holes would quickly run out of fuel as this action tipped the fuel tank and limited the amount available.

Fuel was carried in a 3-pint capacity rectangular tank with a flat, square back that served as a number plate, a separate index plate not then being needed. The tank top had slots for straps, enabling the tank to be used as a carrier. Mixture was fed to an Amal 308/5 carburettor with air filter and strangler, with ignition courtesy of Wipac. Contact breaker and spark plug gaps were to be set at 0.018" and 0.020" respectively. All-up, the Cyclaid weighed in at just 19lbs and, according to the manufacturer, could cruise at 18-20mph while giving the regulation 200mpg economy. A couple of further advantages to the Cyclaid belt-drive layout were that no modification whatever was necessary to the bicycle, the installation did not interfere with any existing gears or require different brakes. However, no means of disconnecting the engine from the rear wheel was provided - inconvenient when pedalling with a dead engine. Owners soon discovered it was easy enough to slip the belt off the large pulley, though it would flap around noisily unless tied out of the way. A Cyclaid would cost a prospective purchaser a nice, round twenty quid.

In November 1952 *Power & Pedal* commented *"with the famous name of British Salmson behind it the Cyclaid attachment has a special place in the market and also a special technical interest by reason of its belt transmission … the endless belt [is] smooth, silent and trouble-free"*. So developing this unusual means (for the early 1950s) of power transmission was worthwhile as it seems to have met with universal approval. The press saw the Cyclaid as a well-designed quality product of compact dimensions, rugged appearance and excellent power-to-weight ratio. The power in question was, for a change, transmitted to the road with a modicum of refinement.

For
STURDINESS...
POWER...
ECONOMY...
RELIABILITY...
it's
CYCLAID
all the way!

The CYCLAID power unit is British designed and built throughout to precision limits.

SPECIFICATION :— Motor—Single cylinder, two-stroke. Piston displacement—31 c.c. Compression ratio—1:5·6. Cylinder—Aluminium with special cast iron liner. Cylinder head—Aluminium detachable. Ignition—Wipac Series 90 Magneto with lighting coil. Carburettor—Amal. Total reduction ratio—1:18·5. Power transmission—Belt drive by endless rubber reinforced V belt. Fuel tank—capacity about 3 pints. Fuel—1 part oil to 25 parts petrol. Continuous output—0·7 h.p. at 3,500 r.p.m. Maximum speed—18-20 m.p.h. Fuel consumption—250 m.p.g. (approx.). Weight of the total installation—18-20 lbs. approx. Complete with tank and all accessories.

Retail Price **£24** No Purchase Tax

BRITISH SALMSON CYCLAID LIMITED

SALES : 76 VICTORIA STREET, S.W.I. TATe Gallery 9138/9
WORKS : Larkhall, Lanarkshire

A fair number survive fifty years after they were manufactured, though the probable total production run of little over 6,000 units between 1950 and 1956 would have been nothing like enough to ensure the future financial health of either the Cyclaid company or British Salmson Aero Engines Ltd.

British Salmson CYCLAID

BELT DRIVEN CLIP-ON

Power & Pedal magazine published its first full Road Test Report on the Cyclaid in June 1954, opening the article thus: *"The tester finished his first test ride of the Cyclaid and handed it over to his collegue with the remark 'You can throw away one of your legs when you ride this one'. The statement is almost literally true for there is no machine we have yet seen that can compare with this Scots-built belt-driver for power right down to something like one rev per minute. It is quite an exceptional performance in the cyclemotor world".*

"The quality of material and high precision engineering workmanship are exceptional and this is reflected in the performanc ... The Cyclaid is not fast, top speed on the machine tested being a trifle under 20mph but within this range the performance was high all the way. Minimum speed was impossible to judge, the machine apparently coming to a standstill and getting away again without pedals and without any sign of snatch from the transmission. The belt drive and the shock-absorbing spring on the rear engine mounting combined to provide a drive that was smooth and dead silent at all speeds." The Cyclaid designers' decision to use V-belt transmission was entirely vindicated on the road. *Power & Pedal* continued enthusiastically *"As might be expected, the quality of low-speed pull combined with low gearing makes the machine an exceptional hill-climber. Hills which normally require pedal assistance on most cyclemotors were taken without moving the pedals at speeds of 12-15mph. London readers who know that famous brute Muswell Hill, with its awkward approach, long drag and fierce bit of 1 in 7 ½ near the top will be impressed to know that the tester climbed this easily, riding all the way up with one hand in his pocket. Traffic handling was delightful, the light weight of the unit left the light roadster-type cycle handling exactly as it would without an engine fitted, except there was no need to pedal if the machine was moving enough to be balanced at all"*

Following a paragraph headed **"Not Yet Perfect"**, the magazine commented *"As an instrument of powered cycling, particularly in towns and hilly or even mountainous districts, the Cyclaid is quite outstandingly good but there are some mild criticisms to be made".* Few in number and mild indeed; because of the low overall gearing (a distinct plus, see below) when the engine was on the over-run down hills some vibration could be felt and as there was no means of disconnecting the engine, this had to be put up with. Other comments were of a minor nature, the twist-grip throttle and decompressor lever could have been combined in one control *à la Mobylette*, to allow one-handed control and, perhaps surprisingly, that the appearance of a Cyclaid-equipped bicycle was old-fashioned. *"The belt drive is wonderfully efficient and very nearly the ideal drive for cyclemotor use but it does look old fashioned and this in utter nakedness combined with the appearance of the rather prim-looking flat tank do seem too reminiscent of the 'Good Old Days' to belong in the present cyclemotor era."*

The Road Test Report concluded *"The Cyclaid is a first-class job from every angle and provides the complete answer for those who need an attachment unit that requires no special cycle or fitments to give of its best ... it is unbeatable in presenting cycling with all the work taken out of it. At £24 complete, the Cyclaid is excellent value for money".* *Power & Pedal* for once actually bettered a factory-claimed fuel consumption figure, overall consumption during their test worked out at 212mpg.

179

During the course of the Cyclaid's production life British Salmson promoted its clip-on with series of original and humorous press adverts published in several motor cycling magazines; samples of these will appear throughout this chapter, starting with this one dating from March 1955.

Readers will have noticed several discrepancies between 1950 and 1955 facts. The price of a Cyclaid is now £19 instead of £20, whereas according to Stone & Cox £20- was correct from 1950 to 1952, the price then going up to £24 between 1952 and 1954, then down to the bargain-basement level of £16 in 1955. Apparently this 33% reduction was due to *"improved production methods"* (*The Motor Cycle*, November 1954). A further reduction to £15 was made in 1956, deliberately undercutting Mini Motor and Power Pak prices in an attempt to shift unsold units and making a Cyclaid amazingly good value compared to less sophisticated but more expensive competitors. Stone & Cox printed the curt phrase *"Manufacture discontinued"* after 1956

There was also evidently some press confusion over certain aspects of the Cyclaid's specification; early reports quoted all-up weight of the unit to be 15lbs. According to *The Motor Cycle* in its Earls's Court Show report dated 20th November 1952, the price also appeared to be different, £24, so no wonder customers weren't entirely sure what they were buying or for how much.

The very low speed which the Cyclaid could be ridden down to without the engine stalling was exceptional, as pointed out by *Power & Pedal*; this feature combined with a modest 20mph top-speed and light weight meant the Cyclaid was ideal transport for either elderly or disabled riders. Those unable to pedal much or cope with complicated controls were less challenged by a Cyclaid than by other marques with more brutish characteristics.

In use the Cyclaid provided low cost, reliable and undemanding (for the rider) transport for many users, though the almost over-simple transmission by belt did have its drawbacks. In the correspondence columns occasional gripes were aired, such as Mr A Moore of London N1 who noted that *"I think the Cyclaid unit would be much better with a clutch, also a larger petrol tank, also when one pedals they have the engine to drive when the engine is not working. I may add the British Salmson Cyclaid Ltd are very good in answering any letters that you may write to them"*. On the whole though, Cyclaid owners did not inundate Letters to the Editor pages with complaints and the one cited above is a rarity, confirming the qualities of the original Cyclaid concept.

Servicing a Cyclaid was not too difficult, the factory suggested drive-belt tension be checked every 200-300 miles by pressing the front or back of the belt inward and observing if the engine unit moved downward against the pressure of the spring loading. If not, it should be adjusted. At around the same mileage both plug and magneto points needed examining and resetting if necessary. Decarbonising, it was recommended, should only be carried out by a mechanic.

"A product is known by the company it keeps" says George.

CYCLAID

Ignition by

WIPAC

of course!

Insist on genuine WIPAC spares

Wico-Pacy Sales Corporation Ltd., Bletchley, England

Wipac (Wico-Pacy Ltd) was not slow to capitalise on its association with the Cyclaid. The company provided sparks and light for a great many British-manufactured cyclemotors. The 'George' illustrated in the advert popped up in almost all Wipac's publicity, usually expressing some pithy comment on the superiority of Wipac magnetos over all other brands. He looks more like a farmer than an engineer. At least Wipac never earned the *"Prince of Darkness"* jibe from customers that Birmingham's own Joseph Lucas most justifiably did in the 1950s. The best that can be said of Joe Lucas's electrics is that they worked moderately well most of the time, except when you most needed sparks or light, then they were often infuriatingly absent. Ask any American who owned a 1950s MG or Triumph motor car.

The Cyclaid seems to have been one of those clip-on units that, once the initial novelty of the design and transmission layout had been fully discussed and commented upon in the press, road tests carried out and a fair number sold to customers, simply disappeared off the motor-cycling press radar. Factory adverts continued appearing regularly in *Power & Pedal*, *Motor Cycling* and *The Motor Cycle* but write-ups or long-term use articles there were none. Surely British Salmson Cyclaid deserved a little more editorial attention than it received for its well-engineered cyclemotor engine? It spent enough on advertising to warrant a plug or two in addition to the brief few words of description that accompanied each year's Earl's Court Show issue. Perhaps this low profile was the result of the Cyclaid being a singularly reliable, quiet and pleasant machine to use, which therefore excited neither condemnation nor over-enthusiasm. In which case it perfectly fulfilled the role it was designed for.

183

184

THE CAIRNS *Mocyc*

So far in this survey we have dealt with cyclemotor units fitted inside, alongside, above and in front of a bicycle rear wheel and driving it via roller, chain or belt. Now we turn to our first front-wheel mounted and front-wheel drive clip-on unit, a layout much more widely followed in Europe, where millions of VéloSoleXes and tens of thousands of Berini, VéloVap, Le Poulain, Vélorève, Baby Star, Kid etc. were made, either as a complete cycle & motor combination (for example Solex & VéloVap) or as a clip-on attachment for an existing cycle-frame (many others).

1952
VéloSoleX
45cc autocycle

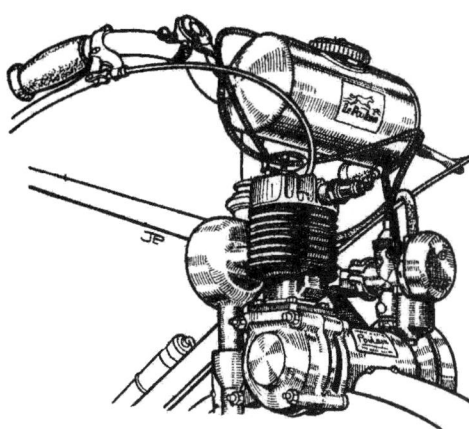

LE POULAIN

The 32 cc Berini

There are many advantages to fitting both clip-on and built-in motors above the front wheel when compared to rear-mounted equivalents. To name a few: inherent stability is a well-known advantage of front-wheel drive vehicles of all kinds, good cooling airflow for air-cooled engines, uncomplicated fitting (no bicycle drive chains, pedal cranks etc. in the way), unobstructed rear carrier space, excellent accessibility for plug cleaning etc. and the ability to make engine adjustments from the saddle. Equally, there are a few notable disadvantages to having an engine immediately in front of the rider; most importantly, noise, oil or petroil leaks unerringly sprayed onto trousers and a high centre of gravity, rendering steering slightly cumbersome through inertia.

(© Mortons Motorcycle Media Ltd.)

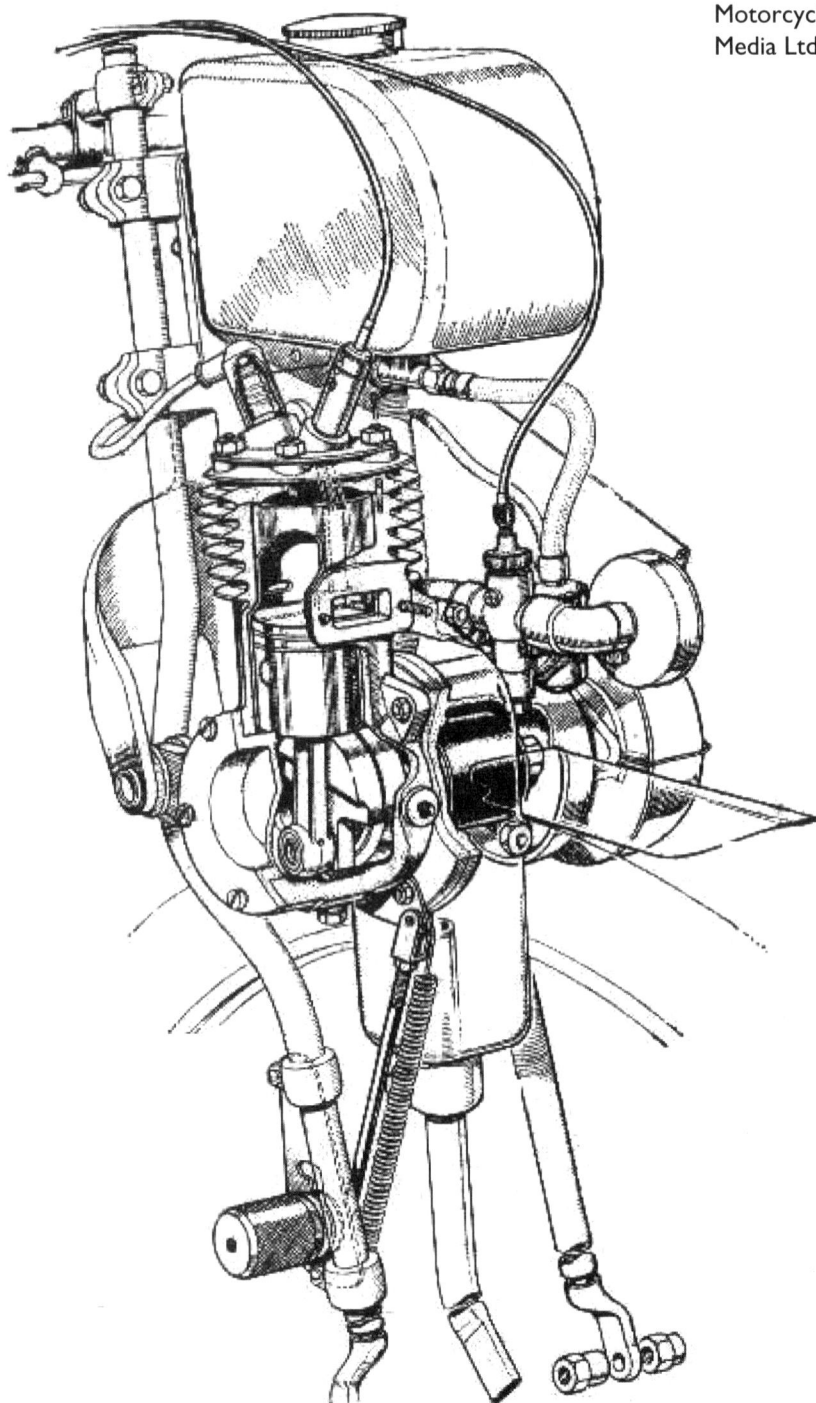

186

The Cairns Mocyc originated in Bournemouth, Hampshire, where it started life in June 1949 as the GYS from the GYS Engineering Company Ltd. In its review of "Your Motor Attachment" dated 18th May 1950, *The Motor Cycle* magazine introduced the GYS, as it was then known, as *"the first all-British unit on the market"* and then went on to describe salient features as follows. *"The GYS drives directly onto the front tyre through a carborundum roller. The unit slides on a frame attached to the handlebar and front wheel spindle. The arrangement is such that no stress is imposed on the front fork of the machine, which is free to flex normally. Contact of the roller with the tyre is maintained by the weight of the engine aided by spring tension, and is controlled by an adjustable friction-type shock damper to obviate bounce. There is, of course, a raised position for the unit. A single lever control on the handlebar operates both decompressor and throttle."*

The designer charged with the GYS had, once it was decided to go ahead with a front-mounted FWD clip-on unit, taken a long, hard look at the hugely popular French VéloSoleX autocycle which, by 1950, had been commercially successful for nearly six years. The Solex was a prime example of how less is more; as a design it was near perfect, the absolute minimum of parts to do the job made of good-quality materials and capable of reliably surviving years of use and abuse. Marcel Mennesson's design was simplified to the *n*th degree, function was everything and because of this excellence, the Solex became an icon. Without indulging in straightforward Solex-copying (for an example of this, look no further than the British-built Cymota; beneath that ugly cowling lurks a crude carbon-copy Solex engine) GYS had incorporated several elements: the outrigged one-sided crank on the right, carborundum drive roller in the middle and magneto overhung the left side of the wheel. Thereinafter paths diverge.

An early factory photo, left, of the GYS clearly showing, despite poor photographic quality, the general layout. Very obvious is the large cast-aluminium silencer in front of the cylinder, which is devoid of finning below the exhaust port. Two cables are connected to the handlebar control lever: turned clockwise this would operate the throttle, with the throttle closed further movement anti-clockwise operated the decompressor.

Also identifiable are the handlebar to wheel spindle engine support tubes and cast-alloy support frame and spring-tensioned damper knob projecting from the right-hand support tube.

Early GYS units such as this had a cast-aluminium fuel tank, soon superseded by a slightly squarer fabricated steel equivalent.

GYS produced an elegant one-piece alloy die-casting combining both crankcase and lined cylinder. This was bolted to a large-diameter aluminium roller housing that carried the single large ball bearing supporting the crank. At the other end, a smaller ball bearing supported the tapered tail-shaft driving the magneto. Unusually, the big end con-rod bearing was a plain bronze bush rather than a roller bearing; as a result the fuel to oil ratio was recommended at 16 to 1, using SAE30 engine oil, rather than the more conventional 25 to 1. The con-rod itself was of aluminium alloy. Another design anomaly inside the GYS concerns sealing arrangements between the crankshaft and crankcase. Most similar engines used ball main bearings with lip-seals outboard of the bearings, which maintained compression within the crankcase, rather important in a two-stroke. GYS however saw fit to simplify this and instead relied on minimal clearance between the crankshaft and crankcase, backed up by a felt seal in a cup-washer to contain pressure. All good and well but with age and many miles or poor component quality, the ball bearing wore, allowing contact between the crankcase and shaft. The resulting wear increased clearance, allowing crankcase compression to escape and consequently reducing power output. Many GYS units were no doubt relegated to the back of a shed in disgrace because of this design flaw.

The GYS was a classic 49cc two-stroke engine with a bore and stroke of 40mm × 40mm producing an unstated power output, most likely 0.7bhp. A deflector-top piston was used, perhaps again influenced by the Solex design. The piston, cylinder liner and rings were of Wellworthy manufacture. Fuel was supplied from a ⅓ gallon tank situated above the engine to a tiny Amal 308 carburettor that sat, facing forward, on top of the drive-roller housing. Ignition was by the inevitable Wico-Pacy flywheel magneto, advance being set at 25° btdc. Initially a small diameter 10mm Champion sparking plug was fitted but subsequently this was replaced by a more readily available 14mm equivalent. On the exhaust side of the engine one innovation was the fitment of a large cast aluminium silencer which could be easily removed for decarbonising by undoing two nuts and two long bolts screwed into the crankcase. Aluminium also offered the advantages of not corroding at great speed and damping sound, unlike more normal, noisy steel silencers. In deciding to create a front-mounted attachment, GYS then compromised some of the engine's advantages of simplicity and lightness by having to design an imposing and complicated tubular and cast aluminium support structure to carry the engine and relieve the host bicycle front forks of stresses.

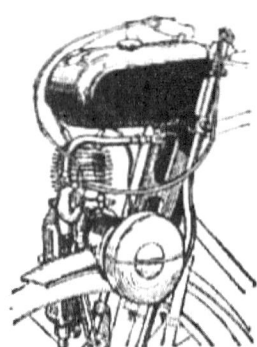

One company that thought the GYS had a future was Cobli Autos of 74 Dawes Street, Walworth, London SE17. They considered the GYS a good unit but misplaced over the front wheel. *The Motor Cycle* magazine published an interesting but brief report in its news review of 26th April 1951 entitled *"GYS Engine Mounting"* in which they described a new installation of the

GYS unit thus: *"Instead of being mounted over the front wheel the engine is attached at a point just below the saddle and roughly parallel with the front down tube. The rear seat stays of the cycle frame are removed and replaced by the supporting tubes - the sub-frame - utilised when the engine is in the orthodox position above the front wheel. The tops of these tubes have been modified to suit the bicycle frame and are fixed at the top to the lug under the saddle. The free movement of the tubes is eliminated by locking the sliding portion with bolts."*

A separate tubular carrier was made to support the GYS fuel-tank, now divorced from the sub-frame, behind the saddle. Only one known photograph exists of this installation, reproduced below, but sadly it is of very poor quality. It nevertheless does give an idea of the unfamiliar position a GYS engine found itself in with a Messrs Cobli installation. The carburettor had to be repositioned and the inlet pipe lengthened as the fixed angle of the engine was reversed when compared to the original front-wheel fitment. *The Motor Cycle* continued: *"A test substantiated the claim for roadholding capabilities; it was possible to ride hands-off with complete confidence at any speed above 4mph, and the bicycle would turn in a 12ft road with ease. There was no trace of frame whip at any speed and the machine was extremely well balanced"*. But nothing came of it, no price seems to have been published and the prototype tested by the magazine was very likely the only one ever made.

£5·11·3 IS YOUR *YEARLY* PETROL BILL
for 8,000 MILES *of Motorised Cycling*

THE GYS
MOTAMITE

GLANFIELD LAWRENCE

is the complete answer to the increased petrol tax giving you a year's motorcycling for a total petrol expenditure of £5.11.3! These sturdy little 49 c.c. machines can be fitted in 15 minutes to any standard bicycle, ladies' or gents', being attached in such a way that cycle and rider are insulated from all vibration and road shocks. Steering is not affected and road holding is improved. Note these special features:—

★ **Petrol Consumption**—225 miles per gallon
★ **Cruising Speed** 15-20 miles per hour
★ **Only one control** (plus choke for starting)
★ **The ideal machine** for the beginner or as an auxiliary mount

ONLY **21** GNS

LONDON 407 High Rd., N. Finchley, N.12
CARDIFF - - - 2-10 City Road
BRISTOL - - - 47-53 Bath Road
PORTSMOUTH - - 147 Fratton Road
SWANSEA - - - Handel Davies Ltd
230 Oxford Street

This 1951 press advert is the first appearance of the GYS 'Motamite' as opposed to simply a GYS. The company goes one better than most other clip-on manufacturers in claiming 225mpg rather than the accepted industry-standard 200mpg. According to its calculation of £5.11s.3d to buy 35.55 gallons of fuel (8,000 miles at 225mpg) the price of petrol would have been approximately 0.16p a gallon. Note the registration number on the fuel tank, JLJ 58, the same number appearing often in factory photos (see previous page 3), presumably this was one of the first production units. It also appears to be fitted to a Cairns Roadster cycle frame, an indication of things to come.

Price of the GYS Motamite was fixed at twenty-one guineas, the all-up weight of the unit claimed to be 22lbs.

"A product is known by the company it keeps"
says George

THE GYS
MOTAMITE

Ignition by
WIPAC
of course!

Insist on genuine WIPAC spares

Wico-Pacy Sales Corporation Ltd., Bletchley, England

"George" from Wipac thought the GYS Motamite had a future too, though he probably didn't realise then how short that would be.

The photo used for this advert is probably an early GYS with an aluminium fuel tank rather than a steel-tanked Motamite. It was painted black and was meant to carry a registration number on the side: this position was not ideal for the Constabulary who no doubt ticked off GYS riders for poor registration number visibility.

Many subsequent Motamites had a metallic blue painted tank with a multi-coloured "GYS Motamite" transfer across the front, though not all did and it is impossible to say for certain when the change from black to blue tanks took place.

A small announcement in *The Motor Cycle* magazine, dated 1st December 1949, revealed the shape of things to come:

GYS ATTACHMENT

49c.c. Cycle-Power-Unit Attachment

To Be Made in North

"Manufacture under licence of the GYS 49cc two-stroke front-wheel-drive cycle attachment is being undertaken by the Cairns Cycle and Accessory Mfg. Co. Ltd., Stoneswood, Todmorden, Lancs." (It was, in fact, made by a Cairns associate company, Automotive Components Ltd, also at Todmorden.)

A year later, in its issue dated 4th December 1950, the same magazine noted that geographical distribution of the Motamite would be as follows:

Northern: Cairns Cycle & Accessory Mfg Co Ltd, Stoneswood, Todmorden, Lancs (who are manufacturing under licence).
Southern: Glanfield Lawrence, 407 High Road, North Finchley, London N12 (and branches) [see advert reproduced on page 190.]
Warwickshire: The Birmingham Garage Ltd.

An article relating to cyclemotors and entitled *"Buzzing Around Box Hill"* was published in *The Motor Cycle* on 8th March 1951 (already referred to in the Power Pak chapter). This told *"The Tale of a Gathering of the Micro-motor Clan in Surrey: The Motor Cycle meets the Manufacturers and Tries their Products"*.

The editorial brief was to try out a range of different makes of clip-on unit attached to a variety of common-or-garden pushbikes. As a result of *"this line of thought: bicycle propulsion units – micromotors or clip-ons to those who are fascinated by a single, expressive word – are being produced in ever-increasing quantities; the number of makes in the list creeps up until, if we cheat just a wee bit, we can call it a round dozen"*. Their list included the VéloSoleX that was, strictly speaking, an autocycle and only ever sold as a complete machine with matched engine and frame. The weather on the test day was predictably foul; rain pelted down relentlessly. However the testers were made of stern stuff and sallied forth. The GYS Motamite was there along with most other manufacturers' products: the Bikotor, Cucciolo, Cyclaid, Cyclemaster, Cymota, Mini-Motor, Mosquito, Power Pak, VAP and VéloSoleX were all put through their paces by John Mills, Arthur Bourne, Roy Morton, Hugh Burton and Harry Louis himself.

At the conclusion of their test, *The Motor Cycle* staff offered a variety of opinions on their day's labours. Roy Morton commented *"amazement at the climbing powers of these tiny engines … when climbing [the Alpine road up Box Hill] only an occasional twirl of the pedals was needed to keep the engine happy. Even when the speed was allowed to drop to little more than a walking pace, so that the engine was on the point of stalling, only the lightest of pedal assistance was required to pick up speed again, this on a gradient almost impossible to climb by pedalling alone."*

Hugh Burton wrote *"These mustard-hot engines took us up the winding Surrey lanes with great gusto and one added little to one's knowledge of ankling (pedalling)"*.

Without singling out any machine by name for commendation or cursing, the journalists were pleasantly surprised by the performance on offer from such small engines. Remember, these gentlemen were more used to testing large capacity multi-cylinder motor cycles than a push-bike powered by a puny 50cc auxiliary engine, so their positive comments were appreciated by cyclemotor manufacturers.

Nearly a year later, on 15th November 1951, *The Motor Cycle* published *"A Review of the Clip-ons"* which revealed that the GYS Motamite had vanished, being reincarnated as the Cairns Mocyc.

No official announcement seems to have appeared in the press so the assumption has to be that GYS, having already licensed Cairns to manufacture its clip-on, turned over the entire project to its licensee. The reasons why are lost in the mists of time, period motor cycle magazines gave no details. No transfer date was quoted so the best we can say is "sometime in 1951". The recent discovery of a Motamite with engine number 51 0 231 indicates Motamite engines were possibly still being made in February 1951 so the change may have taken place sometime between February and October.

The Cairns Cycle & Accessory Mfg Co Ltd of Stoneswood, Todmorden, Lancashire was a long-established manufacturer of bicycles with a great tradition of quality and craftsmanship.

Its company badge (or logo as we would now call it) was the rather stern-looking Cairns terrier seen on the left.

The Motor Cycle magazine was singularly uninformative, not even mentioning that a Mocyc was formerly known as the Motamite, merely recycling the text it had used a year earlier under the new Mocyc title.

The company 'statement' reproduced above gives a clear idea of the serious way that Cairns saw its mission, to make bicycles *"as near perfect as human skill can make them"*. A very Victorian and admirable attitude indeed, but society had moved on from Imperial days when a bicycle was a major capital purchase and was expected to last for a lifetime. Cairns seemingly still lived in the Imperial world, as the names of the Roadster models illustrated in its early 1950's brochure below indicate. Not only were the *"British East African type"* and *"Malayan type"* listed, there were also the *"India-Pakistan type"* and *"North African type"*. This last featured a double crossbar, possibly because in North Africa the roads were even worse than those of the British Empire? This may well have been the case, given that most of North Africa had been colonised by other European nations (they know who they are) who perhaps regarded decent roads for the natives as a bit of a luxury. Alternatively, North Africans were wont to carry very heavy loads or an entire family on the crossbar. And why did neither the North African nor India-Pakistan type cycles qualify for the enclosed oil-bath chain-case that was standard on other models?

Malayan Type

FRAME: best quality steel tubes, steel lugs, cranked seat and chain stays, size 22". FORKS: best quality steel blades, slotted for quick release, with butted steerer tubes. Chrome plated fork crown top plate. WHEELS: 28" x 1½" Westwood chrome rims, rustless spokes, best quality chromium plated hubs. TYRES AND TUBES: Dunlop Roadster. CHAIN WHEEL AND CRANK: bright plated 46/48 teeth, 6½" or 7" cranks. FREEWHEEL: 18/20 teeth, bright plated. CHAIN: ½" x ⅛" pitch rollers. PEDALS: rubber. HANDLEBARS AND BRAKES: heavily chrome plated, flat type up-turned, with roller lever brakes. SADDLE: best quality leather. MUD-GUARDS: Speedwell G.64 (or similar type) with white enamelled tail-piece. FINISH: best quality jet black stoved enamel, lined in red or gold as required, complete with oil-bath gear case.

British East Africa Type

FRAME: best quality steel tubes, steel lugs, cranked seat and chain stays. Size 24". FORKS: best quality steel blades, slotted for quick release, with butted steerer tube. Chrome plated fork crown top plate. WHEELS: 28" x 1½" Westwood chrome rims, rustless spokes, best quality chromium plated narrow barrelled hubs. TYRES AND TUBES: Dunlop Roadster. CHAIN WHEEL AND CRANK: bright plated 48 teeth with 7" crank. FREEWHEEL: 18/20 teeth. Bright plated. CHAIN: ½" x ⅛" pitch rollers. PEDALS: rubber. HANDLEBARS AND BRAKES: heavily chrome plated flat type upturned, with roller lever brakes. SADDLE: Brooks B 33, best quality leather. MUDGUARDS: heavy gauge "U" pattern, deep valanced, with white enamelled tailpiece. FINISH: best quality jet black stoved enamel, lined red and gold, or double gold as required. Complete with pump, tool-bag, tools, bell, rear reflector and oil-bath gear case.

India-Pakistan Type

FRAME: best quality steel tubes, steel lugs, cranked seat and chain stays, size 24". FORKS: best quality steel blades slotted for quick release, with butted steerer tubes. Chrome plated fork crown top plate. WHEELS: 28" x 1½" Westwood chrome rims, rustless spokes, best quality chromium plated hubs. TYRES AND TUBES: Dunlop Roadster. CHAIN WHEEL AND CRANK: bright plated 46/48 teeth, 6½" or 7" cranks. FREEWHEEL: 18/20 teeth, bright plated. CHAIN: ½" x ⅛" pitch rollers. PEDALS: rubber. HANDLEBARS AND BRAKES: heavily chrome plated, flat type upturned with roller lever brakes. SADDLE: best quality leather. MUDGUARDS: "U" shaped heavy gauge roadster pattern deep valanced. FINISH: best quality jet black stoved enamel lined in red or gold as required.

It was very evident from catalogue illustrations that Cairns bicycles, whilst being a tribute to British Craftsmanship and of Superior Quality, belonged to a previous era and were seriously out of date in the UK with their heavy frames, rod brakes and old-fashioned *Vox Populi* handlebars. Perhaps management at Cairns saw salvation in motorising its strong but slow cycles and the fact that a company with such high standards chose to manufacture the Motamite was in itself a tribute to the engineering excellence of GYS's creation. That such a project was undertaken at all by Cairns indicates its desperation: the company was a dinosaur and natural selection (Raleigh in the rôle of furry rodent springs to mind) would see it collapse within a few years.

The GYS, Motamite and subsequent Cairns Mocyc engine numbering sequences were rather baffling until a decade ago, when some astute research by NACC member Derek Rayner shed light on the subject. There seem to have been four, five and even six-figure numbers stamped on surviving GYS and Motamite engines, so a logical numeric progression was not used. It seems that the first two digits might indicated the year of manufacture, the third being the month (October to December having two digits) and whatever followed being the unit number made during that month. For example, 491213 may indicate the year of manufacture as 1949, the month 12 (December) and unit number 13 made that month. It might also mean month 1 - January 1949 - and unit 213 but at that early date it is unlikely that so many were produced. Another example would be 50818: year 1950, August, unit no.18. It has been estimated that around 1,068 Motamites were made before a revised numbering sequence was started when production was transferred from GYS in Bournemouth to Cairns in Todmorden sometime in 1952. From then on, the Motamite became known as a Cairns Mocyc.

THE CAIRNS *Mocyc*

If your interest lies in motorised cycling, the Cairns Mocyc (the first all-British designed and manufactured power-assisted cycle) has earned for itself a reputation second-to-none. FINISH: best quality azure blue stoved enamel, mudguards in ivory. Available also in a range of colours if required at a slight extra charge. EQUIPMENT includes pump, toolbag, tools, rear number plate and hockey stick guard. Usual cycle extras can be supplied.

CYCLE UNIT

Gent's Standard Roadster or Ladies' (as illustrated) specification as given overleaf.

THE "MOCYC" ENGINE UNIT
Precision made to the highest Engineering Standard

Aluminium cylinder and detachable aluminium head. Capacity 49 cc. Liner, piston and rings by Wellworthy. Carburettor Amal. Single lever control. Decompressor. Wico-Pacy Bantamag. Champion 14 mm. plug. Drive: direct on to front tyre. Tank capacity: ⅓ gallon. Cruising speed: 18-20 m.p.h.

NOTE THESE POINTS

1 Up to 225 miles per gallon.	7 Quiet running.
2 Road tax 17/6 per annum.	8 Easily lifted, takes up no more room
3 ENGINE UNIT fits any cycle.	than an ordinary cycle.
4 Engine weight approx. 20 lb.	9 Tyre wear negligible.
5 Only one engine control.	10 Engine can be instantly disengaged
6 Does not affect steering.	for normal cycling at any time.

The Mocyc Engine Unit can be bought separately and fitted to your own cycle, whatever the make in a few minutes.

THE CAIRNS CYCLE & ACCESSORY MFG. CO. LTD.

STONESWOOD, TODMORDEN, LANCS.

Tels. 28 and 617

The Cyclemotor Manual published a useful chapter entitled: *"Maintaining the Mocyc"*

"There is but little maintenance to be done with so simple a unit. The sparking plug should be removed after each 250 miles on the road and it is recommended that after 1,000 miles it should be taken to a garage for sandblasting and re-gapping".

At the same mileage *The Cyclemotor Manual* advised that the contact-breaker points be examined for wear and adjusted if the gap was more than a couple of thou out either side of the 0.018" setting. That great bugbear of all small two-strokes, decarbonising, was tackled next. *"A considerable mileage can be covered before decarbonising is essential and it is recommended that, until a loss of power is evident, the unit be left undisturbed. When it is to be 'decoked' the procedure is to remove the silencer and cylinder head. The piston is turned to BDC and the exhaust port scraped; the tail pipe is detached from the silencer and both cleaned as thoroughly as possible. The piston is then placed at the top of its stroke, where it can easily be cleaned."*

Further advice concerned cleaning everything with petrol (nowadays a very unwise move knowing the vile formulation of unleaded fuel) including the carburettor from time to time. It was also suggested that, once running-in was completed, improved performance could be had by substituting a No 25 main jet for the No 27 originally fitted. No doubt the No 27 gave slightly richer mixture and hence copious oiling of the machinery but it would also tend to make the engine four-stroke under light load.

The Cyclemotor Manual continued: *"Although it is not advisable to 'play with the timing', it is possible to advance or retard the Mocyc's spark by five degrees. To do so, loosen the two cheese-headed screws holding the magneto back-plate to the roller housing and move the back-plate either clockwise or anti-clockwise to retard or advance the ignition.*

That was more or less it, so maintaining a Mocyc was hardly arduous for an owner.

Cairns also developed accessories for cyclemotor owners, one item being the "Auxiliary Petroil Tank" illustrated here, though it did seem rather expensive at nineteen shillings and sixpence, complete with holder.

Road tests of the Mocyc are rather hard to come by in the early 1950s motor cycling press. Little attempt seems to have been made by Cairns to promote and advertise its clip-on unit although it was unlike most others on the market and had some evident advantages. In the Earl's Court Show report dated 20th November 1952, *The Motor Cycle* limited itself to repeating the same copy, virtually word for word, it had published for two years previously, the only difference being that of price: £24.6s.0d instead of £23.3s.0d.

Cairns used a different numbering sequence to the obscure one started by GYS. A simple sequential four-figure number system, apparently began with number 5500 after the transfer of production to Lancashire.

By 1953 Cairns was having trouble selling enough units to keep assembly lines running (if indeed there were such things at Todmorden) and dramatically reduced the price, to sixteen guineas, in an attempt to generate some interest. *The Motor Cycle* had reduced its Show Report (19th November 1953) Mocyc listing to four lines plus Cairns's address details. In comparison, Power Pak had thirty lines, although it had had nothing new to offer since the introduction of the Synchromatic Drive model the previous year. Somebody in Cairns was not very good at PR (Press Relations). Come 18th March 1954, the same magazine featured a

Micromotor Buyers' Guide

The Motor Attachments and Complete Motor-assisted Cycles On the British Market.

"Cycles and cycle-type machines with auxiliary engines—micromotors as they are sometimes called—provide the most economical form of transport. Suitable auxiliary units first appeared on the British market about five years ago and since then, their popularity had become established. Registration statistics which group all these machines in the under-60cc category indicate that around 170,000 are on the roads of Great Britain."

The last couple of lines in this editorial revealed that *"Cyclemotor units sold separately are not subject to British purchase tax."* followed by the usual limited information on the Mocyc but with one difference, the price was now quoted as £14.14s.0d - fourteen guineas. Times must have been hard in Todmorden.

By November 1954 a rock-bottom deal was on offer: a Mocyc could be bought for twelve guineas partially assembled. Presumably, a box of bits was delivered to your door, which you assembled with a bent-wire screwdriver and adjustable spanner before motoring off into the sunset. From the beginning of 1955, the Cairns Mocyc led an ever-more discreet existence, seemingly having disappeared from view of all the popular motor cycling magazines and only appearing in the annual Earl's Court Show listing. Another proof of the Mocyc's continued existence was Stone and Cox, who last mentioned the unit as available in 1956. One intriguing change in *The Motor Cycle's* Show report was a brief mention of *"Also Cairns 49cc moped …(price) not fixed"*. Somebody in Lancashire was still keeping the faith.

That was about it for the Mocyc, no new versions appeared, no publicity, no advertising (the only known adverts appear in this chapter) and no promotions, so presumably the already minimal sales simply dried up.

At some point Cairns must have stopped production but no exact date for this is known at the time of writing, other than it being 1955. If any reader knows better please write to the publisher for amendments to be made in a future edition.

According to engine numbers of survivors from NACC archives, the lowest known four-digit Mocyc number is 5537, the highest 7174, though this information is almost certainly out of date. This leads us to speculate that perhaps 1,700 units were made at Todmorden between mid-1951 and the end of 1955, a very insignificant number when averaged over a five-year period. The GYS/Motamite/Mocyc deserved better: it was a well-engineered unit with a nice flat power curve, sounded good and was able to run at 20mph all day. Unfortunately the high 16-1 petrol to oil ratio (dictated by a plain big-end bush) tended to *"oil the machine and rider ... the odd wipe over of the front rim is a must if you want any braking".* (Derek Langdon in 2003)

As with many clip-on cyclemotor units, the GYS really arrived too late to benefit from the peak of the market. It was insufficiently funded to allow for introducing improvements (crankcase sealing) and new models (despite several name-changes) to keep customer interest alive, so it quietly disappeared, leaving behind a handful of survivors, appreciated and respected by their owners.

Mosquito

The Mosquito clip-on cyclemotor unit originated in Italy from the Moto Garelli Co. Founded in 1913 by Alberto Garelli, the company factory was established at Monticelli Brianza to manufacture a novel motor cycle featuring a 346cc double-piston two-stroke engine designed by Sr Garelli himself. With an initial output of 2.75bhp, this design proved to be very long-lived indeed, being developed through a series of models from 1913 right through to 1935. This established a reputation for Moto Garelli as a maker of sporting two-strokes, which endures to this day. In the early 1920s this machine won many Italian races ridden by young men on their way to fame in the motor cycle world: Ernesto Gnesa, Isacco Mariani, Enrico Manetti and Erminio Visioli. Two other names, both outstanding riders who went on to take motor racing by storm in cars, participated in the history of Moto Garelli: Achille Varzi and Tazio Nuvolari.

Nuvolari, the "Flying Mantuan", honed his legendary machine control skills racing many makes of motor cycle before graduating on to cars and eventually humiliating the Mercedes and Auto Union team cars at Nurburgring in the late 1930s, driving an outdated Alfa Romeo. His reward was a works Auto Union drive, when he again showed his extraordinary talent by simply outclassing most of Europe's finest drivers.

Alberto Garelli's company prospered, the glory and technical benefits resulting from the racing program fed back into series-production touring bikes which no doubt became highly profitable. After all, by 1935 a twenty-year old design and associated tooling costs had long since been amortised.

1935 Garelli 346cc double-piston single.

After the inevitable devastation of World War II (for brief details of the unemployable Austrian painter Mr A Hitler and his influence on Italian affairs, see chapter 5 - Cucciolo) Moto Garelli was faced by the same seemingly insurmountable industrial problems that the likes of Ducati, Moto Guzzi, Gilera and Bianchi had all to tackle. The retreating Nazis ransacked Italian industrial plant for anything valuable they could take with them and blew up most of what they could not, so machine-tools, presses, lathes and welding equipment were all in very short supply indeed. The Garelli company reorganised shortly after the end of hostilities, moving to Milan, at Via Visconti di Mondrone 19, and changing its name to S.p.A. Meccanica Garelli Milano, though its products continued to have "Moto Garelli" cast into engine parts.

Garelli was experienced in the manufacture of small two-stroke motor cycles so, for them, it didn't take a giant leap of imagination to realise the future lay in producing small, cheap clip-on cyclemotor engine units, much as the same thought had occurred to numerous other makers. For Garelli, certain engineering criteria were important when designing its variation on the cyclemotor theme. One of these was stability and roadholding, only to be expected of a company with a long racing history. Accordingly, the Mosquito clip-on engine (for it was baptised thus early on) would be fitted below a cycle bottom bracket, keeping additional weight as low as possible.

One problem immediately presented itself: bicycle pedal cranks are narrowly spaced for rider comfort, usually around 4¼" between inside faces. To allow continued use of the original bicycle pedals, a bottom-bracket engine has to be very narrow indeed, presenting designers with quite a challenge as to how to accommodate engine, ignition magneto, reduction gearing and final drive within a maximum width of just over four inches. In the case of the Mosquito, roller final drive was chosen early on for simplicity. Many engine designers tried gearing their power-units to existing bicycle chain transmissions or creating their own drive systems, but added complication, cost, weight and bulk ruled that roller drive was by far the most practical, if not the most elegant solution in engineering terms.

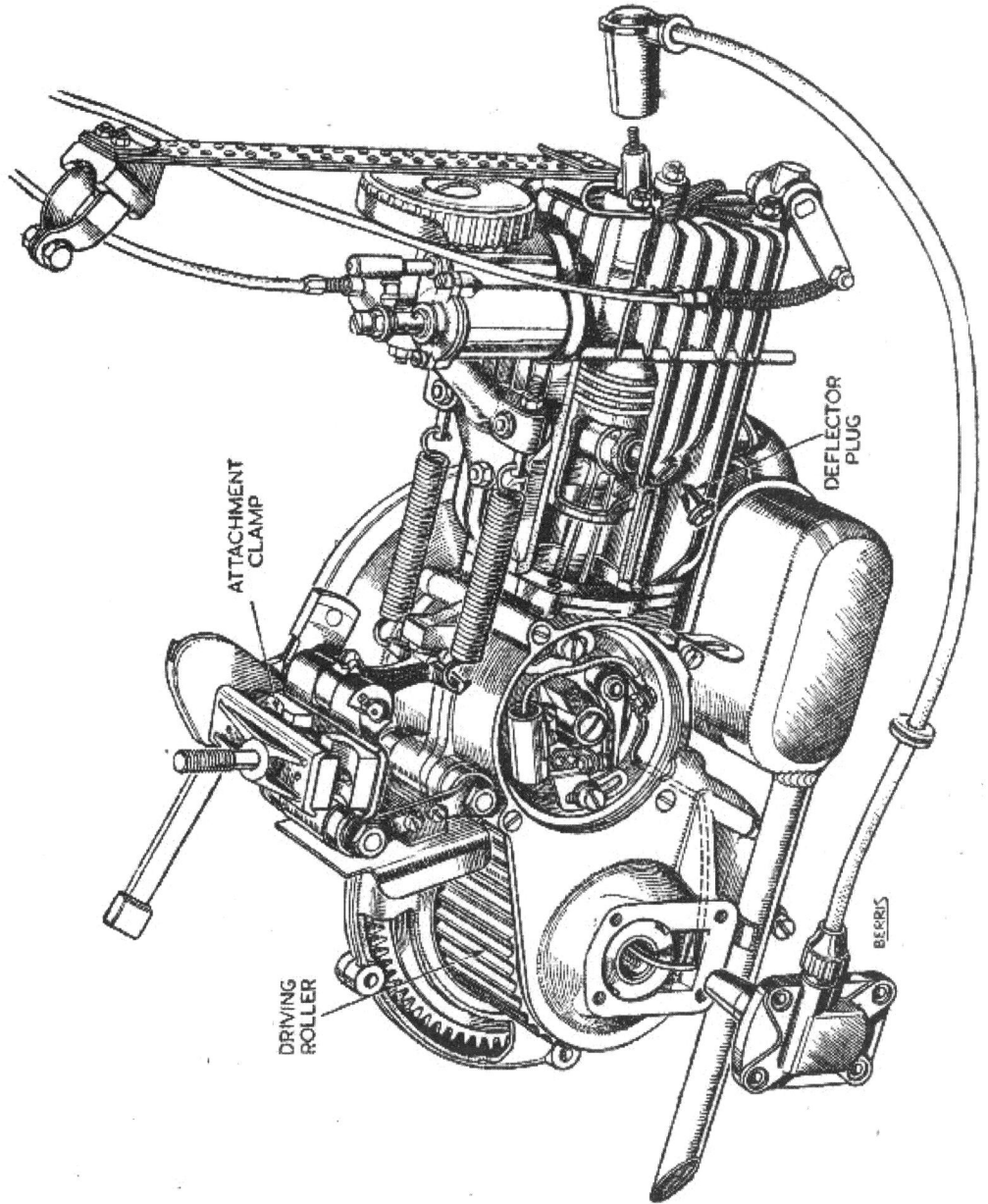

Mortons Motorcycle

ATTACHMENT CLAMP

DRIVING ROLLER

DEFLECTOR PLUG

BERRIS

This sectional drawing, from the incomparable pen of Vic Berris, clearly shows the paths chosen by Garelli to achieve such a compact engine unit. Note the contact-breaker assembly driven from the right-hand end of the crankshaft. Normally magneto windings and a magnetised flywheel assembly would be bolted on the outside, a convenient and simple position if width is not an issue. Garelli's engineers decided to divorce the power-generating function of a magneto from spark timing, but where to put the generator and what would function as a flywheel? In the latter case, a splendidly exposed thin steel disc (affectionately known as a "bacon-slicer") flywheel on the left side fulfilled the rôle perfectly. What then of power generation to provide sparks?

The only space available was inside the drive-roller itself, so Garelli had to squeeze everything else (including HT conversion) except the contact-breaker and condenser in there, in so doing creating a roller twice the normal size and simultaneously the Mosquito's Achilles Heel. Not only did the roller and rotating-magnet magneto run at half engine speed, making reliable sparks (particularly for starting) less likely than usual, the electrickery also lived in the most unpleasant conditions imaginable in wet weather. No wonder many a surviving Mosquito now runs on coil & battery ignition, the magneto windings and their shellac coating inside the roller having long ago given up the ghost.

There was however one incidental benefit to having such a large-diameter drive-roller, the circumference bearing on the rear tyre was correspondingly much greater, the loading per square inch of tyre was reduced and so, hopefully was wear.

201

Power was generated inside the roller, make-and-break took place in the little contact-breaker compartment and the resultant high-tension current fed directly to a Marelli CW 175 spark-plug. It is worth quoting a brief description of the novel Mosquito magneto from Pitman's Book of the Cyclemotor to clarify the set up.

"The stationary coil lead is brought out through the crankcase casting. The high-tension pickup, a spring loaded bush, is pressed into the crankcase face by four screws and thus kept against a carbon contact within the coils. This eliminates all the usual external magneto mounting."

As a result of all this, Garelli managed to make the Mosquito an incredible three & seven-eighths inches wide and it weighed just 21lbs. Few others managed a similar slimline feat, the Miller/Vincent Firefly designer Polisky being one.

A cast zinc-alloy clamp to attach the unit to the very front of the lower rear forks sat immediately above the crankcase, connected via a pair of swinging parallel links to the engine casing. The roller was engaged with the rear wheel by moving a short lever forward, the lower end of which bore onto a vertical plate behind the rear link, tension being assured by a pair of horizontal springs. The weight at the front of the engine was supported by a perforated spring-steel strip clamped to a cycle-frame front down-tube.

Garelli opted for a smaller than 50cc capacity swept volume, so 38.5cc came from long-stroke 40mm × 35mm bore dimensions, output being quoted at 0.9bhp @ 4,200rpm, torque being 0.56mkg at the same revs. The first version engine was given Type 307 designation. Somebody at the factory was unconcerned by high inertia loads because not only was the Mosquito engine a long-stroke unit, having higher piston velocities and accelerations than a short-stroke motor, but, very unusually, Garelli fitted a light cast-iron 3-ring piston, made from a variety known as "Perlitic" iron. This made the piston rather heavier than the normal alloy affair but there was a very good reason for this decision.

This Mosquito parts-list drawing shows how slim the crankshaft assembly had been made in the interest of obtaining a narrow unit, including use of short roller main bearings (20) running directly on a hardened crank track, rather than the more customary ball-races.

The steel flywheel (22) was riveted to the small 32-tooth helical reduction gear. The larger 64-tooth gear drives the ribbed roller, giving an overall ratio of 2:1. Lubrication was by grease contained inside the main alloy castings. The cast-iron cylinder has radial fins, as has the alloy cylinder head.

Also revealed is the decompressor mechanism (which factory-translated instructions describe as *"the blow-off lifter"*) and the drive-roller, number 30.

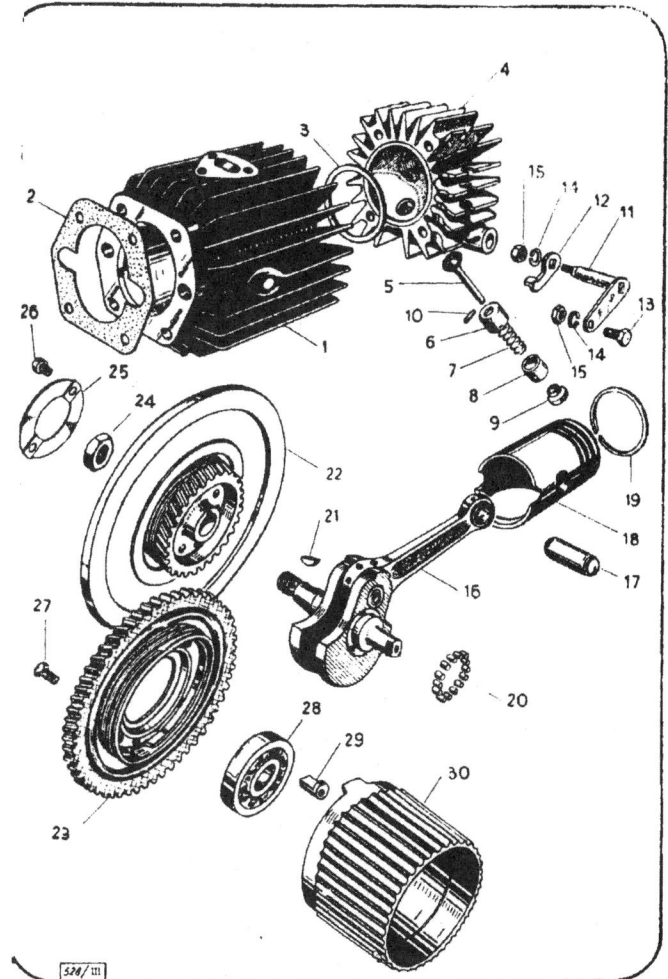

Aluminium has a much higher coefficient of heat expansion than most ferrous metals, including iron. Two-stroke air-cooled engines were notorious for seizing up under demanding conditions of use, when heat build-up within an engine working hard (for example, climbing a long hill on a hot summer's day) exceeds the ability of cooling fins to dissipate it. An aluminium piston running inside a cast-iron cylinder expands at a much greater rate than iron as temperatures rise and sooner or later running tolerances are reduced to the point where the oil film between piston and cylinder (deposited from the oil mixed with petrol and, in the early 1950s, of pretty poor quality) breaks down, resulting in metal-to-metal contact. This can also occur on a long downhill gradient when the throttle is shut and the engine on overrun: heat is not the problem, the fuel supply is cut off and so is the oil, leading to a similar result as above.

The consequences of overheating are immediate and dramatic: the engine usually locks solid and, depending on the robustness of everything between piston and back tyre, the rear wheel stops dead and either drags the bike to a snaking halt or something upstream is overwhelmed and breaks. With luck, once the engine has cooled down again and running tolerances are restored, it can be restarted. Without luck, the piston will have friction-welded itself to the cylinder wall and the piston and cylinder are scrap, as might well be the con-rod and crank, depending on their ability to absorb an inertia shock-loading of several thousand rpm to zero in a fraction of a second.

The thinking at Moto Garelli was that, if both piston and cylinder were made of ferrous materials, no matter what sort of abuse was handed out by rider or climactic conditions, the engine would be unlikely to seize from overheating. *"By making these two components of the same hard-wearing material, piston-cylinder troubles should be reduced to a minimum"* (Pitman's Book of the Cyclemotor). The same ruse was also used by another long-established two-stroke specialist, dear old Villiers, who fitted iron pistons in the cylinders of its often sorely tried industrial engines.

The rest of a Mosquito's engine specification was conventional and similar to most other sub-50cc two-strokes: petrol to oil ratio of 16:1, fuel consumption was stated to be *"at least 250mpg"*, hill-climbing ability was claimed to *"take an adult up a gradient of 1 in 10 without pedalling and 1 in 5-6 with some pedalling"*. Porting was of the inlet-transfer-exhaust variety, with the two transfer ports inclined to deflect incoming mixture away from the exhaust gases without resorting to an even heavier deflector-top piston. Maximum speed was claimed to be 20mph when the engine was running at 4,200rpm.

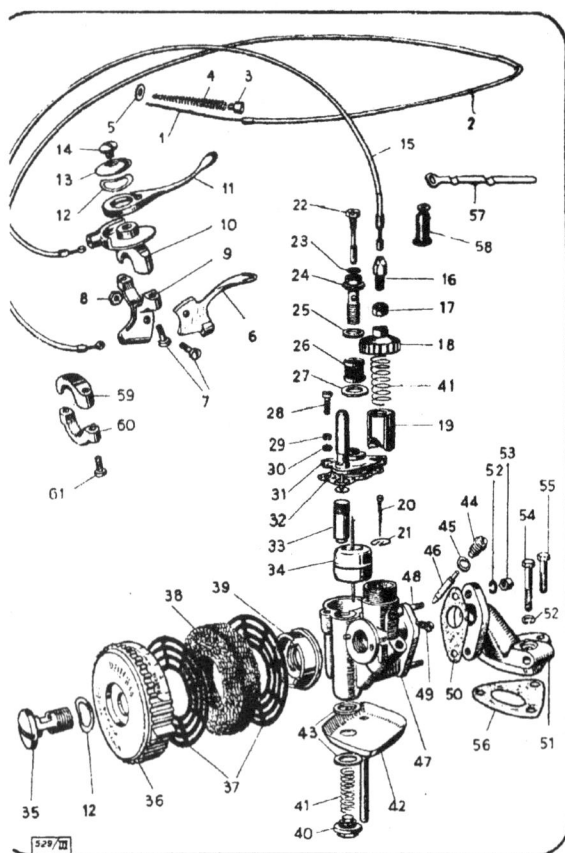

Carburation was courtesy of a single-jet Dell'orto with a small (10mm) choke which nevertheless boasted some useful features. The jet could be cleaned without draining the float-chamber and *"the flooder or tickler does not actuate the float and disturb the needle ... instead, depressing the button operates an extremely small suction pump. This forces fuel up into the mixing chamber. When released, a fresh charge of fuel, ready for the next time, is drawn from the float-chamber."* (Pitmans again).

The carburettor had a small drip-tray complete with drain tube and the air filter rotated to operate the air-strangler (choke). One little refinement was the provision of a small tag extending horizontally to the left from the air filter. Using this a rider could open or close the choke with his toe, or at least that was the theory.

In France, *Chapuis Frères* were manufacturing the Mosquito under licence by 1950 and were selling both clip-on units and complete cyclemotors already fitted with Mosquito engines, the Presto-Sport and Presto-Confort. *Chapuis Frères* was a long-established maker of bicycles, the directors were evidently rather less short-sighted and hide-bound than many would have been under similar circumstances and enthusiastically embraced this new technology. They would not regret their decision.

As can be seen in this illustration, a Mosquito fitted very neatly under a bicycle bottom-bracket. Also to be seen is the engagement-disengagement lever angled toward the rear tyre in the disengaged position and the characteristic Mosquito "bacon-slicer" exposed flywheel.

The left-hand bicycle pedal-crank is not illustrated for the sake of clarity.

Installation of a Mosquito was very simple, the main clamp was fitted over the horizontal rear chain stays, the front support to the bike frame down-tube, the rear carrier complete with fuel tank bolted to theframe, connect up the fuel line, adjust roller to tyre clearance and that was it.

Early European reports on the Mosquito were universally complimentary: *"one of the most remarkable Italian auxiliary motors"* (*Motocycles*, France, February 1950) is a typical example. Most testers found the performance of a Mosquito-powered bicycle unusually lively, despite only having a 38cc capacity. Such performance was, of course, taken for granted in Italy but other European countries were impressed. France led the field when a manufacturing license was taken out by *Etablissements Chapuis Frères* (see above). Garelli were choosy who they granted licences to, demanding high standards of tooling and machining facilities in order to protect the Mosquito's reputation. Chapuis had to build an entirely new factory specifically to make the Mosquito but despite this, early production runs had problems. These were mainly due to the Mosquito's unusual design, which precluded the use of many proprietary components. For instance, a conventional ABG magneto flywheel, readily available and fitted to numerous makes of French cyclemotor engine, could not be used, so Chapuis had to tool up to make the Garelli roller magneto themselves at considerable extra cost.

Inside the Chapuis factory: the assembly area, left, and test-running rig, right.

In Britain, the motor cycle press was far from oblivious of the Mosquito's existence and charms. First off the blocks was Harry Louis of *The Motor Cycle* who, in a report dated January 8th 1948, made known his enthusiasm for Garelli's creation.

"Last March, when at the Swiss Show, I was smitten by the appearance of the Mosquito auxiliary engine. Amongst quite a host of small two-strokes and four-strokes, it was the tiniest engine of its type exhibited. The name of the makers, Garelli of Milan, added to the interest, but the ingenuity and excellence of the design and its solid, practical advantages were the considerations that led me to want to test the Mosquito."

He had some trouble importing a unit (there being no UK distributor or agent in 1948, Lord knows what customs barriers he had to hurdle) but eventually his Mosquito arrived, *"attached to an attractive Hobbs of Barbican bicycle"*. He rode it every day thereinafter as a town hack and was more than pleased with his mount. Garelli claimed the Mosquito could be fitted in an hour, Harry Louis reckoned no more than twenty minutes would be required, and that included the carrier and tank and handlebar controls. With the 21lbs weight low-down and normal bicycle pedal-cranks, *"with the drive disconnected the Mosquito-equipped machine does not feel in the least cumbrous if used as a normal pedal-cycle"*.

"There is real craftsmanship in the engine" was one comment, when the fully machined inlet port was discovered. Transfer ports were carefully angled upward to deflect mixture away from the open exhaust port, they were drilled from outside the cylinder and then plugged with *"meticulously contoured light-alloy deflectors"*. No rough old sand-cast ports for Garelli then. This attention to detail no doubt contributed to the Mosquito's excellent output: *"the machine would buzz along gaily at any speed from a slow walking pace to its maximum on more-or-less level roads of 18-20mph ... The engine was absolutely happy and without perceptible vibration throughout the speed range. It had what I regard as a particularly desirable characteristic - it would keep two-stroking uncommonly well. Carburation was very good and the pick-up and acceleration much better than might be anticipated, bearing in mind that the engine is of only 38cc"*.

In order to test hill-climbing ability, Harry Louis tackled Anerley Hill, Crystal Palace, London *"which is about 200 yards long, has a cobbled surface and a gradient of 1 in 8 at the steepest part. An idea of its severity may be gathered from the remark of an omnibus inspector who assured me that in seven years' duty covering the area he had only once seen a cyclist climb the hill without dismounting. The Mosquito climbed with a total of thirty digs of the pedals - four periods of seven or eight digs to keep the revs up. George Wilson, who is about 28lbs lighter than I, made several climbs with only 20 prods"*. Just for once, fuel economy proved to be better than claimed by a manufacturer, 270mpg under mixed use, including the above hill-climbing tests.

At the time of *The Motor Cycle's* article in 1948, The Sterling Engineering Co Ltd of Dagenham, Essex, with some assistance from George Patchett, was negotiating to make the Mosquito in Great Britain under licence but their efforts came to nought. Sterling Eng Co was probably affiliated to the Sterling Arms Co who *"re-engineered the Sten Gun post-war to make it rather less dangerous to the user's side than the enemy"* [PW]. It is believed an Australian version was called the Patchett and came equipped with a bayonet for serious hand-to-hand fighting.

Bob Sergent from Liverpool won the licence and soon after became sole importer for the Mosquito in Britain, probably helped by his business being a well-established motor cycle and autocycle distributorship, not a wishful-thinking engineering outfit with a thin order book.

Bob Sergent LTD

BOB SERGENT'S AUTO-CYCLE RALLY
~ JUNE 1939 ~

AN AMAZING PERFORMANCE

Here are a few of Bob Sergent's satisfied customers, taken 10 years ago. The 200 riders at this rally covered the 125 miles without mishap and under the worst of weather conditions. Still more today, Bob Sergent can give unfailing service to "Villiers" owners.

MOORFIELDS, LIVERPOOL, 2
PHONE: CENTRAL 7398

The chap circled in white is presumably Bob Sergent himself. Note how only the first few rows of 'satisfied customers' can be seen holding auto-cycles, the rest are just standing around with their hands in their pockets and are most likely passing pedestrians press-ganged into posing, thus expanding numbers impressively for the photograph. A crowd whipper-in is standing upper-left, his head hidden behind Bob Sergent's banner which has very obviously been drawn in after the photo was taken.

Once formal importation and distribution arrangements were signed between Garelli and Mosquito Motors Ltd, a company set up specifically for this rôle (1950 is the date Stone & Cox first list the Mosquito as officially on sale in the UK) the unit soon gained a name as a high-performance, reliable clip-on cyclemotor.

Sole Manufacturer and Distributor for the U.K. and British Commonwealth

MOSQUITO MOTORS L^{TD.}

(Bob Sergent of Liverpool)

MOORFIELDS LIVERPOOL

CENtral 2829   Telegrams MOSQUITO, LIVERPOOL, 2

As was often the case, it fell to *Power & Pedal* magazine to publish the first properly comprehensive road test.

ROAD TEST REPORT

PERFORMANCE

The 38 c.c. Mosquito

"We have been eagerly waiting for an opportunity to try out a specimen of this famous Italian engine. Sheer performance is much of the fascination of the machine. Hill climbing, that makes the pedals unnecessary and real acceleration right from standstill to maximum are something of note in the cyclemotor field, but there is more to it than that. There is the compactness of the unit, less than four inches wide and snuggling out of the way under the bottom bracket, the light weight that makes the engine completely unnoticeable when the cycle is being pedalled and the extraordinary way the engine compliments instead of overshadowing the cycle itself."

*Power & Peda*l also pointed out that *"The three-ringed piston is of cast iron, rather long in the skirt and because of its relatively low coefficient of expansion, able to fit closely into the also cast iron cylinder."* This had several benefits; consistent compression in both the combustion chamber and crankcase and relatively quiet operation when cold. The normal wide running-tolerances between aluminium pistons and iron cylinders (essential due to different rates of expansion) before optimum operating temperatures were generated always produce a lot of mechanical clatter.

On the road, *Power & Pedal* found that *"starting was dead certain at all times. The petrol tap turned on (obvious, but often forgotten) the 'tickler' pressed a couple of times and the choke set in the 'rich' position meant a start in three pushes of the pedals from cold ... Once running the engine had a fascinatingly purposeful way of getting at its work, more than willing, even eager".*

From almost a standstill and without touching the pedals, it would accelerate straight up to its mean speed level road maximum of about 22mph, taking all normal gradients in its stride. The exhaust note was modest, although still a shade loud (oh no, here we go again...) by the pernickety standards of *Power & Pedal*, but it was quieter than many and from the saddle could hardly be heard against a breeze. It was found that some mechanical noise emanated from the reduction gearing, *"a Spitfire whine"* according to *Power & Pedal*.

The magazine was also favourably impressed by the *"careful attention to engine design and particularly the iron piston, the Mosquito will stand full-throttle flogging indefinitely. During the test period we encountered the gales that devastated so much of the Eastern parts of Britain and one ride was undertaken straight into the teeth of the blustering wind. The throttle was parked wide open for mile after mile with the speed never above*

15mph and gusts bringing it down to around 8mph but the pedals were not used and it was the rider who demanded a rest, not the engine. Speeds of up to 30mph were reached on a number of occasions and held as long as the rider's conscience permitted, without any sign of distress from the engine and without any burning or whiskering of the plug points". Hard men, those testers from *Power & Pedal.* They concluded that *"it is difficult to find serious criticisms of this excellent engineering combination* (part of the same test was on the Alfa spring fork).

The *Power & Pedal* road test quoted above began with a reference to *"reading the account of that remarkable performance at Pau, when a Mosquito engine ran for fifty-five days and nights in the hands of eight riders".*

This wonderful stunt, in the great French tradition of amazing endurance feats (M François Lecot once drove a 4cv Rosengard 100,000kms without stopping, in 1930) was cooked up between Garelli and Chapuis Frères in the summer of 1952 and bears repeating as it was truly extraordinary. A press release circulated by Garelli and translated from Italian into English in the most charming way describes the event as follows:

"Milan, 31st October 1952."

"Performance of a Resistance Trial on 40,000 Kilometers by one 'Mosquito' auxiliary engine for bicycle."

"In Pau, town in the South-west France, well renowned for its racing traditions, a bicycle equipped with a 'Mosquito 38cc' achieved successfully on Saturday October 25th, a sensational endurance trial on 40,000 Kilometers (25,000 miles) equal to the length of the Globe's circumference. The trial has been effected on a country ring road of 1 Km and 765 meters of length (1 mile and 174 yards); which has been passed 22,762 times, totalizing 40,175 Kilometers. It was initiated on August 31st at 17 hours lasting after 1,324 hours. This time contains of course all necessary stops for having the supply to be done, tires change, some reparations to the vehicle and the revisions admitted for the engine.

Public interest remained lively throughout the test—This picture was taken on the 35th day

The general average speed reached Km/h 30.343 (19mph) *is very high if one keeps in mind the modesty of the means employed, the immense distance covered, the atmospherics adversity, the peculiarity of the circuit that was open to the traffic and its configuration compelling a continuous slackenings. Eight leaders alternated themselves for 55 days and nights without pause in leading the motorized-bicycle, facing long periods of bad time, during which were registered also proper hurricanes and snow-storm."*

"It was also registered road-incidents to be due to serious injury to the tires and to collision with other vehicles." The engine was a standard Chapuis-manufactured unit, *"the crankcase was sealed in order of not to be permitted its opening; the head, the cylinder and the piston were punched in order that the substitution of the pieces was not possible, only being permitted the dismounting for periodical cleanliness. The pedal and chain were taken away from the bicycle, thus hindering absolutely to the engine of being helped by the leader".*

This was all printed verbatim in Power & Pedal, January 1953, So It Must Be True. A translation such as this would probably have been produced by the unfortunate 16 year-old offspring of a Garelli director who happened to be studying English at school. He or she was no doubt greeted one evening with *"here, you're good at English, translate this, it'll give you some practice".* This sort of thing does happen and the translation is really very good.

To continue: *"Two judiciary-officers of the City of Pau alternated themselves in the aim of following the trial and verbalizing everything in order to control the regularity and to authenticate the results. This manifestation has been followed with much interest in the whole of France. The end of the test was attended by journalists, radiochroniclers and cinematographic-operators from Paris and Toulouse. The Mosquito leaders and the organisers have been keenly feasted by the people of the town and were congratulated from the Pau's highest authorities and those of the near Juracon."*

"The trial has proved in the most brilliant manner the big possibilities offered to the users, by a modest and economical vehicle as the motorized-bicycle, and chiefly evidencing the length of duration and robustness of an engine well studied and constructed too. The 'Mosquito' has always run day and night for nearly two months to the limit of its possibilities."

On l'adapte EN QUELQUES MINUTES
On l'essaye UNE HEURE
On l'adopte POUR TOUJOURS

"One fits it in a few minutes. One tests it for an hour. One adopts it for ever".

Sans fournitures supplémentaires

Sur toutes bicyclettes

Mosquito

MOTEUR AUXILIAIRE ★ CHAPUIS Frères_NEUILLY Seine

SALON DU CYCLE — PORTE DE VERSAILLES — STAND N° 60

Chapuis was already producing around 100 units a day by October 1950, dealers were selling them as fast as they were shipped.

A very unusual frame built for the Mosquito was exhibited at the 1948 Milan Show, it looks small and low (the scale of the spectator - Fab tweed coat, man - indicates this) and had the engine mounted above the bottom bracket in view of the small wheels and low ground-clearance.

Elegant girder forks complete a good-looking machine.

The manufacturer appears to be "Cycli Coven".

Another interesting frame made specifically for the Mosquito, this time from Garelli themselves and sold as a complete autocycle under the name BMG (Bici Mosquito Garelli).

Front forks are again girders but made from pressings rather than of tubular construction. The rest of the frame is simple: a large-diameter tubular V structure combines the main structure and fuel tank, rear forks are swing-arms suspended by coil springs.

The BMG was exhibited at *le Salon de Paris* in 1951 on the Chapuis-Mosquito stand and also appeared at the Ideal Home Exhibition, Olympia, the same year. Details of this model follow later in the chapter.

Also on display on Chapuis' stand at the 1951 Salon was a lightweight bicycle fitted with a standard Mosquito unit which held an economy run record. It used just half a litre of fuel to travel 59.5 kilometres.

Meanwhile, back in Blighty, the Mosquito was making a lot of new friends, Mosquito Motors Ltd was basking in some reflected glory via its adverts claiming *"already over 200,000 in use"*, on mainland Europe, of course.

Signor Garelli must have been very pleased with the success of his creation, for by 1953 the Mosquito was being made in vast numbers in Italy at Garelli's Milan factory and in France by Chapuis. In Holland, it was imported by A Knibbe, Amsterdam and in Britain by Bob Sergent, Liverpool. This success amply justified the care that was put into the Mosquito's design and construction.

213

In April 1953, *Power & Pedal* published one of its periodic reports entitled: *"The Service Department Says - A monthly feature provided by manufacturers' service departments on machine maintenance."*

Mosquito Motors started off by reminding owners that *"Every new motor is supplied with a detailed Instruction Book, profusely illustrated, and given a thorough perusal before opening the tool-box, will save much time and temper! The unit is a first-class Italian precision-engineering job and will give lasting satisfaction for intelligent handling and regular care and attention."*

Under the sub-heading *"Running"* some important insights into adjustments were given; *"Do use mixture control marked 'Avviam' (rich) and 'Marcia' (weak), put to rich for starting and hill climbing, find best operating position on the road. (Please note, this attachment is not a car-type choke but a true variable mixture running device, and should be used as such). Do not ride below 4mph under power, the gears will last a lot longer if you don't. 4-20mph is the range under power. Some owners say up to 30mph, but we turn a 'blind eye' to that- and praise Italian workmanship!"*

Under *"Maintenance"* more good advice was on offer: *"This section of your Instruction Book should not be 'skipped', dear reader, but inwardly digested. To save your pennies; DO clean the plug properly and regularly (150-200 miles). DO clean the filters (two), one in the tank, on the end of the fuel tap, the other in the carburettor top (300-500 miles). DO examine and adjust, and clean contact breaker points 0.020", (300-500 miles) if required. DO keep tyres hard. DO keep fuel pipe away from frame parts, a small clip is cheaper than a new pipe. DO decarbonise the unit, don't put this really simple job off, it has been done in half an hour by an ordinary owner like yourself! DO have the gears cleaned out and slightly smeared with fresh grease, if used every day in wet weather."*

The final sentence of servicing advice that follows leads us on to the next stage in this chapter: *"Owners of English (Crossley) units who desire to change the original Bletchley Carburettor for an Italian Dell'orto, can do so under the special exchange scheme now in operation."*

English, Crossley-made units are an important part of this story, so a little background history here would not go amiss in order to put things in context.

Crossley Motors Ltd began life in Gorton, Manchester, as Crossley Brothers Ltd, founded 1904. The company was the first in Britain to manufacture Otto-principle four-stroke internal-combustion engines, they made Daimler motors under licence and soon became renowned builders of gas-fuelled stationary engines. The first Crossley car was made at Manchester in 1904, a chain-drive 22hp 4-cylinder model, shaft-drive appeared in 1906 and front-wheel brakes were fitted to some cars from 1909. Crossley Brothers changed to Crossley Motors Ltd in 1910, this coinciding with introduction of a new 20hp 4 litre car designed by A W Reeves which proved durable and popular, especially as a staff car with the Royal Flying Corps during World War I. The chassis was sufficiently robust to be bodied as an ambulance and light truck and a great number were made in various guises. Post-war, the substantial 25/30hp version was well received by the British Royal Family who owned several.

Crossley grew rapidly in diverse directions through the 1920s and 1930s, manufacturing military vehicles, building the Willys-Overland Model 4 under licence and, an unlikely foray, attempting to make the Type 22 Bugatti in England, though only a handful were completed. The Willys-Overland-Crossley venture even spawned an operation building the Austin Seven under licence in Germany. Crossley's own cars were worthy, well-engineered and durable but rather lacked charisma. The Crossley brothers seemed to have an affinity for unusual projects; none more so than the manufacture of the 1934 Crossley-Burney 2-litre rear-engined car which was much too far off the beaten track for most 1930s car buyers, even dedicated Crossley men.

(National Motor Museum, Beaulieu)

Only 25 Crossley-Burney cars were built and quickly acquired the unique reputation for being able to boil at both ends in traffic (the radiator was at the front). A costly mistake.

However, trucks, bus chassis, engines and bodies, coaches, trolley-buses and large stationary diesel engines continued to be successfully and profitably made by Crossley Motors Ltd. Car manufacture was finally abandoned in 1937 in favour of commercial and public service vehicles and military equipment.

Post World War II, Crossley were in the same situation as many enlarged engineering concerns, no work and huge overheads. By June 1947, the Manchester sites of Gorton Lane and Crossley Street had been sold, yielding a surplus of £145,250, work now being concentrated at a site in Stockport. In 1948 Crossley merged with bus manufacturer AEC

The following information is sourced from Crossley Motors Ltd Minute Book, June 1947 to July 1954, documenting Company Directors' meetings & decisions.

At the Meeting of Directors on Monday 12th December 1949, Mr A W Hubble, Managing Director, *"stated that the order position was causing anxiety* [this referred to future bus chassis deliveries]. *The normal enquiries from Corporations had not been received ... in consequence, there will be a gap in the machine shop unless orders are forthcoming almost immediately".* Severe competition within the bus manufacturing industry meant that traditional customers were now shopping around. For instance, early in 1950 Crossley, Guy, Daimler and Metro-Cammell were all bidding for just one contract to supply buses to Birmingham City Transport. Outside work was desperately being sought and *"a number of promising enquiries have been received".* Some of these came from AEC, English Electric Engineering Co and Ferranti. Not helping matters was an unofficial machine-shop strike which lasted from 8th January to 20th March 1950, called when a Shop Convenor was made redundant. To the barricades, Brothers.

Many different ways of raising revenue were tried: part of the factory space was sub-leased to Tyresoles Ltd [tyre retreads] and outside work bid for included designing a prototype 4-cylinder

80hp diesel engine for Rotary Hoes Ltd, reconditioning 40 American Air Force vehicles a month and machining work for Massey-Harris Tractors. Desperate times indeed.

"Meeting of the Directors of Crossley Motors Ltd."

"Tuesday 25th April 1950"

"Chair- Sir K.J.Crossley, Mr. Leslie Shaw, A.W.Hubble (Managing Director), A.W.Alexander (Secretary)."

"Item 132, 'Mosquito' Motor Units for use on bicycles."

"The Managing Director reported that he had been approached by Mr.Sergent, the holder of the rights to manufacture and sell 'Mosquito' Motor Units in the British Isles, India, Pakistan and the British Commonwealth, excluding South Africa. The Managing Director had had numerous interviews with Mr.Sergent and the proposal he now wished the Board to consider was the manufacture by this Company for Mr.Sergent of 1,000 units at £15- each, 50% of the value of the order to be deposited on the placing of the same and the balance to be paid as and when units are delivered."

Bob Sergent was no doubt an astute businessman who may have known of Crossley's problems, recognised their abilities and realised the potential for sales and profitability of British-made Mosquito clip-on units. He probably thought he could cut a deal.

"Mr.Sergent is also to pay on placing the order 50% of the estimated tool cost, amounting to £2,650. Delivery to commence in approximately six months from the date of receipt of the order at the rate of 100 units a week. The estimated cost of manufacturing 'Mosquito' units & equipment is as follows:"

Material	£6-0s-0d
Labour	£2-5s-0d
150% overhead	£3-7s-6d
TOTAL	£11-12s-6d
10% profit	£1-3s-3d
COST	£12-15s-9d

"The above price is based on the assumption that the magneto can be purchased at 30/- and the carburettor at 11/-, which prices are now being investigated. The Managing Director was authorised to proceed with negotiations on the forgoing lines."

Tuesday 27th June 1950

Managing Directors Report, 141d: *"Mr Hubble reported that he had now been able to purchase in this country a carburettor for the 'Mosquito' engine … but he had not been able to find a supplier in this country for the magneto."* Hardly surprising, it being completely different from any other magneto and situated inside the drive roller. Wipac's representative probably ran from the boardroom when asked if Wipac could make it. The carburettor referred to was the BEC made by Bletchley Engineering Co which was also fitted to the Power Pak (page 100) amongst others.

"The order for the 1,000 engines had been accepted from Mr Sergent on the basis that he would supply the magneto for the first 1,000 engines with a reduction of 30/- in the sale price quoted of £15-."

Monday 23rd October 1950

Managing Directors Report, 159d: *"The Mosquito engine was being produced according to plan but not yet due for delivery. The licence holder of this engine was in negotiation for the sale of a half-share of his licence to a small engineering firm and if successful it was unlikely further orders would be obtained. It was felt that this Company* (Crossley) *should not invest money in a proposition of this nature".*

It seems certain that the planned first batch of one thousand units was the probable total number produced by Crossley Motors for Bob Sergent, who appears to have rather pulled the rug from under himself. Crossley was apparently perfectly prepared to gear up for producing the Mosquito in quantity and did so, but took a very dim view of Bob Sergent's shenanigans and were not prepared to continue long-term. From December 1950 on, no further mention of Mosquito engines is made in any Crossley Motors Ltd Minute Book, so the presumption must be that just 1,000 units were made and delivered as contracted.

By the end of December 1950, A W Hubble (Managing Director) reported *"insufficient work in the shop at present … in consequence* (we were) *trading at a loss".* At the 40th AGM of Crossley Motors Ltd on 17th December 1951, *"There is, for the time being, insufficient work to keep the machine shop and indeed the men we have available, fully employed".* By June 1952, *"the financial statement for the month of April 1952 was submitted and considered in detail. … [an arrangement had been made] with William Deacons Bank Ltd for an overdraft of up to £150,000 for 6 months, interest at ½% over bank rate with a minimum of 3½%".*

The vultures would soon be gathering.

"MOSQUITO, THE CURE FOR ALL HILLS!"

MOSQUITO THE KING OF CLIP-ONS
38 cc
20 m.p.h.
250 m.p.g.
ALL SPARES IN STOCK
CARR. PAID
£31.10.0 COMPLETE
ITALIAN MADE
IMMEDIATE DELIVERY
Send for List
GENEROUS TERMS AND TERRITORY AVAILABLE
MOSQUITO MOTORS LTD., MOORFIELDS, LIVERPOOL, 2

The Crossley-manufactured Mosquito engine-numbering sequence seems very straightforward and almost certainly followed a progression, this assumption is based on known engine numbers of surviving units. CML (Crossley Motors Ltd) followed by 1 (the figure one was probably intended to signify batch one), then a three figure number such as, for example, 418, indicating the unit in question is number 418 of the first 1,000 unit batch. This machine's engine number would therefore appear as CML 1418. There are anomalies however; several surviving Mosquitos with CML prefixes have completely different six-figure engine numbers, beginning with 394 and followed by three digits, such as 909 or 875. These numbers are a cluster and lead one to suspect that Bob Sergent passed a small batch of Italian-numbered Mosquitos to Crossley for evaluation and use in developing production jigs and tooling. These units were most likely given CML prefixes and sold on to willing customers, as pre-production units sometimes are.

Bob Sergent Ltd, a separate trading name from Mosquito Motors Ltd, acted as importers for a very fine Italian-made spring front-fork, the Alfa, which was often supplied to customers in conjunction with a Mosquito clip-on unit for the not outrageous price of 79/6d (£3.19s.6d), reduced from nearly five pounds.

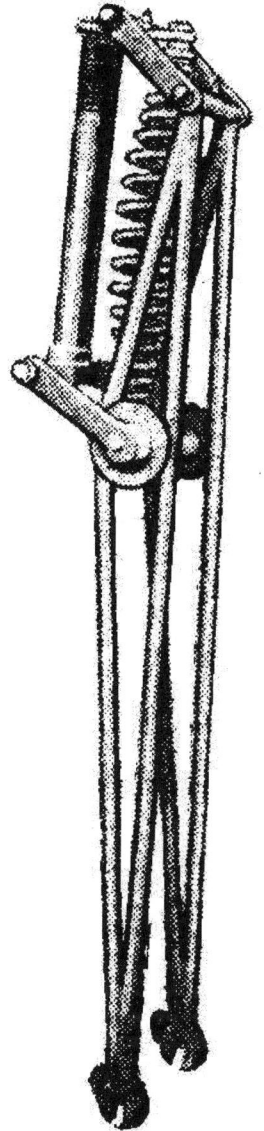

The Alfa girder front fork was probably the lightest and best designed of this type of front suspension, which dates back to motor cycling antiquity, but was sadly eliminated by the advent of simple, cheap, dynamically-compromised 1950's telescopic forks.

Girder forks are a nice idea because they do not involve sliding legs within tubes with bushes which require frequent lubrication. Wear is less of an issue, brake reaction torque does not lock the front suspension solid, adjustments are easier and, best of all, a rider can watch it all moving up & down under his or her nose, which is distracting but interesting. The Alfa forks were, according to *Power & Pedal* in March 1953, *"light, efficient* [and] *immensely strong, much more so than any standard cycle fork and really beautiful to look at. It adds an air of purposeful grace to the machine without obtruding itself in any way. Let it be said here and now that we have nothing but unqualified praise for this delightful fitment. The Alfa fork ... offered perfect 'hands-off' steering at any speed. It was only the occasional shock of a mighty smack under the* **back** *wheel that provided the reminder of the good work the forks were doing in taking really big bumps in their stride. Safety ... in the tremendous addition to front-wheel adhesion under the brakes was greatly enhanced and we suggest that, even without motors, serious cyclists both touring and racing might find the extra couple of pounds weight of the spring forks worth carrying for the real advantage in braking and road-holding."* The magazine evidently thought highly of Alpha forks.

The next evolution of the Mosquito was foreseeable and inevitable: an increase of capacity from 38.5cc to 49cc was made achieved by the usual simple and cheap expedient of increasing bore size, in this case from 35mm to 40mm. The stroke was also reduced slightly to 39mm, bore &

stroke ratio was now oversquare, rather than the previous long- stroke dimensions. Output rose to one brake horsepower at the same revs, no doubt torque was also correspondingly improved but no figure for this seems to have been published. Garelli took the opportunity at the same time to enclose the 'bacon slicer' exposed flywheel within a cast-alloy cover, the engine crankcase being redesigned accordingly. These changes coincided with the appearance of Garelli's BMG autocycle mentioned earlier, a handsome *avant-garde* (with the exception of girder forks) machine of very clean-cut design.

Moto Garelli

As can be seen from the rather poor photo above, a BMG Mosquito was an unusual design: the main frame down-tube and saddle-pillar were fabricated from large oval-section steel tube and doubled as the fuel reservoir, the screw filler-cap hides under the saddle. Drum brakes are evident front and rear, as are the rather old-fashioned girder front-forks. Less evident is the fact that rear suspension is also present, the complete rear wheel & mudguard and engine assembly is supported by trailing arms which pivot around the bottom bracket axis, the good old 'garden gate' swing-frame suspension much beloved of Moto Guzzi (Cardelino) amongst others. Suspension medium was a short horizontal spring in compression. The magneto (still inside the roller) now supplied lighting current via a rectifier to head & tail lamps in addition to current for sparks.

The BMG design was homogenous and clean for 1952, compare this with the contemporary Norman Cyclemate (page 36) or Elswick Trojan (page 63) for a view of the differences between British and Continental designs at the time.

The Motor Cycle magazine describes the new Garelli product thus: *"a big-brother of the 38cc unit, a luxury autocycle of 49cc now makes its appearance. Priced at £80, the new model attracts much attention at the Mosquito Motors Ltd stand … A maximum speed in the region of 28mph and an average fuel consumption of 200mpg are claimed".*

Starting procedure with the new 49cc engine was slightly different to the 38cc clip-on: the engine was engaged with the rear tyre and the decompressor activated via a left-hand twist-grip, the autocycle was given a (claimed) half turn of the pedals and off it went, apparently. It is difficult to ascertain how many BMG Mosquito autocycles, if any at all, were imported and sold in the

UK by Mosquito Motors Ltd. It is believed the BMG autocycle was only manufactured for one year, 1952. One existing machine carries frame number 0015842, so apparently at least 16,000 were made.

The clip-on market had not been forgotten however. The original 38cc Mosquito clip-on soldiered on, continuing to sell well. Signor Garelli was quoted by *The Motor Cycle* in February 1953 as saying the company had sold *"several hundred thousand"* of his beautiful little power units all over the world. It was a huge success but thoughts at Garelli were already turning to a future, different version of the original concept. Bottom-bracket mounting of an exceptionally narrow clip-on would continue without question but many of the 38cc unit's characteristics were to be changed in the light of experience. First to go would be the infamous magneto inside the drive-roller, which on the whole worked well but was costly to make and prone to water ingress and ensuing ignition failure. The 2:1 step-down gearing was also costly to machine and required periodic maintenance; improvements to fuels and engine design allowed Garelli to design a direct-drive engine of greater simplicity without reduction gearing.

Meanwhile, Moto Garelli had become S.p.A. Meccanica Garelli, now at Via Visconti di Modrone 19, Milano.

New Mosquito
Model from Italy Equipped
with Centrifugal Clutch

In 1953 a new model was announced in Italy, it arrived in the UK in 1955. Coded the 38B engine, it was effectively a brand-new design that owed little other than general layout and the cylinder & piston to its predecessor. Bore and stroke were the same 40mm × 39mm as the BMG Mosquito autocycle, giving a 49cc capacity, the compression ratio was low at 5.5:1, output being quoted as one brake horsepower at the considerably lower revs of 2,800rpm (a type 307 38cc unit gave of its best at 4,200rpm). The 38B was a much simpler engine with the drive roller bolted directly to the crank, without resorting to reduction gearing, hence the power output came at reduced revs. It was mechanically a much quieter engine that did not suffer from *"the Spitfire whine"* from gears noted by *Power & Pedal* in its 38cc unit road test. It also possessed a flywheel magneto bolted onto the opposite end of the crank from the drive-roller. So far, how very conventional.

Moto Garelli designers put a lot of unconventional thinking into the new engine that was, after all, similar in layout and function to many other roller-drive clip-on units. An under-4 inch width was achieved, despite having a crankshaft-mounted magneto, by two means. Firstly, the crankshaft itself was unique: quite unlike the usual assembly of forged throws bridged by a big-end. Garelli made theirs from two very thin steel plates riveted together inside the inner track of an amazingly large diameter but very narrow roller-bearing big-end. So large was the big-end that it overlapped the main bearing shaft centreline, this was geometrically inside the con-rod eye periphery, almost like an eccentric. The con-rod itself was a very thin steel forging, centred within the crank assembly by two lugs overlapping the edge, opposite two slim, riveted-on counterweights Two advantages of this superb design were not only the stiffness but also the lightness of the whole rotating structure, without recourse to conventional strong but weighty lumps of metal. Inertia had been cut down to a minimum with many consequent advantages.

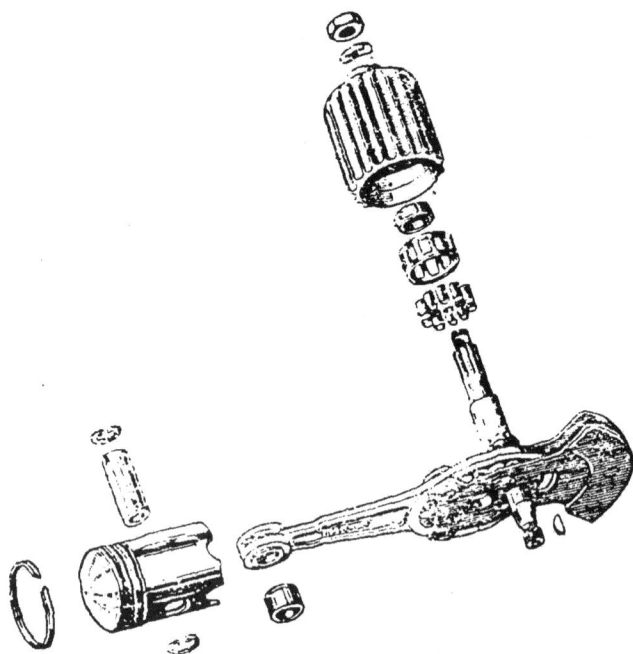

The illustration alongside, from a poor copy of Moto Garelli's 38B parts list, at least shows how exceptionally narrow the whole bottom end was compared to conventional designs. The fluted drive roller, similar in shape to the earlier 38cc engine, is bolted direct to the splined right-hand crankshaft end. Also visible is the narrow caged-roller main bearing housed between the crank and roller.

The second means of keeping the new 38B unit narrow can be seen below; the magneto has been made very compact indeed by the simple expedient of situating both ignition and lighting coils outside the rotating magnets of the flywheel. Their locations in the alloy crankcase half can be seen. The contact breaker and condenser assembly (circled) remained inside the flywheel.

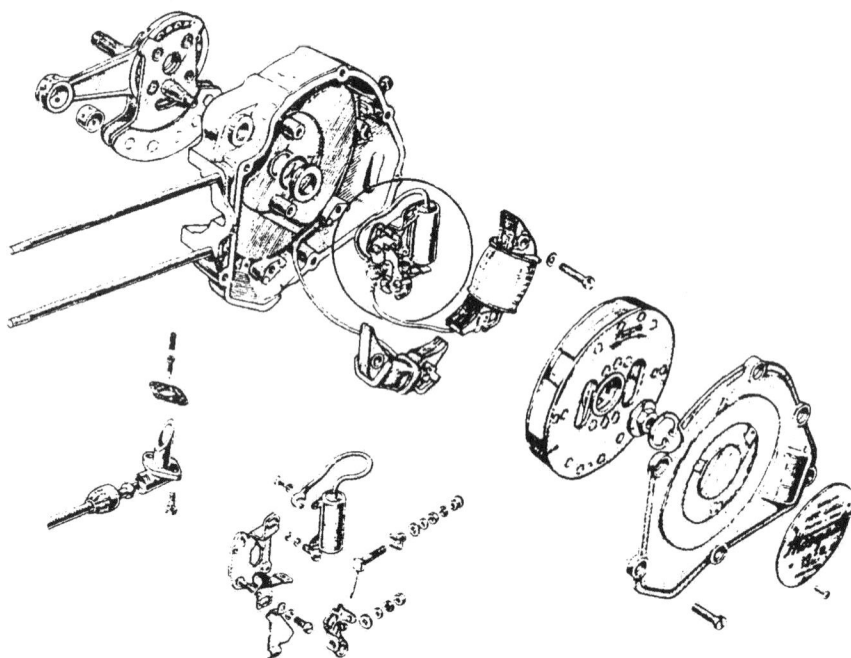

Garelli had maintained its high engineering standards of construction whilst finding novel and effective solutions to the problem of making a bottom-bracket unit narrow enough to fit between standard bicycle pedal-cranks. It was a technical *tour de force* for a humble clip-on cyclemotor engine. Typically Italian, they love engines.

Besides the crank and magneto, other new mechanical parts featured in the 38B:

- A compact but effective expansion-chamber exhaust was made by coiling the outlet forward from the port, then round and back, keeping ground-clearance to a maximum.

- A new modernised type of Dell'orto carburettor was specified, the T10FE, still with a 10mm choke size.

- The lighting coils provided current of 6 volts, 5 watts.

- A Bosch W 175 T1 spark plug was recommended, electrode gap adjusted between 0.5mm and 0.6mm.

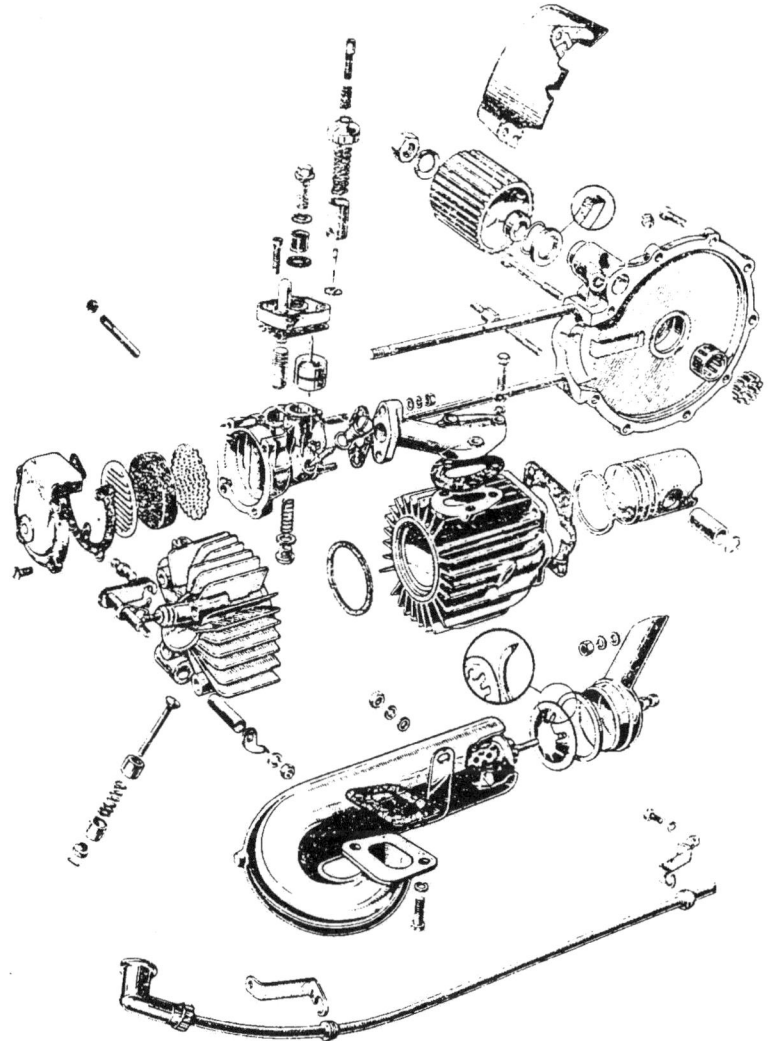

Ah, yes, we haven't mentioned the clutch so far. Read on...

The standard model featured above was accompanied by another model known as the Mosquito-Centrimatic, which boasted a newly designed centrifugal clutch.

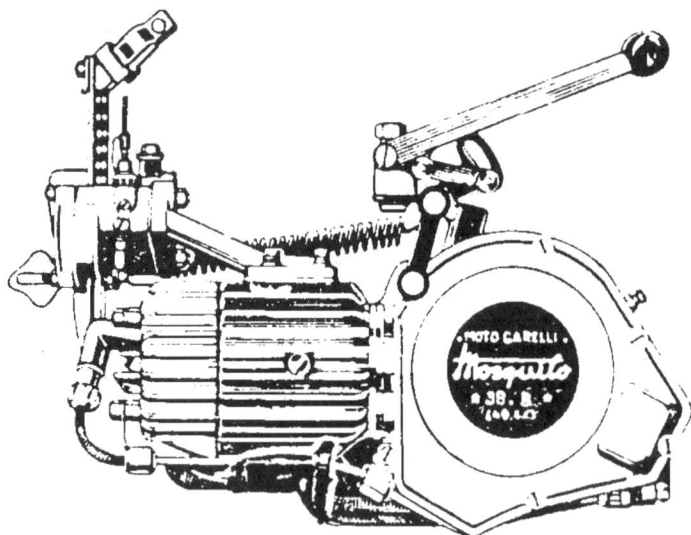

MOSQUITO 38-B

The Motor Cycle published its first review of a Centrimatic-equipped engine on 15th September 1955 and briefly described the mechanism as follows: *"The neatly-enclosed Centrimatic clutch is mounted on an extension of the crankshaft and is located on the right of the driving roller i.e. on the side of the roller remote from the crankcase …[the] dished and flanged end cover carries the clutch shoes. As the speed of rotation rises, centrifugal force acting on the shoes overcomes [a] spring tension and brings the shoes into contact with a drum. The drum forms the driven member of the clutch and is coupled to the driving roller."*

(Power & Pedal)

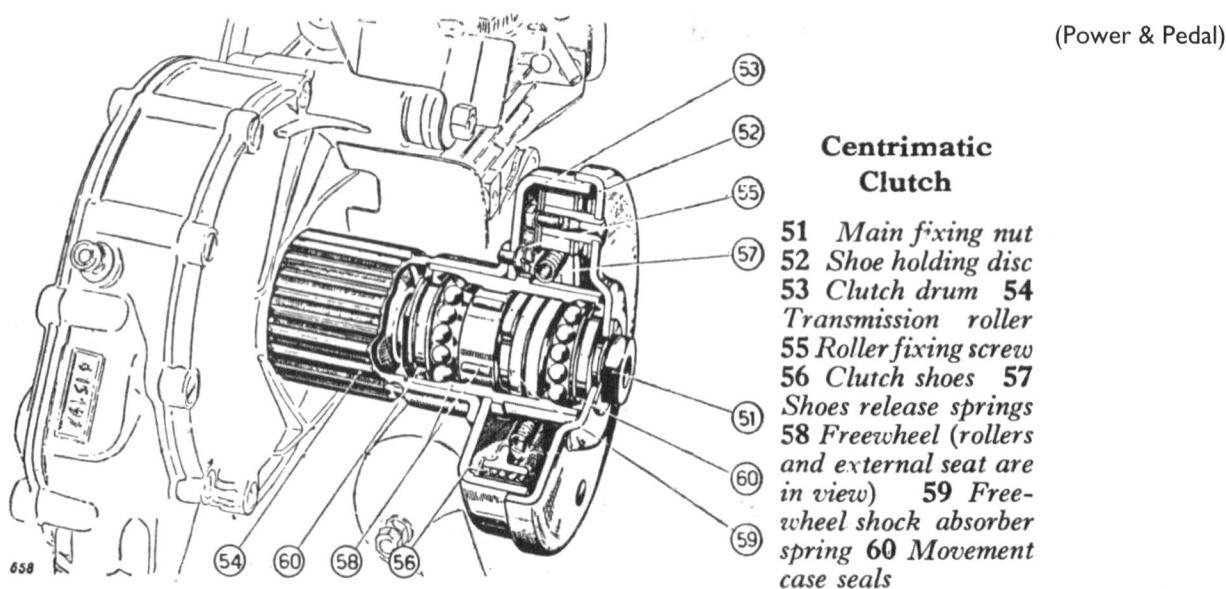

Centrimatic Clutch

51 Main fixing nut
52 Shoe holding disc
53 Clutch drum **54** Transmission roller
55 Roller fixing screw
56 Clutch shoes **57** Shoes release springs
58 Freewheel (rollers and external seat are in view) **59** Freewheel shock absorber spring **60** Movement case seals

A centrifugal clutch is a fine addition to any cyclemotor engine but a rider has to be able to start his engine via the bicycle pedals. Garelli designed a neat solution; a small unidirectional roller free-wheel was fitted between the crank output shaft and inside the drive roller, working independently from the main clutch. Pedalling a cycle forward turned the drive roller against the free-wheel, locking this up and turning the engine over. Once an engine fired, the free-wheel automatically disengaged and all further power transmission duties were passed back to the clutch.

The Motor Cycle of 27th October 1955 published the following road test report on an *"Easy-to-Control Italian Cyclemotor Incorporating a Centrifugally-operated Automatic Clutch"*.

"The de-luxe version is equipped with a simple centrifugal clutch which is entirely automatic in operation … drive is taken up when engine speed reaches a given level … disengagement of the drive is likewise automatic when engine speed drops below that level." Full engine braking was naturally also available at all speeds with the clutch engaged. *"Riding the machine was extremely simple. When the throttle was opened, the clutch took up the drive smoothly from a standing start without pedal assistance, and acceleration was equal to that of a cycle pedalled normally up to a speed of about 8mph. Above that speed the machine could hold its own in city traffic. At a cruising speed of 18mph the exhaust produced no more than a subdued purr; and although it rose to a high-pitched buzz when the machine was travelling downhill on a wide throttle opening, the noise never became obtrusive."*

"Maximum speed was in the region of 24mph on a level road with a 12½ stone rider in the saddle. The happiest cruising speed lay between 18 and 20mph. Normal main road hills were no obstacle to the Mosquito, indeed, the machine climbed a 1 in 13 hill about 350yds long without pedal assistance and without the speed dropping below 9mph. Steeper climbs demanded light pedalling but only gradients steeper than 1 in 9 caller for real physical effort".

The 38B Mosquito without clutch was put on sale at £36.10s, the Centrimatic unit at £39, including Purchase Tax. Both new units were imported from Italy, Bob Sergent's experiments with British manufacture under licence having ended. The old 38cc unit was still available, also an import, being sold at £27-10s in 1955.

Power & Pedal magazine weighed in with its report in February 1956.

"Mosquito Motors Ltd of Moorfields, Liverpool have introduced a new model which is likely to stimulate fresh interest at a time when attachments in general are losing ground against the competition of the mo-ped. … The advantage of the 'centrimatic' clutch is felt immediately on starting … the machine can stand still with the engine ticking over until wanted, then a touch of the throttle lever brings in the very smooth clutch to take the machine away without any jerk, drag or vibration at all … the sensation of smooth gliding away was almost uncanny. The greatest advantage of this type of drive is felt where power assistance is most needed in getting away on up-grades. Stop and restart tests on even steep hills demonstrated the effortless manner in which the machine and a heavy-ish rider could be moved off with only easy pedal work, the engine and clutch taking all the grind out of what is normally the hardest part of cycling."

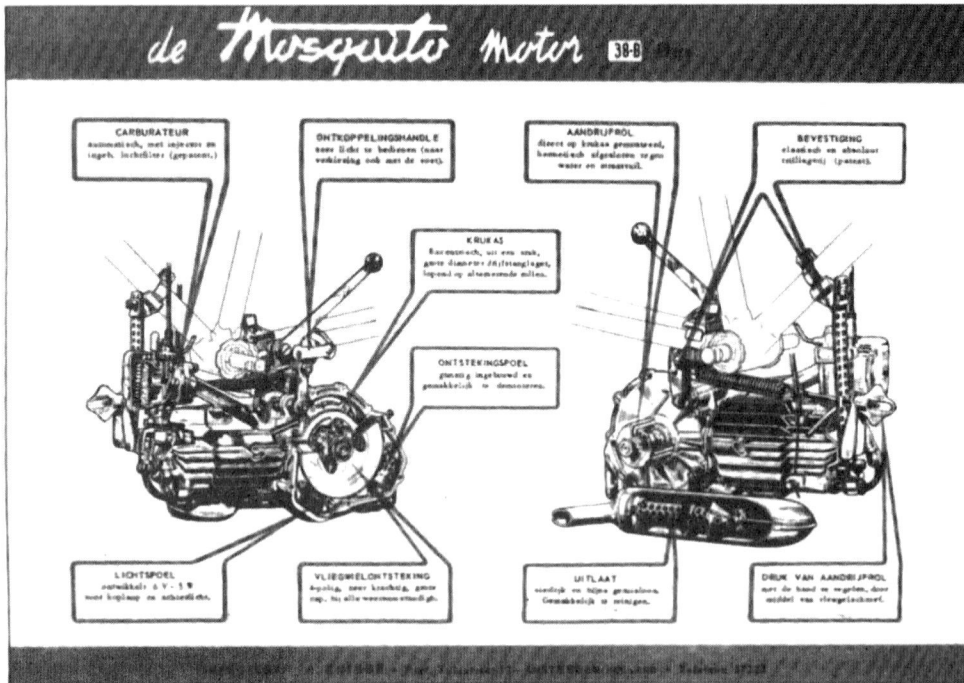

The Netherlands was an important market for the Mosquito and, being an open-minded country with civilised legislation relating to sub-50cc cyclemotors, benefited from a wider range of products than Britain. Garelli again showed its hand early in the career of the 38B series by introducing another well-conceived autocycle sold with the 38B engine unit already fitted. The company had experience with the BMG autocycle in 1952, the new model, Velo-Mosquito, was introduced in 1954.

Velo Mosquito

De bromfiets met de meest eenvoudige en gemakkelijke bedieningsorganen

- Elegant model van standing
- Uiterst stevige constructie uit geperst staalplaat, onder röntgenologische controle electrisch gelast
- Gemakkelijke hantering
- Grootste zekerheid in het verkeer

PRIJS COMPLEET
f. 495.—

(voor Centrimatic extra f. 30.—)

It was a handsome, modern and compact machine, the frame was pressed steel *"very robust construction … and electrically welded under permanent X-ray control. The moped with the simplest and easiest controls … easy handling … best security in traffic … an elegant model showing great class"* according to the Dutch text above. In fact the Velo-Mosquito was so homogenous in appearance it looked an integrated design and, without knowing in advance the motor was originally conceived as a clip-on unit, it was difficult to tell this was not the case. With hindsight, Garelli obviously intended this model to be but an interim one, as less than a year later the company launched a true moped with strong links to the Velo-Mosquito, including using some assemblies such as the front end with handlebars and a lot of the rear end. The new moped centre frame section was larger and heavier-duty, it also accommodated a higher capacity fuel tank; bigger front & rear brakes were now inside full-width hubs, proper rear suspension was fitted and a brand-new unitary engine with integral clutch and 3-speed gearbox took pride of place where once buzzed a humble clip-on unit.

The transformation was complete by December 1955 when the moped went on display at the Milan Show, *The Motor Cycle* commented on a new, elegant and *"most tastefully styled machine … has a commendably well-balanced appearance and the unmistakable stamp of Garelli craftsmanship"*.

From the foregoing it is easy to see that clip-on Mosquito engine units were doomed to an ever-declining role in Garelli's plans as the company prospered by supplying what customers really wanted, sophisticated miniature motor cycles that could be ridden under cyclemotor legislation. No doubt a rump market in rural areas still existed in parts of Italy and France where money was tight, but this would not sustain substantial profits and sooner rather than later the bean-counters' axe was bound to fall.

(Meccanica Garelli)

Surprisingly, the demise of the Mosquito came somewhat later than many expected, Sr Garelli's 1940s creation outlasted a great many competitors and was still being listed by Stone & Cox as available in 1960. The dear old 38cc reduction-gear unit was on sale at £30.9s.7d while the much younger 38B 49cc direct-drive engine sold for £35.6s.6d, the Centrimatic for £38.4s.6d. The 49cc reduction-gear encased-flywheel unit of the BMG had vanished in favour of the 38B. After 1960 a laconic *"importation discontinued"* comment appears. No accurate production totals are known but we think a fair answer would be "a lot"; upwards of 300,000 all told between Garelli in Italy, Chapuis in France and other licencees is a rough guesstimate but, whatever the exact figure, there is no denying that the Mosquito was one of the best engineered and most successful of all clip-on cyclemotor units. Many survive to this day as a result.

Mosquito engines pop up in the most unlikely places. A Spanish aviation engineering company from San Jeronimo, Seville, *Industrias Subsidiarias de Aviación SA,* had a licence in the early 1960s to manufacture the Mosquito 38B as a power source for small 12 volt DC generators. These were well designed and had a purpose-made support frame, an adapter to unite the 38B engine to a FEMSA-built car dynamo which carried a cooling fan and rope-start pulley at the other end. A standard Mosquito fuel tank was used, which supported the control box. Note how the exhaust has been made to turn left rather than right, as on a cyclemotor Mosquito. The company now forms part of the CASA group (*Construcciones Aeronauticas SA*), which makes parts for the Eurofighter, so from small beginnings…

Much of Spain in the early 1960s was rural, poor and isolated; many remote settlements and farms lacked mains electricity so most relied on truck batteries to power a few lights and the television. A Mosquito-powered generator was an ideal way to recharge batteries after an evening watching Pipi Langstrom prancing about in yet another episode of *La Casa de la Pradera.*

The Rest

This is the end of our survey in Episode 1 of the most popular cyclemotors from the 1950s ... but what of the less popular and hence less successful ones? There are eleven more in the list on page 9. It will take another book adequately to describe them all properly, *The Stinkwheel Saga - Episode 2* is in preparation, but until publication at least we can show you what they looked like:

Cymota

A streamlined engine cowling certainly gives the Cymota a distinctive look -but in use it was a nightmare of flapping, resonating metal with few survivors today still so equipped. It also serves to hide the fact that the engine beneath it was a blatant copy of the French VéloSoleX, only not as reliable or so well thought-out. The Cymota flopped - serves them right.

Berini M13

A close cousin of the Cyclemaster, the 32cc Berini never achieved the same popularity in the UK as it did in its home country: The Netherlands. It was nonetheless a very smartly styled roller-drive engine that produced an excellent 0.75bhp with the aid of a rotary inlet-valve.

Teagle

THE *Teagle Cyclemotor*

Produced by a firm of Agricultural Engieers in Truro, Cornwall, the Teagle was a well-built unit, much admired by the few customers who bought one. Prolonged factory development and testing meant it reached the market in 1955, too late to achieve the success it deserved. The engine was of all-alloy monobloc construction and was available with or without fan cooling.

The Teagle company survived however and is still in business today

Lohmann

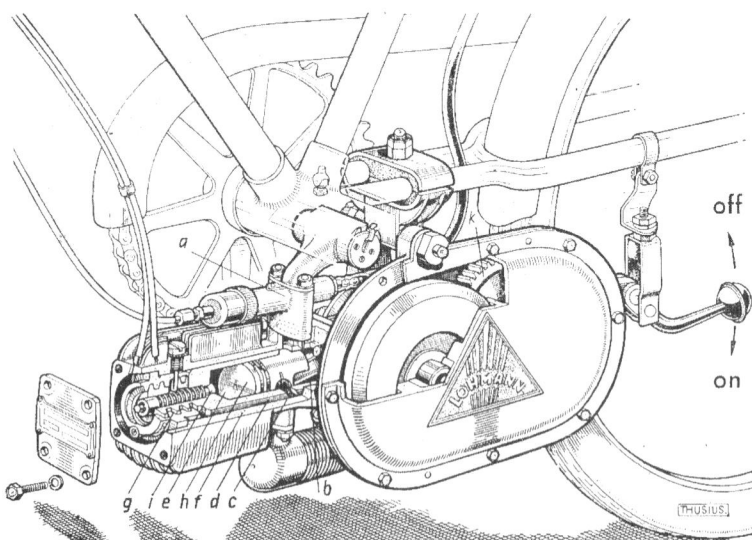

A compression-ignition engine of only 18cc makes the German-designed Lohmann the smallest of cyclemotors available in the UK during the 1950s. When on song it seems to work quite well. Nowadays fuel formulations have become a mysterious and exotic science, often featuring ingredients like Belgian Lamp Oil. The secret of a running Lohmann is known to only a few, fiercely loyal initiates and true believers who have to swear special oaths.

ABG VAP

A very popular French motor, the VAP3 & VAP4, like the Berini, were cyclemotors that never achieved the same success in Britain as on the Continent. Manufacturer ABG was a prime supplier of flywheel magnetos and auxiliary engines to French cyclemotor makers and had the production capacity to cater for demand. The VAP was attached to an extended wheel spindle, transmission was initially by toothed ring (screwed to the spokes) & roller gear, then on later models by conventional chain and sprocket. It even ended up with a clutch.

Tailwind

The Tailwind had two speeds arranged by sliding the engine sideways, thus bringing a larger roller to bear on the tyre. The five prototype machines evolved the design through three stages. At least one 'semi-production' machine was also produced. Despite a lot of attention from the motor cycling press, the Tailwind didn't make it into full production.

Busy Bee

The Busy Bee was a do-it-yourself engine, designed by Edgar T Westbury. A considerable amount of engineering skill was needed to transform the purchased set of castings into a complete motor, hence the almost total absence of survivors. Nevertheless, at least four are believed to exist.

Itom

The 48cc Itom was of Italian origin and yet another example of a highly successful cyclemotor in Europe which never sold well in Britain, despite complimentary press road tests. This roller-drive unit produced an extraordinary 1.4bhp and soon gained a reputation as the high performance mount of choice for sporting Continental *cyclomoteuristes*. Not only high performance but apparently a paragon of reliability, according to a main distributor. Why did it not succeed in the UK? Find out more in Stinkwheel, Episode 2.

TI Powerwheel

Very clever ... but over complicated and would have been both hugely expensive to make and of dubious reliability in use. The TI Power wheel hub contained a single cylinder 2-stroke rotary engine, the crankshaft was a fixed, stationary axis while the rest of the engine spun around it 14 times faster than the rear wheel rotated. It never got past the prototype stage but one unit was made and is reputed to survive to this day. The flat tyre in the factory show picture alongside says it all.

Ostler

Another do-it-yourself machine for the technically competent, the Ostler Mini Auto was designed by a model engineer from Ipswich. Sold as a set of plans for 10/6d, a customer was expected to fabricate and machine all parts to produce his own 27.7cc engine. The unit was effectively a model aircraft motor writ large.

Never sold commercially as a complete, running cyclemotor, so few were completed it is a miracle any survive at all, but one or two do.

ABJ Auto Minor

Produced by A B Jackson (Cycles) Ltd of Birmingham, the short-stroke 49cc Auto Minor drove the front wheel via a carborundum-faced roller *à la SoleX*. It was only ever sold fitted to an ABJ bicycle and seems to have been commercially available for only one year, 1953, according to Stone & Cox. By 1954 manufacture had been discontinued.

Bantamoto

DIRECT DRIVE TO REAR WHEEL HUB

The 40cc Bantamoto (or Bantomoto - both spellings were used) was bolted to an extension of the rear wheel spindle and drove a gear clamped to the wheel hub, rather than the spokes as on a VAP Transmission was by a train of pinions and a rotary inlet valve featured. It was marketed by Cyc-Auto.

THE CONNOISSEUR'S CHOICE

Bikotor

Perhaps the most ephemeral of all the British cyclemotors, a description of the Bikotor appeared in *The Motor Cycle* on 14th December 1950. Production was promised for *"next spring"*… and it was never heard of again.

Tailpiece

So many of the adverts that we discovered in various newspapers and magazines to illustrate this book were fascinating we have included a final chapter reproducing the best of them.

Prime source for adverts has been the cyclemotorist's very own magazine, Power & Pedal, an invaluable part of this work. A little history of the magazine itself parallels the way in which the clip-on cyclemotor market boomed and changed in a short span of four to five years. Power & Pedal was launched in 1952 and, as the title suggests, was aimed specifically at the clip-on cyclemotor user.

Vol. 1   No. 1   **POWER & PEDAL**   November, 1952

Editor : FRANK L. FARR

Editorial and Advertising Offices :

197 Temple Chambers, London, E.C.4   Telephone : Central 5424

However, two years later the magazine's emphasis was already changing to include the new scooter craze from Italy and accommodate an expanding readership; *Power & Pedal* now incorporated *The Scooter* and included the masthead *The Cyclemotor and Autocycle Journal.*

Not only that but the internal page makeup began to change. The first issue to include *The Scooter* carried just one page of "Scooter Topics".

POWER & PEDAL

Founded 1952

with
THE SCOOTER

Editor : FRANK L. FARR

Vol. IV   No. 9   **August, 1956**

A year later in January 1956 *The Scooter* had become a separate 10-page section within the magazine and, more significantly, the inside title page had dropped any reference to cyclemotors, becoming simply *The Autocycle Journal with The Scooter.*

POWER & PEDAL

THE AUTOCYCLE JOURNAL with THE **SCOOTER**

Editor : FRANK L. FARR

Vol. IV   No. 2

January, 1956

By August 1956, even *The Autocycle Journal* reference had been dropped and *The Scooter* section took up nearly half the pages in the magazine.

The following are a sample of the adverts that appeared in Power & Pedal between 1952 and 1956.

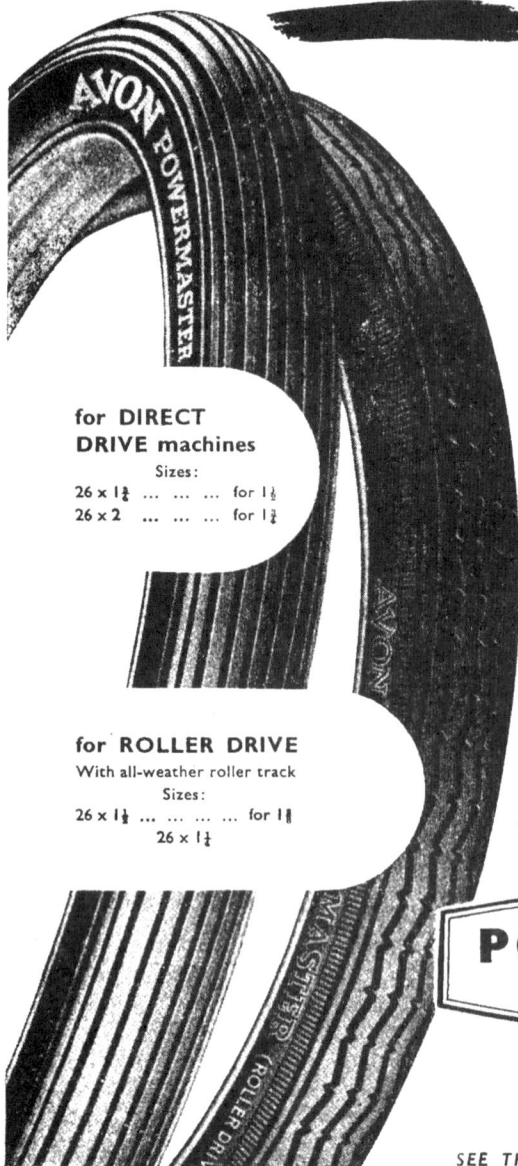

Availability of tyres with roller-drive tread was crucial to expanding the popularity of clip-on cyclemotor units with this transmission. Normal bicycle tyres would wear too quickly, especially as roller-slip was common in the wet with early clip-ons. Both Avon and Dunlop sold a wide range of suitable ones.

Many makes of clip-on cyclemotor were fitted with miniaturised Amal carburettors, Amal being world-renowned for its rather old-fashioned, but simple and effective, motor cycle carburettors. Right through the 1940s and 1950s the vast majority of British-built motor cycles were so equipped, making servicing and repairs so easy for the home mechanic.

239

One competitor surfaced in the form of the B.E.C. monobloc carburettor which claimed to eliminate all fuel leakages. The somewhat summary balancing of rotating masses within small two-stroke engines allowed high-frequency vibrations to build up, often intolerable at certain revs for a rider and equally so for anything attached to the engine. Some carburettors were notorious for disassembling themselves, with obvious consequences to fuel economy.

Oil companies were quick off the mark in offering specially blended oil suitable for fast mixing with petrol.

240

Most oil and additive manufacturers oriented their sales pitch toward a higher mileage between decoking an engine and, more importantly, a reduction in the frequency of whiskered spark-plugs. To a rider that sudden hesitation, splutter, occasional pick-up but more usual total loss of power as that vital spark vanishes heralds a whiskered plug. A grain of something mineral grows between the electrode tip and earth lug, rapidly reducing the air-gap from 0.025" to next to nothing and strangling the spark at birth.

Removing a whisker is not difficult but is a drearily familiar process to most cyclemotorists; the plug is more often than not red-hot (whiskers tend to form during high-speed runs) so burned fingers are a bonus inconvenience, a penknife blade is slid between electrodes and the whisker is gone. Under certain circumstances this procedure had to be carried out every few hundred yards, much to the detriment of a rider's composure and verbal rectitude.

Decoking was and is another of life's little horrors, though with modern oils it is a less frequently required task than of yore. A good proportion of two-stroke lubricating oil burns up and passes through the exhaust port *en route* to the silencer. Carbon deposits soon build up in the port, on the piston top and cylinder head and clog the exhaust system, reducing power to the point when a decoke is essential. It was and is a messy business, avoided until the last moment if possible, hence all those magical oil formulations or additives designed to put off the evil day as long as possible.

Bicycle stirrup brakes were notoriously inadequate in stopping power, unless Fibrax 144 Brake Blocks were substituted for the rather ineffectual original items.

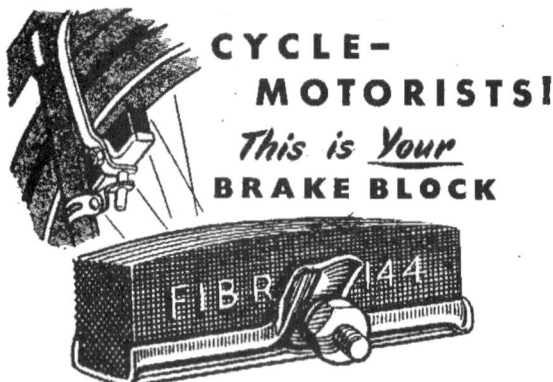

Sooner or later a cyclemotorist would feel the urge to accessorise and adorn his mount. Medieval knights were wont to do this with their horses. Some accessories seemed practical enough, others (and there were many) were a complete waste of money.

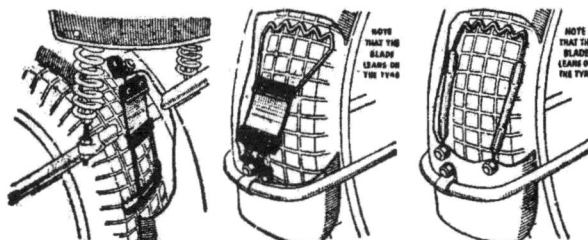

243

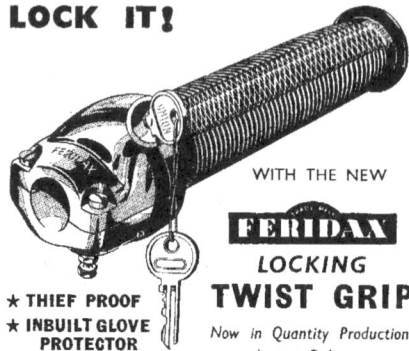

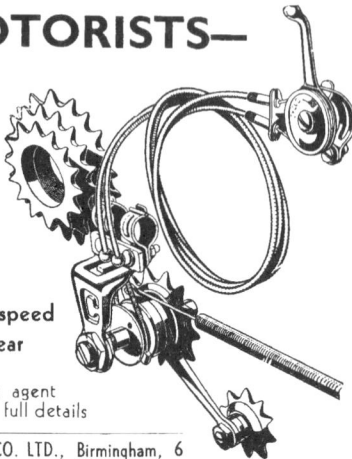

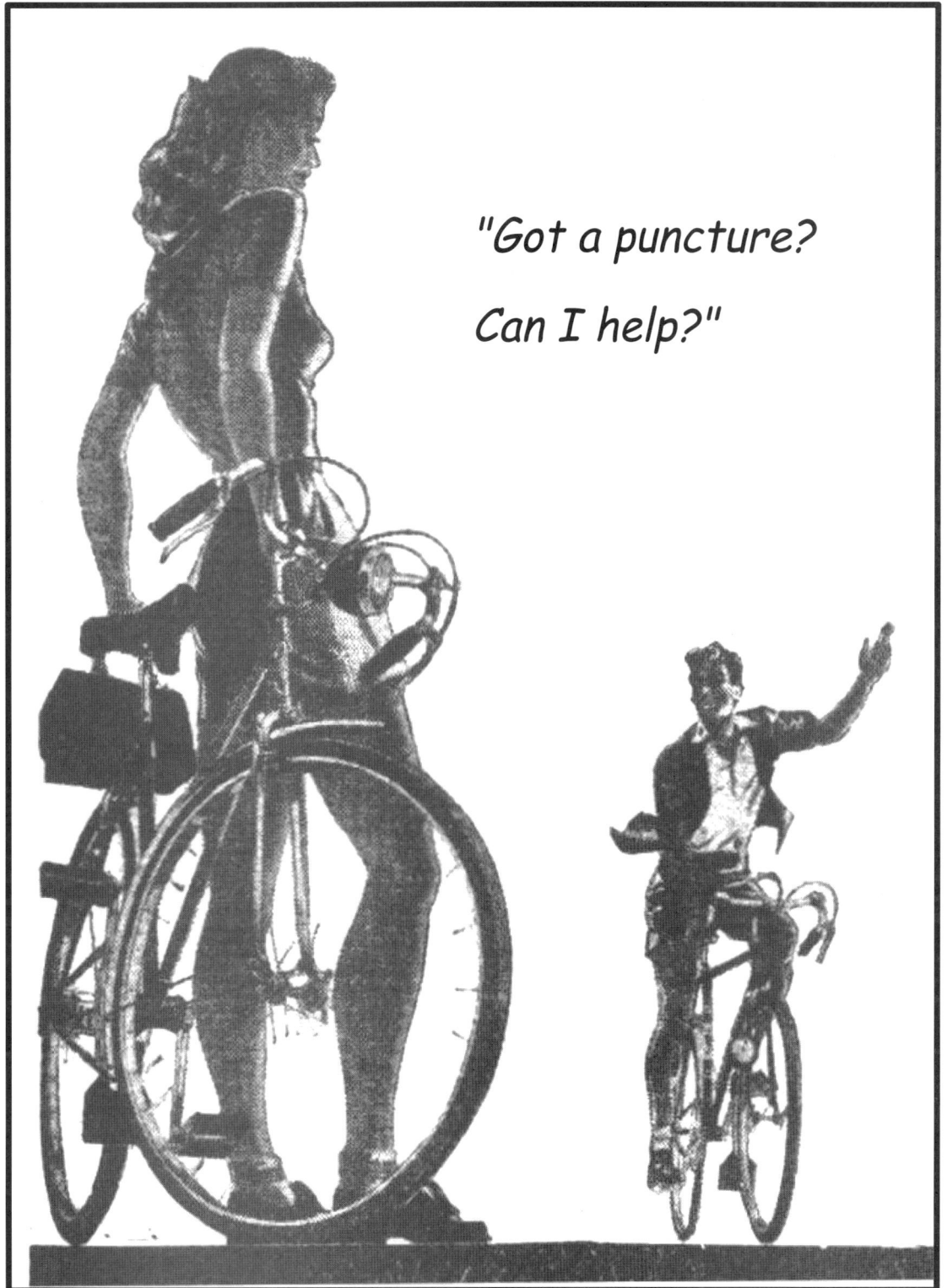

And here we are, back in the summer of 1954 (courtesy of Halfords) when most of us were still young, vigorous and handsome, with an illustration of what male cyclists hoped might happen one day.

In your dreams, boys.

Accessory manufacturers proliferated to satisfy a cyclemotorist's urge, once good money had been parted with for the latest bolt-on crudity, to add a few extras to perk up a usually drab and basic bicycle. Halfords catered for both cyclists and cyclemotorists; remarkably they still do, though scooters have now replaced cyclemotors.

Waterproof, warm outer clothing was much in demand, as were gloves. Not items of great sartorial elegance but they kept you dry

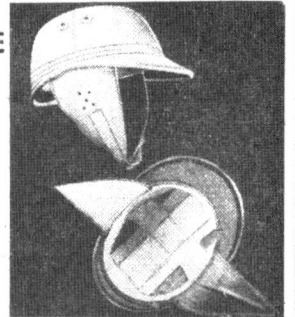

The discovery of clear plastic film technology enabled manufacturers to supply *motards* of all kinds with eye-protection that didn't look like something a WW2 fighter-pilot would have worn.

And in conclusion, a dealer advert......for a moped, the shape of things to come.

Bibliography

The following magazines were a principal source of information and quotations on the cyclemotors described in this book.

- Buzzing (NACC club magazine).

- Motocycles,

- The Motor Cycle,

- Motor Cycle & Cycle Trader,

- Motor Cycling,

- Moto Revue,

- Power & Pedal,

- Revue Technique Motocycliste,

- Scooter et Cyclomoto,

- La Vie de la Moto,

The following books were consulted for technical information and background history.

- The Cyclemotor Manual,

- Stone & Cox Motor Specifications & Prices,

- Motos Peugeot (Bernard Salvat),

- Le Temps des Mobs (Jean Goyard),

- Illustrated Encyclopedia of Motorcycles (Erwin Tragatsch),

- The Complete Encyclopedia of Motorcars (Nick Georgano),

- Le VéloSoleX de mon Père (Franck Meneret).

The NACC website at **www.buzzing.org** was absolutely invaluable.

The Crossley Motors Archive at the University of Warwick Modern Records library provided valuable information for the Mosquito chapter

Original factory manuals, sales brochures, instruction books, advertisements and other period literature were loaned for reference and reproduction by a great many people, thanks to all of you for helping with this project.

Index